Innovative approaches to contemporary trends in education

Alina Felicia Roman, Evelina Balaş, Tiberiu Dughi, Dana Rad,
Alina Costin, Henrietta Torkos, Editha Coşarbă. (eds.)

Innovative approaches to contemporary trends in education

PETER LANG
Berlin - Bruxelles - Chennai - Lausanne - New York - Oxford

Library of Congress Cataloging-in-Publication Data
Names: Roman, Alina Felicia, 1971- author. | Balaş, Evelina, 1978- author. | Dughi, Tiberiu, author. | Rad, Dana, author. | Costin, Alina, 1976- author. | Torkos, Henrietta, 1988- author. | Coşarbă, Editha, 1983- author.
Title: Innovative approaches to contemporary trends in education / by Alina Roman, Evelina Balas, Tiberiu Dughi, Dana Rad, Alina Costin, Henrietta Torkos, Editha Cosarba.
Description: New York, NY : Peter Lang Publishing, Inc., 2025. | Includes bibliographical references.
Identifiers: LCCN 2025000320 (print) | LCCN 2025000321 (ebook) | ISBN 9783631922293 (paperback) | ISBN 9783631934173 (ebook) | ISBN 9783631934180 (epub)
Subjects: LCSH: Educational innovations. | Educational technology. | Education and state. | Educational change.
Classification: LCC LB1027 .C865 2025 (print) | LCC LB1027 (ebook) | DDC 371.102—dc23/eng/20250130
LC record available at https://lccn.loc.gov/2025000320
LC ebook record available at https://lccn.loc.gov/2025000321

Bibliographic Information published by the Deutsche Nationalbibliothek
The Deutsche Nationalbibliothek lists this publication in the Deutsche Nationalbibliografie; detailed bibliographic data is available in the internet at http://dnb.d-nb.de.

ISBN 978-3-631-92229-3 (Print)
ISBN 978-3-631-93417-3 (E-PDF)
ISBN 978-3-631-93418-0 (E-PUB)
DOI 10.3726/b22698

Published by Peter Lang GmbH, Berlin (Germany)

info@peterlang.com - http://www.peterlang.com/

This publication has been peer reviewed.

Contents

The Creative Mindset and the Growth Mindset: Approaches from An Educational Perspective

Alina Felicia Roman and Nicoleta Chioncel

Abstract: This chapter aims to provide an introductory account of the creative growth mindset in relation to good educational practices. Throughout the chapter, the contextual framework of the study of creativity is discussed, as well as its connection (or lack of connection) to educational and developmental psychology theories. Ultimately, these considerations lead to implications for future educational methods, encouraging readers to question the current value, understanding, and applicability of creativity.

Keywords: creative mindset, growth mindset, creativity training, educational methods.

Context

Creativity is a complex concept, as evidenced by the numerous definitions variants proposed by different psychologists. Instead of adhering to a specific definition, I came across a quote from Nobel laureate P. W. Anderson's seminal article "More is different" about emergence:

> The ability to reduce everything to simple fundamental laws does not imply the ability to start from those laws and reconstruct the universe. In the new sciences of complexity, the whole becomes not only more than but very different from the sum of its parts. (Anderson, 1972, p. 393)

This comment can be interpreted as a scientific analogy for the concept of creativity, suggesting that the capacity to create is not just a matter of recombining previously existing ideas, but rather a result of a more complex and dynamic *process* that emerges from the interaction of various elements.

The 1950s saw the birth of creativity as a new research domain in Western psychology, determined by the concurrent development of self-realization psychology and multiple intelligence testing, pioneered by prominent figures such as J. P. Guildford and E. P. Torrance. These developments led to the introduction of two distinct approaches to the study of creativity: the humanist and the instrumentalist approaches. In a detailed review of the field's history, Bycroft (2012) classifies the humanist approach as part of the self-growth movement, distinguishing it from the instrumentalist approach, which emphasizes the quantification and application of creativity.

On the same lines, the cultural sociologist Andreas Reckwitz (2017) remarks that the 1950s represented a substantial structural transition in psychological techniques, with the focus shifting from psychic pathology to improvement of psychic capacities. As a result, while the study methodologies and theoretical underpinnings of the humanist and instrumentalist creativity branches can be distinctly separated, the two are united in the shared goal of enhancing creative capacity.

The Creative Process

When discussing creativity, one of the main focus areas is to analyze the creative thinking process rather than characterize the final creative product. From a humanist perspective, the construct of the creative process sets out to achieve a higher understanding of ideational thinking, similar to cognitivist research. On the other hand, the instrumentalist perspective identifies and highlights reproduceable patterns that lead to creative outputs, with emphasis on the deliberate use of creative practices.

Beginning in the 20th century, social psychologists such as Wallas (1926/2014) and Wertheimer (1945) have delved into the origins of novel ideas by analyzing autobiographical accounts (empirical observations) of polymaths (such as Henri Poincaré). The proposed models of the creative process follow a stage-like structure, consistent with developmental theories. For exemplification, the well-known model pioneered by Wallas (1926) defines the structural elements of a creative process into four *stages of control*: *preparation* (researching), *incubation* (unconscious processing of the information), *illumination* (experiencing a sudden insight), and *verification* (evaluating and refining the idea).

Jean Piaget propounded the constructivist theory of cognitive development in his book *The Psychology of Intelligence* (1952), where he introduces the biological term *ontogenesis* in the context of psychology. In his theory, *ontogenesis* refers to the individual's gradual development of knowledge and cognitive abilities, which he argues to be a continuous process that begins at birth and advances throughout the lifespan (Piaget, 1970). He proposes that the *active* process proceeds in a series of stages: *sensorimotor, preoperational, concrete operational*, and *formal operational*, each particularized by distinct ways of thinking and understanding the world, proportional to the different levels of cognitive complexity and abstraction. The main hypothesis is that the child constructs new schemas in order to adapt to their current understanding of reality, suggesting that each construction is not only the result of knowledge build-up, but rather a *transformation*, that is, "a complete reorganization of thought" (Sawyer, 2003, p. 13).

With regards to creativity, Piaget notes, "The real problem is how to explain novelties. I think novelties constantly intervene in development" (Piaget, 1971, p. 192). In his later work "Genetic epistemology" (1970), he introduces the interplay between individual development and scientific advancement (*phylogenesis*). He identifies *disequilibrium* situations as the driving force behind knowledge acquisition, which can stem from internal (personal) or external disturbances. Therefore, the accumulation of knowledge is a constant and active process of readapting *disequilibrium* to *equilibrium*: "Knowledge ... is a system of transformations that become progressively adequate" (Piaget, 1970, p. 15).

The book *Creativity and Development* (2003) constructs a powerful theoretical foundation on the connection between developmental psychology and the creative process, arguing the importance of implementing developmental methodologies for a more rigorous study of creativity. In addition, it suggests that the traditional application of creative practices may be used to support yet unanswered problematics of cognitive development.

Implications in Education and Creativity Training

With regards to the adaptation and application of Piaget's developmental theory in creative problem-solving, *Creativity and Development* (2003) opens with a quote from the pioneering creative psychologist Howard E. Gruber:

> Piaget, working with children, found that the growth of their ideas is a process spread over years. Now that we are learning about adult creative work in this new way, we can compare two radically different development processes that have some important points in common. Each will illuminate the other.

Piaget's developmental theories have been widely applied in preschool and primary school methodologies. More recently, studies such as Gelbach's (1991) research suggest that designing lesson plans and playground activities based on the cognitive development of children can have a powerful impact on the future creative capacity of the adult individual.

Growth Mindset in relation to Creative Processes and Education

The fixed mentality is a method of thinking that originates from the assumption that our traits are a product that does not change. A growth mindset is a way of thinking that is founded on the concept that we can change our basic traits by employing desire and effort.

When people enter a thought pattern, they are essentially entering new worlds: the world of fixed characteristics, where success is determined by our ability to prove that we are smart, talented, or creative and receive validation of who we are, or the world of changing qualities, where success is determined by our ability to broaden our horizons in order to learn something new and develop (Dweck, 2017).

Thought patterns are powerful beliefs, but they are a part of our minds that can be altered. Knowing these patterns allows us to start thinking about and responding to requests in new ways. Each pattern produces a world, and the essential thing to remember is that individuals have the ability to select whatever world they want to live in (Dweck, 2017).

People with a development mentality are willing to take chances, overcome obstacles, and persevere. They have no problem absorbing truthful facts about their talents since they feel they can grow. The concept that talent can be developed helps people to attain their full potential (Dweck, 2017).

The degree to which students perceive their intellect or creativity to be malleable affects their ideas, behaviors, and, ultimately, their academic achievement. Understanding student mentality development is thus of significant importance to educational scholars interested in establishing methods for student achievement.

Understanding that our talents are malleable and that we may support a habit of thinking that fosters their development has far-reaching consequences for education. Even the tasks that instructors set to their pupils function as a means for teachers to communicate with their students. In mathematics, for example, if students are given short-answer (yes/no) questions and make mistakes in their answers, it will be difficult for them to believe that they can only succeed if they put in time and effort, but when the demands are more open, creative, and present opportunities for learning, students can see that it is possible to make progress and be more successful (Boaler, 2013).

Teacher intervention strategies have a significant impact in establishing effective teaching practices, quality relationships with students, and a positive classroom and school climate. It is essential that teachers discuss and examine the mood of effective students who are engaged and motivated to determine how to improve mood in the classroom. The focus on social-emotional development and student well-being is not an additional curriculum that takes time away from academic study of skills and content, it overlaps the curriculum with practices that promote motivation and stimulate creativity (Brooks et al., 2012).

Students who acquire a growth mindset believe that intelligence and creativity are adaptable and expanding. Students that exhibit this pattern have a desire to accept difficulties, like problem-solving, and are resilient in the face of failure. Those with a "fixed mindset," on the other hand, feel that talents are permanent attributes. When youngsters with this perspective fail or make errors, they assume they are not smart or creative enough, lose confidence, and give up. These pupils forgo regular difficulties in favor of easy, routine work in which they are confident of success (Boaler, 2013).

Conclusion

In conclusion, the intertwining studies of developmental psychology and creativity research, though contemporaneous, suffer from a lack of integration as social modeling tools, hindering a cohesive affiliation. This observation prompts a dual call to action: firstly, to scrutinize societal and cultural expectations and the pressures imposed on individuals to foster creativity, thereby influencing the perceived value of creativity itself. Secondly, it urges a reconsideration of implementing a more robust educational foundation, inspired by developmental methodology, for the effective application of creativity training. The pivotal role of mindset is underscored, impacting various noncognitive factors such as students' goals, attributions of successes and failures, and their coping mechanisms. As ongoing research delves into the intricate development and evolution of student mindsets, its potential benefits in adapting educational methods and fostering heightened creativity continue to be a focal point for future exploration and improvement in educational practices.

References

Anderson, P. W. (1972). More is different: Broken symmetry and the nature of the hierarchical structure of science. *Science*, *177*(4047), 393–396.

Boaler, J. (2013). Ability and mathematics: The mindset revolution that is reshaping education. *The Forum*, *55*, 143–152.

Brooks, R., Waters, J., & Wilson, H. P. (2012). International education and the employability of UK students. *British Educational Research Journal*, *38*(2), 281–298. <https://doi.org/10.1080/01411926.2010.544710>

Bycroft, M. (2012). Psychology, psychologists, and the creativity movement: The lives of method inside and outside the cold war. In M. Solovey & H. Cravens (Eds.), *Cold War Social Science* (pp. 197–214). Palgrave Macmillan.

Cohen-Cole, J. (2014). The creative American. In *The open mind: Cold war politics and the sciences of human nature* (pp. 35–62). Chicago: University of Chicago Press. <https://doi.org/10.7208/9780226092331>

Dweck, C. S. (2017). Mindset. O nouă psihologie a succesului [Mindset: A new psychology of success]. Bucureşti: Curtea Veche Publishing

Dweck, C. S. (1999). *Self-theories: Their role in motivation, personality, and development*. Psychology Press.

Dweck, C. S. (2017). *Mindset. O nouă psihologie a succesului* [Mindset: A new psychology of success]. Bucureşti: Curtea Veche Publishing.

Gehlbach, R. D. (1991). Play, Piaget, and creativity: The promise of design. *Journal of Creative Behavior*, *25*(2), 137–144.

Heine, S. J., Kitayama, S., Lehman, D. R., Takata, T., Ide, E., Leung, C., & Matsumoto, H. (2001). Divergent consequences of success and failure in Japan and North America: An investigation of self-improving motivations and malleable selves. *Journal of Personality and Social Psychology*, *81*(4), 599–615. https://doi.org/10.1037/0022-3514.81.4.599.

Hoyert, M., & O'Dell, C. (2008). Goal orientation and the aftermath of an academic failure. *International Journal of Learning*, *15*(3), 245–251.

Piaget, J. (1952). *The origins of intelligence in children*. (M. Cook, Trans.). W. W. Norton & Co. <https://doi.org/10.1037/11494-000>

Piaget, J. (1970). *Genetic epistemology*. (E. Duckworth, Trans.). Columbia University Press.

Piaget, J. (1971). *Biology and knowledge: An essay on the relations between organic regulations and cognitive processes.* (B. Walsh, Trans.). Edinburgh University Press. (Original work published 1967).

Piaget, J., & Garcia, R. (1989). *Psychogenesis and the history of science.* (H. Feider, Trans.). Columbia University Press. (Original work published 1983).

Reckwitz, A. (2017). The psychological turn in creativity: From the pathological genius to the normalization of the self as a resource. In *The invention of creativity: Modern society and the culture of the new* (pp. 127–153). Polity Press.

Rose, N. (1988). Calculable minds and manageable individuals. *History of the Human Sciences, 1*(2), 183–189.

Sawyer, R. K. (2003). Emergence in creativity and development. In R. K. Sawyer, V. John-Steiner, S. Moran, R. J. Sternberg, D. H. Feldman, J. Nakamura, & M. Csikszentmihalyi (Eds.), *Creativity and development* (pp. 12–60). Oxford University Press.

Stoltz, T., Piske, F. H. R., de Freitas, M. D. F. Q., D'Aroz, M. S., & Machado, J. M. (2015). Creativity in gifted education: Contributions from Vygotsky and Piaget. *Creative Education*, 6(01), 64.

Wallas, G. (2014). *Art of thought* (reprint ed.). Solis Press. (Original work published 2014).

Wertheimer, M. (1945). *Productive thinking.* Harper & Brothers.

Factors Predicting Academic Success in Preschool Children

Ion Albulescu, Cristian Stan, and Marta Gana Mutaşcu

Abstract: Academic success in early childhood lays a foundation for lifelong learning and development. This chapter explores the multifaceted landscape of factors that contribute to the academic achievement of preschool children. Drawing on a comprehensive review of empirical studies and theoretical frameworks, this chapter identifies key predictors that play a pivotal role in shaping children's early academic experiences. Factors such as socioeconomic background, parental involvement, cognitive and language development, teacher quality, and classroom environment are examined in depth, highlighting their intricate interplay and influence on preschoolers' academic outcomes. Furthermore, this chapter delves into the significance of early interventions and educational programs in harnessing these predictors to foster optimal academic growth. By gaining a holistic understanding of the factors that contribute to academic success during the preschool years, educators, parents, and policymakers can collaboratively design strategies and initiatives that ensure a strong academic foundation for young learners. This chapter underscores the importance of recognizing and addressing these factors to empower preschool children with the tools they need for a successful educational journey.

Keywords: preschool children, academic success, predictors, socioeconomic background, parental involvement, cognitive development, language development, teacher quality, classroom environment, early interventions, educational programs.

Introduction

Academic success in early childhood is a crucial milestone that lays the foundation for lifelong learning and development (Duncan et al., 2007; Magnuson & Duncan, 2016). The significance of achieving positive academic outcomes during the preschool years has garnered increased attention from educators, researchers, and policymakers alike. This focus on early academic achievement stems from a growing body of evidence highlighting its enduring impact on subsequent educational attainment, cognitive development, and socioeconomic well-being (Heckman, 2006; Camilli et al., 2010).

The aim of this chapter is to explore the multifaceted landscape of factors that contribute to the academic success of preschool children. This exploration is rooted in the recognition that early childhood education plays a pivotal role in shaping cognitive, social, and emotional development (Blair & Raver, 2015; Raver et al., 2011). The preschool years represent a critical period during which children begin to acquire foundational skills and knowledge that form the basis of their educational journey (Bierman et al., 2008).

To achieve this aim, we will draw upon a comprehensive review of empirical studies and theoretical frameworks. By synthesizing existing research, we aim to identify and elucidate key predictors that influence preschoolers' academic outcomes. These predictors encompass a range of domains, including socioeconomic background, parental involvement, cognitive and language development, teacher quality, and classroom environment.

The significance of each of these factors cannot be overstated. Socioeconomic disparities have been consistently linked to variations in academic achievement (Duncan & Magnuson, 2012). Parental involvement is recognized as a critical ingredient for fostering early learning (Desimone, 1999; Fan & Chen, 2001). Cognitive and language development, as fundamental building blocks of academic success, warrant meticulous examination (McClelland et al., 2007; Hoff, 2013). Teacher quality, encompassing educators' pedagogical skills and abilities to engage and motivate young learners, plays a vital role in shaping the educational experience (Pianta et al., 2008; Hamre & Pianta, 2005). Finally, the classroom environment, as the immediate context in which preschoolers learn and grow, has been shown to significantly impact their academic progress (Mashburn et al., 2008; Curby et al., 2009).

In addition, this chapter will delve into the importance of early interventions and educational programs in harnessing these predictors to foster optimal academic growth. Recognizing the potential of early childhood education as a powerful tool for mitigating disparities in academic achievement (Reynolds et al., 2010), we will explore evidence-based practices that have yielded promising results in promoting school readiness and enhancing academic outcomes for preschool children.

By gaining a holistic understanding of the factors that contribute to academic success during the preschool years, educators, parents, and policymakers can collaboratively design strategies and initiatives that ensure a strong academic foundation for young learners. This chapter underscores the importance of recognizing and addressing these factors to empower preschool children with the tools they need for a successful educational journey, ultimately shaping the trajectory of their future educational endeavors.

Literature review

Academic success in preschool children is influenced by a complex interplay of various factors that encompass socioeconomic background, parental involvement, cognitive and language development, teacher quality, and classroom environment. This section provides a comprehensive review of existing literature on these key factors, offering insights into their significance and impact on preschoolers' academic outcomes.

Research has consistently demonstrated the substantial impact of socioeconomic background on academic success during the preschool years (Duncan & Magnuson, 2012; Duncan et al., 1998). Children from lower-income families often face challenges related to limited access to educational resources, quality childcare, and early learning opportunities (Heckman, 2006). These disparities in access to resources can contribute to differences in school readiness and subsequent academic achievement (Magnuson & Duncan, 2016).

Recent studies have highlighted the enduring nature of these effects, with socioeconomic disparities influencing not only early academic performance but also long-term educational trajectories (Duncan et al., 2007). It is important to note that while socioeconomic background is a significant predictor, it does not determine a child's destiny. Intervention programs and targeted support can mitigate the impact of economic disadvantage (Reynolds et al., 2010).

Parental involvement plays a pivotal role in shaping preschoolers' academic development (Fan & Chen, 2001). Studies have consistently shown that parents who actively engage in their children's learning by providing a stimulating home environment, reading to them, and engaging in educational activities positively impact their cognitive and language development (Desimone, 1999; Hoff, 2013).

Furthermore, parental involvement extends beyond the home and into early education settings. Collaborative partnerships between parents and educators have been associated with improved school readiness and academic success (Pianta et al., 2008). Effective communication and involvement in school activities create a supportive learning environment that enhances children's educational experiences.

Cognitive and language development represent foundational skills for academic success in preschool children (McClelland et al., 2007). Cognitive abilities, including executive functions and problem-solving skills, are crucial for tasks such as numeracy and literacy development. Language proficiency is similarly essential for communication and comprehension in educational settings (Hoff, 2013).

Numerous studies have emphasized the role of early cognitive and language development in predicting later academic achievement (Blair & Raver, 2015; Bierman et al., 2008). Early interventions that target these domains, such as quality preschool programs, have demonstrated significant benefits in promoting school readiness and reducing achievement gaps (Camilli et al., 2010).

Teacher quality is a vital factor in preschool education and can significantly impact academic outcomes (Hamre & Pianta, 2005). High-quality teachers possess the skills and knowledge to create engaging and developmentally appropriate learning environments. They can effectively facilitate learning, provide individualized support, and foster a love of learning in young children.

Research has consistently indicated that teacher–child interactions characterized by warmth, responsiveness, and instructional support are associated with improved academic and social outcomes for preschoolers (Pianta et al., 2008; Raver et al., 2011). Consequently, efforts to enhance teacher quality and professional development are essential for optimizing the early educational experience.

The classroom environment serves as the immediate context in which preschoolers learn and develop. Factors such as class size, classroom materials, and the overall organization of the learning space can impact academic success (Mashburn et al., 2008; Curby et al., 2009).

Recent studies have highlighted the importance of creating stimulating and inclusive classroom environments that foster exploration, curiosity, and peer interactions (Mashburn et al., 2008). Classrooms designed to support these principles have been associated with positive academic outcomes, as they provide opportunities for active engagement and learning.

In summary, a comprehensive review of the literature underscores the multifaceted nature of factors predicting academic success in preschool children. Socioeconomic background, parental involvement, cognitive and language development, teacher quality, and classroom environment all contribute significantly to early academic outcomes. Understanding the intricate interplay of these factors is essential for designing effective interventions and strategies that ensure a strong academic foundation for young learners.

Socioeconomic background

Socioeconomic background refers to the economic and social conditions in which a child is raised, encompassing factors such as parental income, education, and occupation. It profoundly influences preschool children's academic success (Duncan & Magnuson, 2012). Research indicates that children from lower socioeconomic backgrounds often face disparities in access to educational resources and opportunities, leading to differences in school readiness and later academic achievement (Sirin, 2005).

Recent studies have reaffirmed the significant impact of socioeconomic factors on educational outcomes. For instance, a study by Noble et al. (2015) found that family income is closely linked to brain structure in children, affecting cognitive functions that underlie academic success. Similarly, a longitudinal study by Heckman (2006) emphasized the persistent influence of early socioeconomic disadvantage on later-life outcomes, including educational attainment.

Socioeconomic disparities affect academic achievement through various mechanisms. Limited access to quality early childhood education, fewer educational materials at home, and reduced exposure to stimulating environments can hinder cognitive development (Rouse & Barrow, 2006). In addition, chronic stress associated with economic hardship can negatively impact children's attention, memory, and self-regulation (Evans & Kim, 2010).

Parental involvement

Parental involvement encompasses a range of activities, from assisting with homework to engaging in school-related events. It plays a pivotal role in predicting academic success during the preschool years (Hill et al., 2004). Actively engaged parents can create a supportive home environment that fosters early learning and skill development (Henderson & Mapp, 2002).

Recent research highlights the positive correlation between parental involvement and preschoolers' academic performance. A study by Dearing et al. (2016) demonstrated that parent–child engagement in early literacy activities significantly predicted later reading skills. Similarly, Epstein and Sanders (2002) found that family involvement in schools positively influences student achievement.

Promoting effective parental involvement involves strategies such as regular communication between educators and parents, workshops on supporting children's learning at home, and involving parents in school decision-making (Pomerantz & Moorman, 2010). These strategies enhance children's early learning experiences and contribute to their academic success.

Cognitive and language development

Cognitive development, including executive functions, memory, and problem-solving abilities, lays the foundation for academic success in preschool children (Diamond & Lee, 2011). Language skills, such as vocabulary and communication, are equally crucial as they enable children to engage effectively in educational activities (Lonigan et al., 2008).

Recent research highlights the significance of early cognitive and language development. A study by Carlson et al. (2013) demonstrated that executive functions, including inhibitory control and working memory, predict early math and literacy skills. In addition, Hoff (2013) found that children's language proficiency in preschool is a strong predictor of their later reading comprehension.

Play-based learning and interactive experiences are instrumental in fostering cognitive and language development (Dore et al., 2017). These activities engage children in problem-solving, creative thinking, and language acquisition, facilitating the acquisition of essential skills for academic success.

Teacher quality and classroom environment

Teacher quality and classroom environment significantly impact preschool children's academic outcomes. Skilled educators who provide meaningful learning experiences and individualized support contribute to improved academic and social development (Mashburn et al., 2008). A stimulating classroom environment with adequate resources enhances the learning experience (Pianta et al., 2008).

Research demonstrates the positive impact of high-quality teachers. A study by Early et al. (2010) found that preschool teachers who engage in professional development and create enriched classroom environments foster early literacy skills in children. Moreover, Hamre and Pianta (2005) highlighted the importance of teacher–child interactions characterized by warmth and instructional support in promoting academic success.

Creating an enriching classroom environment involves practices such as providing age-appropriate materials, organizing learning centers, and fostering positive peer interactions (Curby et al., 2009). These practices facilitate active engagement and support academic and social development in preschool children.

Early interventions and educational programs

Early interventions and educational programs play an indispensable role in mitigating potential barriers to academic success among preschool children, especially those hailing from disadvantaged backgrounds (Heckman, 2013). These programs are thoughtfully designed to provide targeted support and enrichment, recognizing that the early years are a critical developmental period when foundational cognitive, socioemotional, and academic skills are established.

Recent research has illuminated the effectiveness of evidence-based interventions and programs in bolstering the educational prospects of young learners. One notable example is the Abecedarian Project, a pioneering initiative explored by Campbell et al. (2012). This project implemented high-quality early childhood education alongside comprehensive support services, leading to remarkable cognitive and socioemotional benefits for its participants. The children who had the opportunity to engage with this program experienced significant gains in cognitive abilities, such as language proficiency and problem-solving skills, as well as substantial improvements in socioemotional development, including enhanced self-regulation and social competence. These gains are vital precursors to academic success, setting a solid foundation for lifelong learning.

Another impactful program is Head Start, a widely recognized initiative evaluated by Puma et al. (2010). This program has consistently demonstrated positive effects on school readiness and long-term academic achievement, particularly among at-risk children. By offering comprehensive early childhood education, health, and family support services, Head Start addresses multiple dimensions of children's development. It equips children with the cognitive and socioemotional skills necessary to navigate the demands of formal schooling successfully.

Incorporating tailored interventions into preschool curricula is a strategic imperative. Programs like Tools of the Mind, thoughtfully examined by Merkley et al. (2023), exemplify this approach. Tools of the Mind places a strong emphasis on structured play and self-regulation activities, recognizing their profound impact on young children's development. By engaging children in activities that promote executive functions, emotional regulation, and social interaction, this program contributes to improved self-control and heightened academic readiness. The intentional integration of these interventions within the preschool curriculum aligns seamlessly with the emergent curriculum approach.

The emergent curriculum approach recognizes that children are active participants in their learning journey. It values individualized, child-centered instruction and acknowledges that children construct knowledge through their experiences and interactions with the environment (Nxumalo et al., 2018). By embracing this approach, early childhood educators create enriched learning environments that are responsive to each child's unique developmental needs and interests. This, in turn, enhances children's learning experiences and fosters their enthusiasm for exploration and discovery.

In conclusion, early interventions and evidence-based educational programs represent indispensable tools in overcoming the challenges that some preschool children may face on their path to academic success. They provide the necessary scaffolding for children to develop essential skills and competencies, ensuring that they enter formal schooling prepared and equipped to thrive. These programs not only bridge existing gaps but also lay the groundwork for a future of continuous learning and achievement.

Discussion and implications

The extensive literature review and the detailed discussions on various factors have illuminated the intricate web of elements contributing to preschool academic success. These factors, including socioeconomic background, parental involvement, cognitive and language development, teacher quality, classroom environment, and early interventions, collectively shape the academic outcomes of young learners (Reardon, 2013). It is crucial to recognize that these factors are not isolated but intricately interlinked, creating a holistic ecosystem within which preschool education operates.

Understanding the interconnections between these factors is paramount for effectively promoting preschool academic success. For example, Nguyen et al. (2016) underscored the synergistic effects of high-quality teachers and supportive classroom environments. It has become increasingly evident that these two elements do not function in isolation but rather interact dynamically to create an optimal learning environment. High-quality teachers possess the pedagogical skills to engage students effectively and adapt their teaching methods to diverse learning needs. When coupled with a supportive classroom environment, which includes ample resources, a positive classroom climate, and opportunities for interactive learning, these combined influences can significantly enhance children's academic trajectories, especially in the crucial early years.

The implications of this research extend far beyond academic circles and have significant implications for various stakeholders, including policymakers, educators, parents, and early childhood program administrators.

Policymakers can draw on this knowledge to advocate for equitable access to high-quality preschool education. Recognizing the profound impact of socioeconomic background on educational outcomes, policymakers can prioritize initiatives aimed at reducing disparities in access to early childhood education. By investing in early education programs that emphasize quality teaching and enriched classroom environments, policymakers can work toward leveling the playing field for all children, regardless of their socioeconomic status.

Educators can tailor their teaching practices and classroom environments to optimize learning for every child. Informed by the latest research, educators can implement evidence-based instructional strategies that cater to the diverse needs and strengths of their students. This includes recognizing the pivotal role of parental involvement and striving to foster collaborative relationships with families. Moreover, educators can advocate for the resources and support necessary to create enriching classroom environments that stimulate curiosity, exploration, and active engagement in learning.

Parents can be encouraged to actively engage in their children's education, recognizing their vital role in the academic journey. Parental involvement goes beyond supporting homework; it includes active participation in a child's learning experiences. This could involve reading with children, engaging in educational activities, and maintaining open communication with teachers. When parents are empowered with knowledge about the factors contributing to academic success, they can provide valuable support at home.

Early childhood programs can integrate evidence-based interventions to provide comprehensive support to young learners. Programs that incorporate elements like structured play, self-regulation activities, and socioemotional development opportunities, as demonstrated in the work of Diamond and Lee (2011) and Rad et al. (2022), can significantly contribute to academic readiness. By adopting a holistic approach that encompasses not only cognitive but also socioemotional development, early childhood programs can lay a solid foundation for future academic achievements.

In summary, the discussions and insights provided by this research emphasize the multidimensional nature of preschool academic success. Understanding how socioeconomic factors, parental involvement, teacher quality, classroom environments, and early interventions interact can inform targeted efforts to enhance early education outcomes. This knowledge empowers stakeholders to work collaboratively toward creating an educational landscape that maximizes the potential of every preschool child, setting the stage for a lifetime of successful learning.

Conclusion

In conclusion, this chapter has explored various factors that predict academic success in preschool children, including socioeconomic background, parental involvement, cognitive and language development, teacher quality, classroom environment, and early interventions. Recent research has provided valuable insights into the influence of these factors.

Understanding and addressing these predictive factors are of paramount significance. Academic success in the preschool years lays the foundation for lifelong learning and development (Heckman, 2008). By recognizing and acting upon these predictors, we can empower young learners with the tools they need for a successful educational journey.

Collaborative efforts between educators, parents, policymakers, and early childhood programs are essential to creating a supportive learning environment. By leveraging the knowledge gained from recent research, we can work together to ensure that all preschool children have an equitable opportunity to thrive academically and beyond.

References

Bierman, K. L., Nix, R. L., Greenberg, M. T., Blair, C., & Domitrovich, C. E. (2008). Executive functions and school readiness intervention: Impact, moderation, and mediation in the Head Start REDI program. *Development and Psychopathology*, *20*(3), 821–843.

Blair, C., & Raver, C. C. (2015). School readiness and self-regulation: A developmental psychobiological approach. *Annual Review of Psychology*, *66*, 711–731.

Camilli, G., Vargas, S., Ryan, S., & Barnett, W. S. (2010). Meta-analysis of the effects of early education interventions on cognitive and social development. *Teachers College Record*, *112*(3), 579–620.

Campbell, F. A., Pungello, E. P., Burchinal, M., Kainz, K., Pan, Y., Wasik, B. H., ... & Ramey, C. T. (2012). Adult outcomes as a function of an early childhood educational program: An Abecedarian Project follow-up. *Developmental Psychology*, *48*(4), 1033–1043.

Curby, T. W., Rimm-Kaufman, S. E., & Ponitz, C. C. (2009). Teacher-child interactions and children's achievement trajectories across kindergarten and first grade. *Journal of Educational Psychology*, *101*(4), 912–925.

Dearing, E., Kreider, H., Simpkins, S., & Weiss, H. B. (2016). Family involvement in school and low-income children's literacy: Longitudinal associations between and within families. *Journal of Educational Psychology*, *108*(7), 1081–1091.

Desimone, L. M. (1999). Linking parent involvement with student achievement: Do race and income matter? *Journal of Educational Research*, *93*(1), 11–30.

Diamond, A., & Lee, K. (2011). Interventions shown to aid executive function development in children 4 to 12 years old. *Science*, *333*(6045), 959–964.

Dore, R. A., Zosh, J. M., Hirsh-Pasek, K., & Golinkoff, R. M. (2017). Plugging into word learning: The role of electronic toys and digital media in language development. In *Cognitive Development in Digital Contexts* (pp. 75–91). Academic Press.

Duncan, G. J., & Magnuson, K. (2012). Socioeconomic status and cognitive functioning: Moving from correlation to causation. *Wiley Interdisciplinary Reviews: Cognitive Science*, *3*(3), 377–386.

Duncan, G. J., & Magnuson, K. (2016). Investing in preschool programs. *Journal of Economic Perspectives*, *30*(2), 159–180.

Duncan, G. J., Yeung, W. J., Brooks-Gunn, J., & Smith, J. R. (1998). How much does childhood poverty affect the life chances of children? *American Sociological Review*, *63*(3), 406–423.

Duncan, G. J., Ziol-Guest, K. M., & Kalil, A. (2007). Early-childhood poverty and adult attainment, behavior, and health. *Child Development*, *78*(1), 306–325.

Early, D. M., Maxwell, K. L., Burchinal, M., Alva, S., Bender, R. H., Bryant, D., ... & Zill, N. (2010). Teachers' education, classroom quality, and young children's academic skills: Results from seven studies of preschool programs. *Child Development*, *81*(1), 280–297.

Epstein, J. L., & Sanders, M. G. (2002). Family, school, and community partnerships. In M. H. Borland (Ed.), *Educating all children: A global agenda* (pp. 97–106). Lawrence Erlbaum Associates.

Evans, G. W., & Kim, P. (2010). Multiple risk exposure as a potential explanatory mechanism for the socioeconomic status–health gradient. *Annals of the New York Academy of Sciences*, 1186(1), 174–189.

Fan, X., & Chen, M. (2001). Parental involvement and students' academic achievement: A meta-analysis. *Educational Psychology Review*, *13*(1), 1–22.

Hamre, B. K., & Pianta, R. C. (2005). Can instructional and emotional support in the first-grade classroom make a difference for children at risk of school failure? *Child Development*, *76*(5), 949–967.

Heckman, J. J. (2006). Skill formation and the economics of investing in disadvantaged children. *Science*, *312*(5782), 1900–1902.

Heckman, J. J. (2008). Schools, skills, and synapses. *Economic Inquiry*, 46(3), 289–324. https://doi.org/10.1111/j.1465-7295.2008.00163.x.

Heckman, J. J. (2013). *Giving kids a fair chance*. MIT Press.

Henderson, A. T., & Mapp, K. L. (2002). *A new wave of evidence: The impact of school, family, and community connections on student achievement*. National Center for Family & Community Connections with Schools.

Hill, N. E., Castellino, D. R., Lansford, J. E., Nowlin, P., Dodge, K. A., Bates, J. E., & Pettit, G. S. (2004). Parent academic involvement as related to school behavior, achievement, and aspirations: Demographic variations across adolescence. *Child Development*, *75*(5), 1491–1509.

Hoff, E. (2013). Interpreting the early language trajectories of children from low-SES and language minority homes: Implications for closing achievement gaps. *Developmental Psychology*, *49*(1), 4–14.

Lonigan, C. J., Burgess, S. R., & Anthony, J. L. (2008). Development of emergent literacy and early reading skills in preschool children: Evidence from a latent-variable longitudinal study. *Developmental Psychology*, *44*(2), 428–442.

Magnuson, K., & Duncan, G. J. (2016). Can early childhood interventions decrease inequality of economic opportunity? *RSF: The Russell Sage Foundation Journal of the Social Sciences*, *2*(2), 123–141.

Mashburn, A. J., Pianta, R. C., Hamre, B. K., Downer, J. T., Barbarin, O. A., Bryant, D., ... & Howes, C. (2008). Measures of classroom quality in prekindergarten and children's development of academic, language, and social skills. *Child Development*, *79*(3), 732–749.

McClelland, M. M., Cameron, C. E., Connor, C. M., Farris, C. L., Jewkes, A. M., & Morrison, F. J. (2007). Links between behavioral regulation and preschoolers' literacy, vocabulary, and math skills. *Developmental Psychology*, *43*(4), 947–959.

Merkley, R., Sernoskie, E., Cook, C. J., Howard, S. J., Makaula, H., Mshudulu, M., ... & Scerif, G. (2023). "We don't have things for counting": An exploration of early numeracy skills and home learning experiences of children growing up in poverty in South Africa. *Journal of Numerical Cognition*, *9*(2), 268–284.

Nguyen, T., Watts, T. W., Duncan, G. J., Clements, D. H., Sarama, J. S., Wolfe, C., & Spitler, M. E. (2016). Which preschool mathematics competencies are most predictive of fifth grade achievement? *Early Childhood Research Quarterly*, *36*, 550–560.

Noble, K. G., Houston, S. M., Kan, E., & Sowell, E. R. (2015). Neural correlates of socioeconomic status in the developing human brain. *Developmental Science*, *18*(5), 713–725.

Nxumalo, F., Vintimilla, C. D., & Nelson, N. (2018). Pedagogical gatherings in early childhood education: Mapping interferences in emergent curriculum. *Curriculum Inquiry*, *48*(4), 433–453.

Pianta, R. C., La Paro, K. M., & Hamre, B. K. (2008). *Classroom Assessment Scoring System (CLASS) Manual, Pre-K*. Brookes.

Pomerantz, E. M., & Moorman, E. A. (2010). Parents' involvement in children's schooling. In B. Laursen, T. D. Little, & N. A. Card (Eds.), *Handbook of developmental research methods* (pp. 341–363). Guilford Press.

Puma, M., Bell, S., Cook, R., Heid, C., Broene, P., Jenkins, F., ... & Downer, J. (2010). *Third grade follow-up to the head start impact study: Final report.* US Department of Health and Human Services.

Rad, D., Redeş, A., Roman, A., Ignat, S., Lile, R., Demeter, E., Egerău, A., Dughi, T., Balaş, E., Maier, R., Kiss, C., Torkos, H. and Rad, G. (2022). Pathways to inclusive and equitable quality early childhood education for achieving SDG4 goal – a scoping review. *Frontiers in Psychology, 13*, 955833. <https/www.doi.org/10.3389/fpsyg.2022.955833>

Ramey, C. T., & Ramey, S. L. (1998). Early intervention and early experience. *American Psychologist*, 53(2), 109–120. https://doi.org/10.1037/0003-066X.53.2.109.

Raver, C. C., Jones, S. M., Li-Grining, C., Zhai, F., Metzger, M. W., & Solomon, B. (2011). Targeting children's behavior problems in preschool classrooms: A cluster-randomized controlled trial. *Journal of Consulting and Clinical Psychology*, *79*(5), 590–600.

Reardon, S. F. (2013). The widening academic achievement gap between the rich and the poor: New evidence and possible explanations. In G. J. Duncan & R. J. Murnane (Eds.), *Whither opportunity? Rising inequality, schools, and children's life chances* (pp. 91–116). Russell Sage Foundation.

Reynolds, A. J., Temple, J. A., Ou, S. R., Arteaga, I. A., & White, B. A. (2010). School-based early childhood education and age-28 well-being: Effects by timing, dosage, and subgroups. *Science*, *333*(6040), 360–364.

Rouse, C. E., & Barrow, L. (2006). School vouchers and student achievement: Recent evidence, remaining questions. *Annual Review of Economics*, *7*, 37–51.

Sirin, S. R. (2005). Socioeconomic status and academic achievement: A meta-analytic review of research. *Review of Educational Research*, *75*(3), 417–453.

Implications of Metacognition in Mentoring

Daniel Mara and Muşata Bocoş

Abstract: Our study aims to examine the relationships between mentoring and metacognition, two intricate and multilayered concepts that are now of particular interest in the field of education. At first glance, it appears that the two ideas are distinct and divergent – mentoring focuses on forming a supportive relationship with another person, whereas metacognition primarily entails introspection and self-discovery of the inner self.

Keywords: mentoring, metacognition, learning-teaching.

Mentoring, Metacognition, and Learning

The interrelationship between mentoring, metacognition, and learning involves a complex process of cognitive, metacognitive, and noncognitive learning, through which affective, psychomotor, and social learning becomes possible in various situations relating to the professional, personal, and social life. Thus, we can see the mentoring process as a construction of a system of learning opportunities for the mentee – opportunities that significantly impact the mentee's teaching style, professional and social behavior, and professional and social development paradigm. These opportunities involve, in a cyclical manner, cognitive and metacognitive (self)reflection; individual and collective learning; cognitive and noncognitive learning; searching; exploratory activities; critical analysis; experimentation with ideas and solutions; monitoring of approaches and processes; critical (re)evaluation of problems, situations, and experiences; and solutions. In practice, mentoring fosters an integrative spiral learning process, increasingly integrating complex and refined cognitive and noncognitive approaches, involving acquisition, practice, deepening, refinement, expansion, etc., with the learning cycle being repeated in different professional and life situations and at different levels of complexity.

The learning opportunities during the mentoring period significantly contribute to shaping the professional profile of the teacher and influencing the learning opportunities that the teacher creates in relation to his/her students. They have major impacts on learning styles, lifestyles, and even sustainable development, which is why the Education Agenda 2030 considers learning as the essential purpose of education. According to the European Parliament and Council's Recommendation – Key Competences for Lifelong Learning 2006/962/EC of 2006, the capacity to actively participate and persist in learning, plan one's own education, and efficiently manage time and information both individually and in groups is known as the learning to learn competence. A framework to evaluate the learning to learn competence has been developed by an expert group (Expert Group established by the European Network of Policy Makers for the Evaluation of Education Systems, 2006). The framework considers two dimensions: cognitive (the capacity to "gain, process and assimilate knowledge," "ability to cope with obstacles") and affective (the desire to learn, motivation, and self-assurance). Experts at the Centre for Research on Lifelong Learning (CRELL) released an updated framework in 2008 that measures competence in learning to learn. This revised framework includes a new dimension called metacognition, which is defined as the body of knowledge we possess about our cognitive functioning, learning abilities, and how to regulate and monitor our own cognitive functioning. Metacognition is thought of as a kind of "control body" for cognition, one that continuously receives information from cognition, assesses it, and then provides feedback about what should be done next.

Educational mentoring is a specific activity that aims to involve the mentee in a process of cognitive, metacognitive, and noncognitive learning and its development, by making use, in a systemic way, of the different learning opportunities corresponding to the mentoring program. In this way, it becomes possible to develop the mentee's metacognitive development – such as metacognitive confidence, metacognitive reflection, and metacognitive acquisitions, including knowledge, strategies, experiences, and skills – as well as the mentor's metacognitive development, such as diversification of metacognitive strategies and improving metacognitive accuracy.

On the other hand, metacognition implies a conscious awareness of one's own cognitive activity, serving as cognitive tool for managing cognitive processes by practicing and educating metacognitions – in other words, it can be seen as self-mentoring.

Main metacognitive acquisitions in the context of mentoring

The psycho-pedagogical values of mentoring are to be perceived in several dimensions of the mentored teachers' personality and, indirectly, in students' personality. The informative and formative dimensions are clearly marked by the support, guidance, and direction provided by the mentor. Mentored teachers accumulate knowledge, develop skills and strategies, and apply ways of solving different problems encountered in different contexts through learning transfer. At the metacognition level, we identify the same categories of changes produced as a result of metacognitive learning activity, changes that involve the accumulation of metacognitive knowledge, the formation and development of metacognitive strategies, and the implementation of metacognitive activities.

1) Metacognitive knowledge

Metacognitive knowledge is related to the declarative aspect of metacognition and refers to the learner's knowledge about cognition, how information is processed, how memory is called upon, how comprehension/understanding of the text takes place, and the products of learning.

Flavell (1987) divides metacognitive knowledge into four categories, considering the elements of reference:

1.a.) Knowledge about human learning in general and knowledge about oneself as a learner, including:

– *knowledge about cognitive processes* in general and *their implications for learning* (motivation, attention, emotional processes, memory)

Examples of mentoring activity: being aware of one's own learning and memory limitations; knowing that emotional involvement increases the quality of professional and social activities; knowing that the output of professional and mentoring activities increases in the morning.

– *knowledge about other learners* to which the subject relates and refers, that is, knowledge about interindividual differences

Examples of mentoring activity: knowing that I learn and develop better with a particular mentor because of their mentoring style; seeing another mentored colleague progressing better than me.

– *knowledge that the subject has about him/herself as a learner*, also called beliefs about intraindividual differences

Examples of mentoring activity: knowledge about the person's attitude to learning: perseverance, consistency, experimentation, collaboration, monitoring, concern for learning from mistakes; knowledge about the functioning of one's own motivational, attentional, and affective processes; knowledge about the most effective ways of solving certain problems; knowledge about the mistakes the person is most likely to make from a particular perspective.

1.b.) Task knowledge: this is knowledge that crystallizes as a result of the person's cognitive experience, based on which comparisons are made with similar learning situations.

Examples of mentoring activity: knowing exactly what needs to be done/what the task requires; quantifying and assessing the difficulty of the task; knowing what kind of effort the task will require; knowing that retaining the spirit of a text is easier than retaining the letter.

1.c.) Knowledge of strategies with a role in achieving autonomy, since possessing it entails understanding which teaching methods, in a certain situation, are successful and which are not; being aware of the strategy the person uses to learn a subject.

1.c.1.) Knowledge of cognitive strategies used in learning tasks.

Examples of mentoring activity: knowledge of appropriateness/relevance, appropriateness, requirements for use/application, effectiveness in particular situations and implications of using particular strategies; rehearsal/exercise strategies (e.g., skills and abilities to develop curriculum documents); knowledge processing strategies (identification of main ideas of a text, summarizing, paraphrasing, memorizing); knowledge organization strategies (corroborating and connecting information, constructing concept maps) (Weinstein & Mayer, 1986).

1.c.2.) Knowledge of metacognitive strategies (Livingston, 1997) used in learning tasks.

Examples of mentoring activity: Knowledge of planning learning approaches (e.g., formulating goals and formulating objectives under them); knowledge of monitoring learning approaches (e.g., formulating (self)questions while reading a text); knowledge of the steps needed to carry out learning actions and to argue the necessity of these steps, taking into account knowledge of oneself as a learner); knowledge of how to control one's own learning (e.g., re-reading a text which has been difficult, not sufficiently understood, in order to understand the text correctly and fully; correlating certain key terms and phrases).

1.d.) Conditional/strategic knowledge concerning the how, where, and why specific cognitive and metacognitive techniques are applied, the criteria for choosing a certain strategy, depending on the work task or the specificities of the proximal or distal learning context, the ability to allocate selective, personalized, intellectual and physical resources, depending on the learning task, the possibility of self-regulating learning.

Example of mentoring activity: The mentee, knowing the mentor's preferences for a particular working strategy, will adapt more quickly and effectively to the requirements of the mentoring program.

2) Metacognitive strategies

Metacognitive strategies are related to the metacognitive procedural aspect and refer to the use and adaptation of metacognitive knowledge in order to manage one's own mental activity, to regulate cognitive activity.

The formation of these strategies is gradual and, once formed, they can be trained and developed through practice. They are applied in articulated and coherent activities by:

- planning, control, and monitoring while completing an educational activity;
- assessment of the moment of achievement of a goal;
- assessment of the degree of achievement of an aim.

The effectiveness of metacognitive strategies in the learning process is ensured by aspects such as:

- the degree of orientation toward achieving learning targets: goals and objectives;
- the extent to which so-called self-oriented feedback is provided;
- the quality of effective use of attentional resources;
- the quality of effective use of cognitive strategies;
- the extent to which the person is aware of the degree of understanding of the material being studied (see, e.g., Suarez Riveiro et al., 2001).

Examples of mentoring activity (Brown, 1987; Lafortune et al., 2000; Pintrich, 2002, etc.):

2.1.) Anticipatory strategies, which involve the "self system" (Marzano, 1998), i.e., the system of values, beliefs, and personal motivations:

- *foresight* – anticipation activities: of the results of cognitive action; of its goals; of the ways to monitor and regulate it;
- *planning the cognitive process* – anticipating the stages of an action; choosing working strategies according to the goal, the evaluation criteria, and possibly other factors;
- *allocation of resources* – time, cognitive effort, attention, etc., to achieve performance.

2.2.) Follow-up strategies, which involve prospective (carried out before and during learning) or retrospective (carried out after learning has taken place) actions (Nelson & Narens, 1990; Hertzog & Dixon, 1994) by:

- *assessment* of effectiveness: action plan, working strategy, quality of use of resources, progress, difficulty of learning, etc.;
- *regular self-testing* to ensure progress;
- *monitoring* of expected performance; sense of knowledge – assessment of the extent to which an item is memorized or can be recognized, confidence in response, etc.

Marzano (1998) talks about monitoring "dispositions," that is, the intellectual and affective readiness of the person involved in the cognitive activity to approach the learning task in a way that enhances the efficiency of the cognitive processes involved. He identifies the following dimensions involved in disposition monitoring:

- monitoring accuracy and precision;
- monitoring clarity of approach and conclusions;
- monitoring impulsivity bias;
- monitoring the intensity of involvement in the work task;
- monitoring the degree of focus on the work task.

Also, one of the learning mediation directions, that of self-regulation and behavioral control in Feuerstein's (2002) Theory of Mediated Learning Experience, is superimposable over the above-mentioned monitoring dimensions.

2.3.) Adjustment/evaluation/control strategies consist of modifying the action steps, following the evaluations made during the course or the final evaluation, according to the monitoring results, in relation to the expectations, the goals, and the action model.

Examples of mentoring: reviewing and reformulating the aims of the mentoring program; reviewing the conclusions drawn at the end of a mentoring activity; reallocating resources to different activities; making corrections to the actions undertaken.

3) Metacognitive experiences

Metacognitive experiences are judgments, that is, experiences of a metacognitive nature that occur in the process of solving a learning task, in relation to how to work, how to achieve learning, learning efficiency, etc. They refer to moments of awareness of metacognitive processes, which are both cognitive and affective in nature (Flavell, 1979) and can occur at any time before, during, or after the unfolding of a cognitive process, especially in challenging knowledge/learning contexts.

Basically, metacognitive experiences involve:

- on the one hand, awareness of concrete aspects in the task solving process:
  Example of mentoring activity: awareness that if the learning activity was continuously reviewed with the help of the mentor, the effectiveness was better and the task was better accomplished.

- on the other hand, experiencing a state of satisfaction or dissatisfaction about the accomplishment of the learning objectives and the nature of the learning process:
  Example of mentoring activity: the mentee experiences a state of satisfaction for participating in a mentoring program designed according to his/her own professional needs.

Metacognitive learnability in the context of mentoring

A highly relevant acquisition for educational sciences is that metacognitions are educable, so it is appropriate and necessary to carry out the metacognitive training of the educable (Bocoş, 2013; Chiş, 2002; Frumos, 2005; Joiţa, 2006, etc.). In the context of mentoring, this metacognitive training is possible if consider its specific metacognitive educability.

In the context of mentoring, the mentee's capacity for learning or self-education from a metacognitive perspective, as well as their potential to be open to the metacognitive support system and the molding effects of metacognitive training, are all considered aspects of their personality that are considered to be metacognitively educable. To help mentees (self)educate from a metacognitive perspective, a "molecular analysis" of the cognitive operations performed as well as the metacognitive acquisitions involved in mentoring processes is required. This is because there is a reciprocal and direct relationship between the level of cognitive development, the quality of cognitive performances, and the quality and functionality of metacognitions.

As mentees develop and refine their metacognitive acquisitions and educate themselves metacognitively, conditions must be satisfied in order for them to acquire metacognitive intelligence. This approach requires that the development of metacognitive acquisition is viewed in a systemic way, integrated across the whole mentoring program, by ensuring that metacognitive education is embedded in cognitive education.

As a result, metacognition is a useful part of mentoring and a cognitive tool for arranging, arranging, structuring, controlling, enhancing, and increasing the effectiveness of cognitive processes (Bocoş et al., 2021). Gradually, this tool becomes increasingly powerful, facilitating the overall involvement of the mentee and the achievement of increasingly higher cognitive and non-cognitive performances.

Metacognition in initial and in-service teacher training programs

Metacognition is a very important component of teacher training. In order to prepare teachers to learn from their pedagogical actions, anticipate them, revise their teaching activity while doing it, and reflect (cognitively and metacognitively) on the outcomes and strategies applied, it is important for them to develop their metacognitive competences during initial and in-service training.

A detailed analysis of national and international initial and in-service training programs shows that there are few courses or topics on metacognition, which leads us to stress the need to introduce a scientific approach to this issue in theoretical and practical research. In the current circumstances, a partial or more extensive solution to this situation can be achieved by addressing the topic of metacognition through educational mentoring programs. The training and development of metacognitive skills in the mentee is aimed not only at knowledge of one's own way of thinking and acting, but also at achieving a higher level of intellectual activity, materialized in continuous training with the aim of improving, enhancing, and optimizing it.

When the mentee becomes aware of his/her own cognitive functioning, both in terms of the informational and formative components, he/she will be able to design, organize, and implement activities aimed at increasing the quality of the educational activities he/she carries out.

In the educational field, mentoring activity is primarily aimed at developing the mentee's competences required for teaching. Metacognitive competences are an important category of transversal competences alongside digital competences, project and partnership design competences, communication and ethical commitment competences, etc. Metacognitive competences are a category of competences that refers to the person's ability to undertake and effectively complete their learning, study, and knowledge processes, and to organize these processes themselves, including through effective time and information management, both individually and in groups.

Metacognitive skills include skills of goal setting, planning, systematic approach, task orientation, selection of working methods and tools, (self) observation, (self)analysis, (self)reflection, (self)control, (self)evaluation of outcome, and giving (self)feedback.

Metacognitive competences, as transversal competences, are interdependent with the fundamental (basic) competences of teachers, such as specialist (scientific) competences, psycho-pedagogical (educational or teaching) competences, psychosocial competences, and managerial competences.

Once formed, developed, and practiced by teachers, metacognitive skills can be cultivated in students. The process of cultivating metacognitive skills in pupils requires a specific attitude on the part of teachers, evidenced by involvement, quality training, and, above all, awareness of the intellectual benefits gained through this approach. In this way, the pupil can continually strive to improve his or her cognitive functioning and the learning process as a whole, which will also be an essential basis for future professional activity.

The training and development of metacognitive skills in school contributes significantly to the achievement of long-term educational, social, economic, and cultural goals. Thus, metacognitive competences are essential for lifelong learning, effective intellectual activity, and ensuring a quality life for the elderly.

Every person has to use metacognitive thinking in order to learn new things constantly and adjust to changing circumstances. Learning is acknowledged as a contribution to social justice, sustainable development, and global citizenship, and Binkley et al. (2012) claim that metacognition is a 21st-century talent (UNESCO, 2019). Metacognition is the term used to describe people's conscious actions of cognitive operations as well as their knowledge, judgments, and beliefs about their cognitive potential (Flavell, 1976; Yerdelen-Damar et al., 2015; Zohar & Barzilai, 2013;).

A metacognitively mature person will know what they want to accomplish and how to do it. Modeling metacognitive thinking requires an understanding of the difference between metacognitive knowledge and metacognitive abilities. The processes involved in controlling and altering the course of cognitive activity are referred to as metacognitive abilities. It includes proactive planning, process monitoring, and assessment while carrying out a cognitive activity (Yerdelen-Damar et al., 2015). These abilities increase the person's awareness of the thought processes that go into the action.

Effective and authentic mentoring activity consists of a series of actions that provide multiple opportunities for educational practice contextualized in the educational reality of the school. Opportunities for practice should be frequent in educational training, including a comprehensive repertoire of learning activities and assessment assignments currently present in in-service training programs, in order for trainee instructors to master teaching. Training instructors may master teaching in safe environments with mentors by progressively tackling the complexity of the subject through the incorporation of practice opportunities in learning activities (Matsumoto-Royo et al., 2022).

At least three fundamental components may be identified, according to the findings of a study that aimed to address the following question: what factors that support lifelong learning and metacognition should be taken into consideration in the learning evaluation procedures of pre-service teachers? The first relates to evaluation activities as practice opportunities that are appropriate, including information and abilities that are often used in the field (authentic), like lesson preparation and role-playing as a teacher. The development of metacognitive planning and monitoring abilities is aided by these exercises.

The second fundamental element relates to the assessment procedures taking into account the earlier dissemination of guidelines and assessment standards to the student teacher. Apart from elucidating the task, the correspondence ought to furnish information regarding its pertinence to the professional milieu, explore potential novel approaches to its resolution, and bolster the organization of goals, tactics, schedule, and assets for its implementation. This element is crucial for helping new instructors become more curious and build their metacognitive planning abilities.

The third element consists of the regular feedback that teacher trainers and peers give both during and after tasks are completed. In addition to encouraging reflective attitudes (through questions) on the desired objectives, performance, and tactics used, this should also emphasize the performance of the instructors in training and support their metacognitive evaluation (Matsumoto-Royo et al., 2022).

The mentoring activity is guided by a multitude of objectives, all of which are convergent with increasing quality in the educational process. Teaching practice mentoring and teaching career mentoring aim at training and developing teachers' core and transversal competences. Metacognitive competencies are a subset of transversal competencies that pertain to an individual's capacity to initiate and efficiently navigate learning, study, and knowledge processes.

This includes the ability to self-organize these processes, including efficient time and information management, both individually and in groups. The main metacognitive acquisitions in the context of mentoring are metacognitive knowledge, metacognitive strategies, and metacognitive experiences.

References

Binkley, M., Erstad, O., Herman, J., Raizen, S., Ripley, M., Miller-Ricci, M., … et al. (2012). Defining twenty-first-century skills. In P. Griffin, B. McGaw, & E. Care (Eds.), *Assessment and teaching of 21st-century skills* (pp. 17–66). Springer.

Bocoş, M.-D. (2013). *Interactive training. Axiological and methodological milestones*. Polirom Publishing House.

Bocoş, M.-D. (coord.), Răduţ-Taciu, R., & Stan, C. (2021). *Dictionary of pedagogy*. Cluj University Press Publishing House.

Brown, A. (1987), Metacognition, executive control, self-regulation and other more mysterious mechanisms. In F. E. Weinert & R. Kluwe (Eds.), *Metacognition, motivation and understanding mechanisms*. L. Erlbaum Associates.

Brown, B. B. (2004). Adolescents' relationships with peers. In R. M. Lerner & L. Steinberg (Eds.), *Handbook of adolescent psychology* (2nd ed., pp. 363–394). Hoboken, NJ: Wiley.

Chiş. V. (2002). *The teacher's activity between curriculum and evaluation*. Presa Universitară Clujeană.

European Union (2006). Recommendation of the European Parliament and of the Council of 18 December 2006 on key competences for education and lifelong learning (2006/962/CE). *Journal Officiel de L'Union Européenne*, *L394*(10). <https://eur-lex.europa.eu/legal-content/FR/ALL/?uri=CELEX%3A32006H0962>

Feuerstein, R. (2002). Preface for English version. In M. Skuy (Ed.), *The experience of mediated learning in the classroom and outside it* (A. Domuţa, trans.). ASCR Publishing House.

Flavell, J. H. (1976). Metacognitive aspects of problem-solving. In L. B. Resnick (Ed.), *The nature of intelligence* (pp. 231–235), L. Erlbaum Associates.

Flavell, J. H. (1979). Metacognition and cognition monitoring: A new area of cognitive developmental inquiry. *American Psychologist*, *34*, 906–911.

Flavell, J. H. (1987). Speculations about the nature and development of metacognition. In F. E. Weinert & R. Kluwe (Eds.), *Metacognition, motivation and understanding mechanisms*. L. Erlbaum Associates.

Frumos, F. (2005). Reconsiderations of didactics from the perspectives of cognitive psychology [unpublished doctoral dissertation]. Alexandru Ioan Cuza University.

Hertzog, C., & Dixon, R. A. (1994). Metacognitive development in adulthood and old age. In J. Metcalfe & A. P. Shimamura (Eds.), *Metacognition: Knowing about knowing* (pp. 227–251). MIT Press.

Joita, E. (2006). Instruirea constructivistă – o alternativă *Constructivist instruction – an alternative*. Bucharest: Aramis Press.

Lafortune, L., Jacob, S., & Herbert, D. (2000). *Pour guider la metacognition*. Presse Universite du Quebec.

Livingston, J. (1997). *Metacognition: An overview*. State University of New York at Buffalo.

Marzano, R. J. (1998). *A theory-based meta-analysis of research on instruction*. Mid-continent Regional Educational Laboratory, Aurora, Colorado.

Matsumoto-Royo, K., Ramírez-Montoya, M. S., & Glasserman-Morales, L. D. (2022). Lifelong learning and metacognition in the assessment of pre-service teachers in practice-based teacher education. *Frontiers in Education*, 7. <https://www.doi.org/10.3389/feduc.2022.879238>; <https://www.frontiersin.org/articles/10.3389/feduc.2022.879238/full>

Nelson, T. O., & Narens, L. (1994). Why investigate metacognition? In J. Metcalfe & A. P. Shimamura (Eds.), *Metacognition: Knowing about knowing* (pp. 1–25). Cambridge, MA: MIT Press.

Pintrich, P. R. (2002). The role of metacognitive knowledge in learning, teaching, and assessing. *Theory Into Practice*, 41(4), 219–225. https://doi.org/10.1207/s15430421tip4104_3.

Suárez Riveiro, J. M., González Cabanach, R., & Valle Arias, A. V. (2001). Multiple-goal pursuit and its relation to cognitive, self-regulatory, and motivational strategies. *British Journal of Educational Psychology*, 71(4), 561–572.

UNESCO (2019). *UNESCO Institute for Lifelong Learning: Annual report 2018*. UNESCO.

Weinstein, C. E., & Mayer, R. E. (1986). The teaching of learning strategies. In M. C. Wittrock (Ed.), *Handbook of research on teaching* (3rd ed., pp. 315–327). New York: Macmillan.

Yerdelen-Damar, S., Özdemir, O. F., & Ünal, C. (2015). Pre-service physics teachers' metacognitive knowledge about their instructional practices. *Eurasia Journal of Mathematics, Science and Technology Education*, *11*, 1009–1026. <https://www.doi.org/10.12973/eurasia.2015.1370a>

Zohar, A., & Barzilai, S. (2013). A review of research on metacognition in science education: current and future directions. *Studies in Science Education*, *49*, 121–169. <https://www.doi.org/10.1080/03057267.2013.84726>

The Impact of Nonformal Education on Student's Social Experiences

Alina Felicia Roman, Horațiu Catalano, and Editha-Margareta Coşarbă

Abstract: Social competence is characterized by the capacity to adeptly navigate social interactions. This concept encompasses an individual's capability to establish and sustain intimate relationships while adapting appropriately to various social contexts. Considering the intricate nature of social exchanges, social competence emerges from an extensive array of cognitive functions, emotional mechanisms, behavioral aptitudes, social perceptiveness, and personal and cultural values pertinent to interpersonal connections. The extent to which social skills are acquired and used determines the degree of social adaptation of the individual. Student behavior is influenced by the expectation of reciprocated benefits, whether received or anticipated. Participants are solely responsible for ensuring their partner's well-being, a responsibility that arises from their social engagements. Therefore, social exchange equates to social interaction.

Keywords: nonformal education, social competencies, social experiences.

Introduction

Nonformal education has evolved into a distinct subsystem within the broader educational framework, primarily focused on identifying and nurturing individual skills. The principal aim of nonformal education – to foster wisdom, achievement, and personal growth – aligns with the goals of formal education (Hoppers, 2006).

Nonformal education encompasses a diverse array of educational objectives, which can be categorized into informational and formative objectives. Informational objectives pertain to the acquisition of new knowledge, the enhancement of existing knowledge, the analysis of content elements, and the reorganization of these elements. Formative objectives, on the other hand, are geared toward developing transferable skills across various aspects of human life, including self-awareness and personal development, effective communication, conflict resolution, collaboration, and creativity.

Since nonformal education is centered on the development of students, it generates flexible characteristics in terms of the processes, objectives, and substances that are instituted and implemented. Consequently, through nonformal education, it is vital to respond to the transformations that may affect the demands of students and implicitly of the community (Zaki Dib, 1987).

Given its scope, nonformal education includes a multitude of educational situations, which in most cases have significantly contributed to the revitalization of educational systems and curriculum and methods, techniques, and training procedures. In relation to the benchmarks of the concept of nonformal education, the analysis of correspondence learning, distance learning, and open systems was carried out, which, due to their characteristics, are included in the area of nonformal education (Murphy et al., 2019).

The sociological approach to nonformal education

The major sociological principles of nonformal education include multisectoral activities, close community relations, and economic development at either the individual or societal level.

The interrelationship within nonformal educational activities plays a significant role in enhancing the social well-being of the community to which we belong. Active participation by community members is crucial for the success of these activities. Individual involvement in the planning and management of every aspect of nonformal educational programs fosters a sense of ownership among participants and increases the relevance of these activities to their needs. Engagement in nonformal educational activities facilitates the integration of education into the procedural and social structures that individuals interact with in their daily lives (Riezen, 1996).

Lewis and Geach (1962) points out that, due to the particularity and significance of nonformal education, there are multiple principles that must be taken into account, so nonformal education must be consistent with the following principles:

1. Nonformal education is accessible to all, regardless of previous educational achievements.
2. Maximum flexibility. Educational institutions can adjust the flexibility of nonformal education during the proposed activities to achieve results or meet the needs of the participants, to the maximum possible extent.
3. The nonformal education model should be learner-centered rather

than teacher-centered.
4. The relationship between teachers and students is informal.
5. Nonformal education is focused on practical skills and knowledge, on the development of creativity.

Nonformal education offers students, young people, and middle-aged people the opportunity to develop their values, skills, and competences, which are different from those developed within the structure of formal education. Skills cover a wide range of competencies such as interpersonal, group, organizational and conflict resolution, cross-cultural awareness, leadership, planning, organizing, controlling, directing, coordinating and practical problem-solving skills, teamwork, self-confidence, discipline, and responsibility (Muro & Jeffrey, 2008).

What is remarkable about nonformal education is that all those involved – beneficiaries and facilitators – are people who show enthusiasm in the process of education and learning. The nonformal learning process requires the creation and development of an environment in which the student himself is the designer of his skills (Nomikou, 2006).

Beyond the factors influencing students' decisions to engage in nonformal educational activities, teachers, leveraging their level of professional training, can significantly enrich the psychological education experience. With an abundance of educational resources, students are likely to participate more responsibly if the activities offered are limited to a select few. Consequently, it is imperative to develop a continuous professional development plan for teachers in the realm of nonformal education. This strategy aims to enhance the quality of nonformal education and positively impact students' personality development (Bradea, 2012).

The involvement of students in structured nonformal education activities organized within educational units is crucial, as it fosters personality development, cultivates positive attitudes toward learning, and enhances skills and problem-solving strategies. According to Feldman and Matjasko (2007), nonformal education activities yield several positive outcomes for students, including:

- improved academic performance;
- reduced school dropout rates;
- enhanced psychological well-being, increased self-esteem, and fewer anxieties about the future;
- decreased feelings of social isolation; and

– lower incidence of delinquent behaviors.

Social competence includes factors such as cognitive experience, communicativeness, the ability to understand the messages transmitted, the ability to solve problems, creativity in thinking and action, communication and interpersonal cooperation in the group, the attitude of confidence in oneself and others, the attitude of overcoming the obstacles that appear in the way of achieving goals, the flexible style of approaching tasks, sincerity, responsibility and empathy in interpersonal relationships, the need for knowledge, affection, and social valorization (Dumitru, 1998). The foundations of social competence are laid in the family, at the youngest ages, to which elements of the personal value system are added, during the years of study, through formal and nonformal education.

Theoretical analysis proves that certain behavioral components are present in the structure of social skills – that is, skills that help the individual to recognize social signals and respond appropriately to them, to behave in a way where the potential to receive support from the environment is maximum (Walker, 2005). Students need to develop social skills in order to be accepted in their environment, solve problems with others, deepen other life skills, help reduce collegial conflicts, and be more enthusiastic. In the following, we identify some qualified behaviors from a social point of view, which facilitate the social integration of the student in the student class community.

Social skills can be classified according to the fields of their development, namely substantiation, interaction, and emotional skills. These are manifested in social interactions and are necessary in order to recognize and be aware of the feelings of others, respectively, for understanding social norms and choosing an appropriate behavior in different situations (Canney & Byrne, 2006).

We consider it reasonable to classify social skills according to their functional areas:

Interactional competence consists of the management and control skills of interpersonal interactions, which include the management of one's own behavior and the skills to manage and control the interaction of others with oneself (e.g., ability to withstand negative effect, etc.).

Communication skills are characterized by their intricate structure, comprising abilities of varying complexity. Analysis of this structure reveals that communication skills encompass multiple levels of complexity. Various authors primarily associate communication skills with the ability to initiate and sustain both verbal and nonverbal contact (Bellack et al., 2004; Gevorgianienė, 1999; Rapee et al., 2000). Furthermore, nonverbal communication skills, which precede verbal communication, hold significant importance. In some instances, such as in cases of speech underdevelopment, nonverbal communication becomes predominant, effectively substituting for verbal communication.

Emotional and social cognitive skills demonstrate integration and overlap, evident in various communication and interpersonal activities. Emotional competencies, as outlined by Gailienė et al. (1996), encompass self-awareness skills. Of particular relevance are emotional expressiveness and emotional sensitivity, which intersect with communication skills.

Emotional competencies serve to enhance and enliven both verbal and nonverbal communication. Emotional expressiveness, situated within the realm of nonverbal information exchange, encompasses not only the ability to articulate the need for communication but also demonstrates an individual's capacity to convey emotions in a manner comprehensible and acceptable to others. Emotional sensitivity involves discerning the emotions of others, while emotional control entails managing and regulating one's emotional states and nonverbal expressions. In addition, it involves masking one's emotional state and averting spontaneous emotional outbursts (Malinauskas, 2004).

The foundation of social sensitivity is formed by skills such as awareness of social norms and recognition and assessment of the emotional state of partners. Both the knowledge of and practical reference to social norms in various social situations require a high level of social and emotional intelligence.

Social cognitive skills reflect the person's orientation in social life, understanding the logic of interpersonal relationships, expectations from the point of view of the surrounding people, and controlling behavior corresponding to expectations. The social competences of each area are revealed by the ability to send and interpret verbal and nonverbal information (body language, facial expressions, emotions) and to control the quality of one's own communication.

In summary, communication skills hold a pivotal position within the framework of social skills. While intricately linked to cognitive and emotional abilities, communication skills manifest in observable behavioral forms, particularly in managing and controlling interactions.

Communication plays a foundational role in fostering the development of various other social skills. It facilitates learning avenues for expressing socially acceptable behaviors and emotions, regulates the expression of behaviors and emotions, facilitates constructive conflict resolution, and fortifies interpersonal bonds. Conversely, communication serves as both a catalyst and a prerequisite for the cultivation of social skills. The development of communication and other social competencies is contingent upon social and educational interactions.

Training of social skills in educational institutions – between necessity and possibility

According to Eccles (1999), students who have attained academic success and honed their social skills view participation in extracurricular activities as a significant aspect of their school experience. Conversely, findings from the study indicate that students who perceive themselves as lacking proficiency in academic, social, or other endeavors are more prone to exhibiting symptoms of depression, social withdrawal, and heightened levels of anger and aggression. Consequently, the author asserts that students' level of social competence functions as a reciprocal influence on their academic achievement, performance, and self-perception.

In any educational program, teachers and students interact in an environmental context. Broadly defined, this context includes the physical structures, objects, and organization of the classroom; temporal organization of routines and activities; as well as the emotional climate of the setting. These elements can be manipulated to create an optimal framework facilitating the development of students' social skills.

The arrangement of the physical environment plays a pivotal role in fostering the cultivation of social competence. Organizing spaces such as classrooms, learning environments, or educational facilities into well-defined areas of interest facilitates group access and sets the stage for the development of interpersonal skills and knowledge. Certain areas of interest, primarily social in nature, afford ample opportunities for the practice of social skills through informal activities. Conversely, other areas may offer secluded spaces conducive to self-regulation. Establishing a private, comfortable space can serve as a retreat for students during times of heightened frustration, providing them with a sanctuary for relaxation (Moore, 1996).

Careful selection of the teaching staff for the nonformal activities can influence the positive self-identity of the students, contributing to the development of the students' sense of social competence, as an adequate programming of the nonformal activities, from the point of view of physical, emotional development, and educational needs of students, and provide them with adequate time to practice planning and decision-making skills on how to use their free time (McClellan & Katz, 2001).

Nonformal education and students' social experiences

Nonformal educational activities are directly influenced by the formation of students' social competence. Their social experiences, as well as the motivational, cognitive, behavioral, and social value components of social competence, can influence the successful implementation of the proposed nonformal activities.

The motivational component of social competence stimulates the student's personality to "assume" the need for the formation of social competence, by reflecting on his own behavior.

The cognitive component presupposes the acquisition by the student of a certain level of social intelligence; knowledge about society, laws, and social relations; knowledge about themselves and their place in life; capacity for self-determination and self-realization; and an understanding of the laws of social life, society, and the world.

The behavioral component is characterized by the presence of social interaction skills and abilities, in the context of productive cooperation with different group partners, playing different social roles and finding compromise and mutual understanding with other people. This component deals with students' attitudes and interactions with peers and their willingness to cooperate and work in a team.

The social value component of social competence refers to students' need to be responsible and to form their own principles, level of tolerance, and other values oriented for the purpose of social and personal progress.

Nonformal education provides a set of necessary social experiences, complementing other forms of education by:

- capitalizing on students' free time, from an educational point of view;
- opportunities for capitalizing on students' life experiences, through a more flexible, open framework and through the diversification of everyday learning environments;
- voluntary, individual, or collective participation;

- flexible ways to respond to students' interests through the wide range of activities it proposes and the possibility for each student to decide which activities to participate in;
- developing skills for life and preparing young people to become active citizens;
- formation of organizational, self-management, time management, critical thinking, decision-making, or problem-solving skills; and
- a framework for practicing and cultivating different inclinations, skills, and capacities, for manifesting talents in art, culture, music, sports, painting, IT, etc.

Social relations of the students

Social relations extend into reciprocity-dependent interactions, where participants increasingly rely on each other. These interactions underscore similarities in attitudes, needs, and values, stemming from social exchanges involving information or goods, rather than mere potential for interaction (Kelley & Thibaut, 1978).

In social psychology, two distinct forms of social relations are noted (Clark & Mills, 1979): communal relations, which encompass affiliations with friends, colleagues, and family members; and exchange relations, which encompass all others. In communal relationships, individuals orient their behavior toward the well-being of their counterparts. In exchange relationships, learners' behavior is guided by the reciprocity of received or anticipated benefits. Participants are bound only by the obligation to ensure each other's well-being, which arises from their social interactions. Therefore, social exchange equates to social interaction.

The term reciprocity encompasses social interactions involving giving and returning or repaying what one has received, though it is not explicitly used in describing social relations. Younnis (1980) delineates two forms of reciprocity:

- Symmetrical reciprocity: Situations wherein two students make equivalent contributions to a social exchange or collegial relationship.
- Complementary reciprocity: Situations wherein the contributions of the two students are not equivalent but are compensatory or complementary.

Any relationship involves mixtures of symmetrical and complementary reciprocity. Although reciprocity may be a defining characteristic of friendships and other social relationships, the construct is both similar and different. Both children and adults use norms of reciprocity in interpreting and guiding their social behavior. Berndt (1977) posits that reciprocity is the fundamental structure of students' collegiate friendships. This reciprocity evolves based on mutual interests, alignment of emotional and psychological states, and shared concern (Selman, 1980).

A social relationship can be broadly understood as an interaction between individuals. More precisely, it is a relationship between individuals as members of a group, between groups of people, or between an individual and a group. The group in question could be defined by ethnicity, kinship, social institutions or organizations, social classes or strata, nations, populations, gender, and so forth. Social relationships are defined by the quality of interactions between individuals within a society. Individuals with active social relationships generally experience higher levels of life satisfaction and happiness. This positive impact on personal well-being can be attributed to several benefits. Primarily, social relationships are crucial in affirming an individual's sense of self, fulfilling the basic human need for belonging, and providing positive affirmation (Deci & Ryan, 2002).

A student's well-being is enhanced by the number of trustworthy individuals with whom they can discuss important issues or problems. Conversely, their well-being diminishes in the presence of adults or strangers (Taylor et al., 2001). The existence of social relationships positively influences a child's mental and physical health, contributing to overall well-being, whereas the absence of such relationships increases vulnerability to suffering.

Friendship among students, like many relationships, is significantly influenced by opportunities, social values, and the decision to form a particular bond. This suggests that friendships often stem from positive interpersonal relationships that hold importance and meaning for the child. Support from friends and colleagues is usually voluntary, supported only by feelings of affection, reciprocity, and love and not motivation or moral obligations (typical of family ties). However, friendships can also play a negative role in a person's well-being through the fear of being criticized or excluded from the group.

The contingent nature of curriculum development in nonformal education

The curriculum in nonformal education is substantiated by the argument that curriculum theory, initially developed within the formal education system, is also applicable to the nonformal sector (McGrath & Kelly, 1986). D'Hainaut (1986) supports the implementation of a curriculum in a nonformal context, defining it as a conscious, organized educational action that does not necessarily need to be formal. He emphasizes that nontraditional forms of education require meticulous preparation.

Eisdorfer and Lawton (1973) emphasize the cultural dimension of the curriculum. They interpret culture in a sociological and anthropological sense, encompassing a broad spectrum that includes knowledge, beliefs, art, morals, laws, and more. Factors such as the well-being of the student, their educational needs, the environment, the structure of the activities, the learning experience, andragogy or pedagogy, the teaching staff or the facilitator of the activity, and the purpose of the activities, all together, determine the need for a curriculum in nonformal education. The student should determine what is taught, how, where and when it is taught. A symbiotic relationship should be created between student/learner and teacher/facilitator (Squires, 1992).

The educational needs of the participants should determine the curriculum. The author identifies a possible conflict between what is seen as individual needs and the needs of society or community, and these do not always converge.

In conclusion, curriculum development in nonformal education must be situational or contingent. This contingent nature results from several factors, including (Hayden & Thompson, 1995):

1. The nature of nonformal education: characteristics of nonformal education, which include flexibility, organized structure, content and diversity of methods, orientation to the student, and life and environment.
2. Characteristics of the clientele/participants: the clientele of nonformal education is heterogeneous, consisting of groups and subgroups with various learning needs. These include literate and illiterate adults, out-of-school youth and adolescents, and the elderly and the unemployed, among others. Learner characteristics are factors that determine curriculum content and methods, in addition to the duration and location of programs.
3. Variability and volatility of the nonformal environment: The nonformal learning environment is subject to constant change due to

> the changing needs and circumstances of learners. Changes in the socioeconomic environment will impact on the nonformal learning environment – for example, technological changes will result in new learning needs and affect the responses that nonformal education can make to its clientele.

The issue of nonformal education has been examined through the lens of variables that influence students' decisions to participate in nonformal educational activities within schools or other institutions. Starting from the premise of student-centered education, the primary variable is the student's interest in the proposed topic. Many students associate nonformal activities with physical exercise, perceiving them primarily as a form of relaxation and subsequently as a means to enhance physical fitness. While it is important to respect students' interests, they should sometimes be guided to choose activities not solely based on immediate satisfaction but also on their potential for long-term success.

Another significant variable in selecting nonformal activities within a school is the educational conditions provided by the institution. The efficacy of nonformal education is substantially influenced by the size and organizational level of the school, as well as its human, educational, and financial resources, and the quality of its educational and teaching processes (Stearnes & Glennie, 2010). In addition, the impact of informal education on students' personality development is a critical consideration. Opinions vary, with some believing that nonformal education is highly effective in achieving comprehensive learning, while others point to the lack of a rigorous methodology for activity implementation. However, research by Okamoto et al. (2013) demonstrates that students with strong academic performance tend to participate more in nonformal activities. The positive impact of nonformal education includes optimizing school performance, increasing student participation in school organizations and NGOs, and reducing deviant behaviors both within and outside the school setting.

Furthermore, beyond the factors influencing students' participation in nonformal educational activities, teachers, based on their level of professional training, can significantly enhance their experience of psychological education. Given the abundance of educational resources, students may engage more responsibly if the available activities are limited to a few options. Thus, it is essential to develop a continuous professional development plan for teachers in the field of nonformal education. This approach aims to improve the quality of nonformal education, significantly impacting students' personality development (Bradea, 2012).

The participation of students in structured nonformal education activities, organized in educational units, is an important element, because it contributes to the development of their personality, helps students to form positive skills toward learning, to acquire skills, problem-solving strategies. According to Feldman and Matjasko (2007), nonformal education activities have positive effects on the student through:

- better school performance;
- lower school dropout rate;
- better psychological state, increased self-esteem, fewer worries about the future;
- reduced feeling of social isolation;
- low level of delinquent behaviors.

Another study examining student performance in relation to their participation in extracurricular activities concludes the following (Eccles & Barber, 1999):

- Participation in all types of nonformal education activities is positively correlated with improved school performance.
- Students who participate in sports, administrative-school activities, and school clubs have a higher probability of enrolling in college by the age of 21.
- Participation in prosocial activities is associated with a lower delinquency rate among the participating students.

Feldman and Matjasko (2005) highlight the positive effect of certain nonformal education activities on the self-esteem of participating students. Receiving appreciation from others enhances teenagers' perception of their abilities, thereby increasing their level of commitment to these activities.

Conclusions

Drawing on the assertion by the American educator Jerome Bruner (1970) that any child, at any stage of development, can be successfully taught any topic in an intellectually suitable form if appropriate methods and procedures are employed, and if the subject matter is simplified to facilitate easier and deeper mastery of knowledge, we recognize that nonformal education activities offer a significant opportunity for knowledge transmission.

Nonformal educational activities conducted within a formal setting, executed with substantial pedagogical and managerial skill, along with the dedication and professionalism of the teaching staff, effectively address the personal, social, and emotional development of learners.

The interrelationship of students in nonformal activities contributes to the improvement of the well-being of the group of students. Students need social skills to make friends and be accepted by their peers, and friendships allow them to learn more effectively. In addition, if we use social interaction with friends to help children learn, we see improvements in academic performance and social interaction with friends. Enrollment in school is a crucial moment in a child's life. The child is in a new social environment and encounters a new circle of social relations, including adults, classmates, teachers who teach in the classroom, and school staff.

Social competence encompasses an individual's ability to establish and sustain close relationships while responding adaptively to social environments. This capacity is shaped by a myriad of cognitive abilities, emotional processes, behavioral skills, social awareness, and personal and cultural values pertinent to interpersonal relationships, owing to the intricate nature of social interactions. The friendships cultivated within groups play a significant role in shaping students' interactions and social behaviors.

Considering the school as an institution, and especially in the context of the teaching process, teachers and students communicate, interact, and develop a relationship through certain circumstances and under specific terms and conditions. So, the learning process is a product of communication.

Social skills are part of the teaching and learning process because they are key parts of the individual's development and are cultivated with appropriate environmental stimuli. So, in the school institution, the facilitator of nonformal activities is the teacher. It is their responsibility to motivate and inspire both the students and the local community in an effective partnership. Teaching staff, by facilitating nonformal, organized, and structured educational activities, can contribute to the development of students' social skills, and the involvement of parents in the design, organization, and implementation of nonformal activities is highly recommended for the achievement and success of these activities.

References

Bellack, A., Mueser, K., Gingerich, S., & Agresta, J. (2004). *Social skills training for schizophrenia: A step-by-step guide*. The Guilford Press.

Berndt, T. J. (1977). The effect of reciprocity norms on moral judgment and causal attribution. *Child Development*, *48*, 1322–1330.

Bradea, A. (coord.). (2012). *Educația nonformală. Modele de bună practică* [Nonformal education: Models of good practice]. Oradea: Editura Universității din Oradea.

Bruner, J. S. (1970). The growth and structure of skill. In K. J. Connolly (Ed.), *Mechanisms of motor skill development* (pp. 63–94). New York, NY: Academic Press.

Canney, C., & Byrne, A. (2006). Evaluating Circle Time as a support to social skills development: Reflections on a journey in school-based research. *British Journal of Special Education*, 33(1), 19–24. https://doi.org/10.1111/j.1467-8578.2006.00415.x.

Clark, M. S., & Mills, J. (1979). Interpersonal attraction in exchange and communal relationships. *Journal of Personality and Social Psychology*, *37*, 12–24.

Deci, E. L., & Ryan, E. M. (2002). *Handbook of self-determination research*. University of Rochester Press.

D'Hainaut, L. (1986). *L'interdisciplinarité dans l'enseignement général* [Interdisciplinarity in general education] (Report No. ED-86/WS/78). Paris: UNESCO. https://www.unesco.org/education/pdf/31_14_f.pdf

Dumitriu, Gh. (1998). *Comunicare și învățare* [Communication and Learning]. București: Editura Didactică și Pedagogică..

Eccles, J. S. (1999). The development of children ages 6 to 14. *The Future of Children*, *9*(2), 30–44.

Eccles, J. S., & Barber, B. L. (1999). Student council, volunteering, basketball, or marching band: What kind of extracurricular involvement matters? *Journal of Adolescent Research*, *14*, 10–43.

Eisdorfer, C. E., & Lawton, M. (1973). *The psychology of adult development and aging*. American Psychological Association.

Feldman, A. F., & Matjasko, J. L. (2005). The role of school-based extracurricular activities in adolescent development: A comprehensive review and future directions. *Review of Educational Research, 75*(2), 159–210.

Feldman A., & Matjasko J. (2007). Profiles and portfolios of adolescent school-based extracurricular activity participation. *Journal of Adolescence, 30*(2), 313–332.

Gailienė, D., Bulotaitė, L., & Sturlienė, N. (1996). *Aš myliu kiekvieną vaiką. Apie vaikų psichologinio atsparumo ugdymą* [I Love Every Child: On Developing Children's Psychological Resilience]. Vilnius: Valstybinis leidybos centras.

Gevorgianienė, V. (1999). Vidutiniškai sutrikusio intelekto mokinių komunikacinių gebėjimų ugdymas [Development of communication skills in learners with moderate intellectual disabilities]. *Specialioji edukacija / Special Education*, 1, 63–74. Vilnius: Lithuanian Centre for Special Education and Psychology.

Hayden, M., & Thompson, J. (1995). International schools and international education: A relationship reviewed. *Oxford Review of Education*, 21(3), 327–345.

Hoppers, W. (2006). *Non-formal education and basic education reform: A conceptual review.* International Institute for Educational Planning.

Kelley, H. H., & Thibaut, J. W. (1978). *Interpersonal relations: A theory of interdependence*. Wiley.

Lewis, J., & Geach, P. (1962). *History of philosophy.* The English Universities Presses.

Malinauskas, R. (2004). Socialinio ugdymo įtaka sporto pedagogų socialiniams įgūdžiams [The impact of social training on the social skills of sports educators]. Vilniaus pedagoginis universitetas. *Vilniaus edukologijos žurnalas / Vilnius Journal of Education*, 12, 1–8. Vilnius: Lithuanian University of Educational Sciences.

McClellan, D. E., & Katz, L. G. (2001). Evaluando la competencia social en los ninos [Assessing young children's social competence]. ERIC Digest.

McGrath, J. E., & Kelly, J. R. (1986). *Time and human interaction: Toward a social psychology of time*. Guilford Press.

Moore, R. (1996). Back to the future: The problem of change and the possibilities of advance in the sociology of education. *British Journal of Sociology of Education*, 17(2), 145–161.

Murphy, I., Scott, D., Villalba-Garcia, E., Endrodi, G., & Souto-Otero, M. (2019). *European inventory on validation of non-formal and informal learning 2018 update: Synthesis report.*

Muro, M., & Jeffrey, P. (2008). A critical review of the theory and application of social learning in participatory natural resource management processes. *Journal of Environmental Planning and Management*, *51*(3), 325–344.

Nomikou, M. (ed.) (2006). *The impact of non-formal education on young people and society*. AEGEE Europe.

Okamoto D., Herda, D., & Hartzog, C. (2013). Beyond good grades: School composition and immigrant youth participation in extracurricular activities, *Social Science Research*, *42*(1), 155–156.

Rapee, R. M. (2000). Group treatment of children with anxiety disorders: Outcome and predictors of treatment response. *Australian Journal of Psychology*, *52*(3), 125–129.

Riezen, K. (1996). Non-formal education and community development: Improving the quality. *Convergence*, *29*(1), 82–95.

Selman, R. L. (1980). *The growth of interpersonal understanding: Developmental and clinical analyses*. Academic Press.

Stearnes, E., & Glennie, E. (2010). Opportunities to participate: Extracurricular activities distribution across academic correlates in high school. *Social Science Research*, *39*(2), 296–309.

Squires, G. (1992). Interdisciplinarity in higher education in the United Kingdom. *European Journal of Education*, *27*(3), 201–210.

Taylor, R. J., Chatters, L. M., Hardison, C. B., & Riley, A. (2001). Informal social support networks and subjective well-being among African Americans. *Journal of Black Psychology*, *27*(4), 439–463.

Walker, S. (2005). Gender differences in the relationship between young children's peer-related social competence and individual differences in theory of mind. *The Journal of Genetic Psychology*, *166*(3), 297–312

Youniss, J. (1980). *Parents and peers in social development: A Sullivan-Piaget perspective*. University of Chicago Press.

Zaki Dib, C. (1987). *Formal, non-formal and informal education: Concepts/ Applicability*. AIP Publishing.

Self-sabotage, Resilience, and Learning in School

Georgeta Pânişoară and Andreea Şiţoiu

Abstract: During a student's learning journey, the aim of which is to foster their development, there may arise some situations where the student becomes their own enemy, thereby limiting their progress. This could be caused either by childhood problems, whose consequences are seen in the long term, or by the impact of student's relationships, such as those with parents, teachers, or other reference persons in their life. This is how self-sabotage appears, representing an adaptation mechanism that students use to deal with stressful situations and past traumas. Although it can provide short-term "security" because the student does not leave their comfort zone, over time it contributes to aggravating problems and limiting the student's ability to evolve in an authentic way (Field, 2023). Self-sabotage occurs not only when the person's behavior creates problems in daily activities, but also when it interferes with the achievement of long-term goals. There are several manifestations of self-sabotage, for example, procrastination of tasks; self-administration of medication even though the experienced symptoms do not always agree with the self-administered medication; emotional eating, also known by the term comfort eating; and last but not least, various forms of self-harm such as cutting or hitting until the skin is bruised (Davis, 2023a). Ho (2020) claims that self-sabotage does not appear out of the blue, but is triggered by several sources, and to detect the triggering sources, it is recommended that students pay attention to how they feel by clearly identifying the thoughts that caused them to feel in a certain way, and the context in which the thoughts and feelings experienced subsequently produced self-sabotaging behaviors. Following such an analysis, Ho (2020) noted that students will become aware of certain patterns of action. They may realize that their thoughts tend to view the task or learning in general in a more dramatic way than it is, causing the mind to emphasize the worst-case scenario that can happen even though the real chances of its occurrence are reduced. Another source of self-sabotage is the situation where the student imposes an exaggerated number of rules and acts according to the principle of "must," and such thinking makes them believe that they do not have the ability to achieve the task of work no matter how hard they try. In the context of school learning, self-sabotage can occur as a result of the student's feeling of ambiguity regarding academic success, and as a result of how past experiences were perceived, of negative self-perception regarding the chances of success and not in the last row of the low level of self-efficacy. In addition, the behaviors of classmates and teachers can act as sources of self-sabotage development (Zhang, 2022).

Keywords: self-sabotage, resilience, learning.

Manifestations of self-sabotage

a) Fear of failure

Fear of failure is operationalized from the perspective of consequences that harm student development. The different manifestations of fear include the fear of experiencing the feeling of shame; the fear of being affected by self-esteem ; the fear of not being secure about the future; and the fear of losing social influence, a consequence more common in the case of students who have passed the period of early childhood; and last but not least, the fear of causing disappointment in loved ones (Nakhla, 2019).

McGregor (2003) and Andrews (1998), cited in Nelson and McDaniel (2023), demonstrated that shame in student' fear of failure is determined by parents' reactions to their behaviors. Despite high levels of parental fear of failure, they set high standards for their children's achievement, although as a result of high parental fear of failure, beliefs emerge that children will not be able to achieve respective standards (Smith, 1969, as cited in Nelson & McDaniel, 2023). At the same time, parents who punish failure and have neutral reactions when children experience success and achievement cause the latter to acquire a high level of fear of failure (Birney et al., 1969, as cited in Nelson & McDaniel, 2023).

Fear of failure is transmitted intergenerationally from parents to children. Withdrawal of parental love, especially maternal love, influences this intergenerational transmission of the fear of failure, and students who generally experience the fear of failure are educated to be aware of the social cues that predict failure but have not developed a high level of awareness of the cues that predict personal success. In their case, success is not given the necessary importance – it is considered insignificant or even nonexistent – while failure is considered to be constantly significant in their lives, with a strong negative impact on behavior and the way tasks are perceived. As a result of the fear of failure, states of anxiety appear, resulting in emotional responses that inhibit students' cognitive functioning and planning skills (Elliot & Thrash, 2002, as cited in Nelson & McDaniel, 2023).

Bartels and Herman (2011), cited in Jacob (2017), state that students who face the fear of failure tend to underuse their cognitive strategies with a role in achieving academic performance and overuse cognitive strategies with a role in increasing the risk of failure. One of the most frequently used cognitive strategies determining a high level of failure is self-handicapping, which involves the imposition of barriers on one's person to protect self-esteem in the face of failure. In this way, the experience of failure is mitigated, but even though the student's self-esteem is protected, in the long term, they will not see an evolution following their potential. Also, students who experience fear of failure often experience a negative mood after projecting the steps they need to take to achieve success (Langens, 2002).

An important step in reducing fear of failure is to set small, achievable goals, the fulfillment of which will contribute to the development of self-confidence. Initiating alternative plans that students can refer to in emergencies and practicing positive thinking can represent other steps that you apply constantly, and contribute to reducing the fear of failure (MindTools, n.d.).

b) Perfectionism

Perfectionism is another form of self-sabotaging behavior, which can be classified into three types, as follows:

1. *Socially prescribed perfectionism* occurs when the student feels a constant need to achieve perfection due to high standards set by significant members of the society. It is a type of perfectionism that can often be fostered by influencers on social media. This can manifest in depression, anxiety, eating disorders, increased tendency toward suicidal behaviors, and reduced adaptation to situations that require change. Students with a high level of socially prescribed perfectionism experience the fear of being negatively evaluated, which is why they find ways to avoid failure (Blankstein & Winkworth, 2004; Neumeister, 2004, as cited in Nelson & McDaniel, 2023).
2. *Other-oriented perfectionism* refers to the imposition of unrealistic goals, with minimal or nonexistent chances of being achievable in the student's case. This type of perfectionism is associated with the individual's expectation that the other person is perfect. It can be found both in the case of the student who expects perfection from those around them, and in the case of parents, teachers, or individuals in general who expect perfection from the student. In the context of this chapter, other-oriented perfectionism will be treated from the perspective of the second situation, noting that the information presented is also

valid for the first situation described. People who have a high level of other-oriented perfectionism make a strict evaluation of the student in the context of achieving the performance for perfection, judging them by using high standards of perfectionism, sometimes in an inversely proportional relationship with the performance of the adult who evaluates the student (Conroy et al., 2007, as cited in Nelson & McDaniel, 2023; Hewitt & Flett, 1991).

3. *Self-oriented perfectionism* involves creating an idealistic image of oneself and setting goals with little chance of being achieved following the student's capabilities, the context, and the conditions available to them. The student who is characterized by this type of perfectionism has a harsh and critical attitude toward their performances or behaviors, believing that only in the presence of such an attitude can they achieve perfection and avoid failure. It has been shown that self-oriented perfectionism is associated with suicidal behaviors, anorexia, depression, rumination, burnout, constant dissatisfaction with individual performance, and, last but not least, experiencing maladaptive emotional responses from the perspective of failure feedback (Besser et al., 2004; Gould et al., 1997, as cited in Nelson & McDaniel, 2023).

Decreasing perfectionism involves correcting inappropriate thinking about oneself, and recognizing and being aware of distorted thoughts is the first strategy to combat perfectionism. Living in the present reduces intrusive and compulsive thinking as well as perfectionism. Practicing mindfulness techniques, focusing on positive thoughts, and accepting that failure is a source of learning are ways to combat perfectionism (Kelly, 2015).

c) Procrastination

In the context of self-sabotage, procrastination allows the student to avoid tasks that generate negative emotions such as anxiety or suffering, providing short-term comfort, but at the same time diminishing the possibility of achieving long-term goals that could lead to experiencing well-being and fulfillment (Davis, 2023b). The unlimited use of technology as a result of strong incentives that cause students to lose control and the absence of a schedule according to which school tasks are completed are factors that encourage procrastination behaviors (Davis, 2023a).

To combat procrastination, it is important to understand the reason behind it and its consequences on the development of the individual. Managing time according to the difficulty of the task and maintaining motivation to continue despite the obstacles encountered are ways to reduce procrastination (Voge, 2007).

How does self-sabotage affect student learning?

Davis (2023a) lists the reasons that can lead a person to self-sabotage. These include excessive food cravings and drinking, but it is recognized that a source of self-sabotage is also the dysfunctional and distorted beliefs that lead the student to not trust their abilities, repress their feelings, and even behave inappropriately toward those around them.

Before examining how self-sabotage affects student learning, Field (2023) draws attention to the difference between conscious self-sabotage and unconscious self-sabotage through the following analysis (see Table 5.1).

Table 5.1 Difference between conscious self-sabotage and unconscious self-sabotage

Conscious self-sabotage	Unconscious self-sabotage
The student wants to achieve the goal of completing the science project, which requires a systematic work schedule of two hours a day for five days. Conscious self-sabotage occurs when the student chooses to play video games for the last two days out of five, disregarding the two hours of work devoted to the project.	The student is aware of the deadline to hand over the model on technological education. Although the suggestions for its completion have been respected, the fear of failure causes the student not to be aware that the homework deadline has not been respected, although at first glance the teacher may consider it a delay. In such a situation, a longer period will be necessary to achieve the objective, during which the student's progress may stagnate.

Tipton (2018) outlines how student learning is negatively impacted by self-sabotage:

1. *Students confuse knowledge with learning* – knowledge is associated with remembering information and not necessarily learning it. For learning to truly occur, students must anticipate the fact that they may experience forgetfulness, which is why learning must be accompanied by reflections on the information acquired in such a way that it is conscious, in

addition to frequent practice so that the knowledge can be recovered. Watching a video showing students the moves needed to match the faces of the Rubik's Cube does not automatically teach the skill of matching the faces of the Rubik's Cube, just as noting steps for efficient matching will not ensure learning, creativity, or innovation. Learning will occur as students actively practice playing with the Rubik's Cube to acquire the skill of face matching.

2. *Students believe they are learning effectively if they use multitasking* – the danger is caused by the fact that multitasking is associated with trying to learn rather than deep learning. Believing that they are multitasking and saving time, students self-sabotage their learning by changing the contexts in which it occurs, oscillating between tasks, dividing time according to the difficulty of the task, and not actually multitasking. The more students focus on multiple tasks, the less likely it is that conscious and deep learning will occur.
3. *Students focus on avoiding failure* – self-sabotaging their learning in this way, students end up with low expectations and imagine the worst-case scenario. In this case, they will not discover development opportunities or develop risk-taking skills. One solution to reduce the self-sabotage of learning by avoiding failure is to divide tasks into stages, the completion of which leads to the achievement of the proposed objective and achievement of success.
4. *Students believe they are subject matter experts* – self-sabotaging their learning by not documenting themselves when the information they know does not agree with what is presented in the classroom or other learning contexts. In this situation, students are advised to document themselves in depth so that all perspectives on a topic can be analyzed and not just the perspective they know best or agree with, and not avoid looking for multiple pieces of evidence to solve problems even if their own beliefs were confirmed. Confirmation of beliefs is not always associated with truth.

Strategies for reducing self-sabotage in learning

What is the need for a self-sabotaging student? A student who is prone to self-sabotage needs support from adults to identify their thinking style and subsequently to build and implement strategies that reduce the impact of negative thoughts and boost self-efficacy to achieve success (Table 5.2).

Table 5.2 Questions about how can students be encouraged to realize if they are self-sabotaging

Parents and teachers can help children learn to be aware of the moments in which they self-sabotage by asking themselves questions. We mention the fact that for better awareness of self-sabotage, it is recommended to adapt the questions to the specifics of the student.	
Does the way I behave help me accomplish my tasks or achieve the goal I set for myself?	Is the discomfort I feel based on what others have told me about my aspirations or dreams, limiting them?
If my behavior is not in line with the proposed goal, what prevents me from taking the necessary steps to change my behavior?	Is the source of this discomfort a fear of failure or a worry that I am not good enough for the goal I have set for myself?
Is my behavior specific to the values I believe in? For example: if taking responsibility is a guiding value, is my behavior responsible?	Is the discomfort I feel based on fear of success and lack of awareness on how I will manage this possible success?
If my behavior does not correspond to the values I believe in, what are the obstacles that prevent me from changing it?	Do I often think that I have better results than would be possible under the given conditions?
Do I feel anxious or uncomfortable when I notice an improvement in my results? If so, it's time to ask yourself why you feel this way.	If I solve work tasks better and better, and the results keep improving, do I think that the success I have achieved is more than I deserve? (Field, 2023)

Davis (2023b) presents several ways in which students can come to avoid self-sabotage:

1. *Practicing self-compassion* – Neff et al. (2007) demonstrate that people who practice self-compassion in situations of failure facilitate the process they have to undergo to achieve the proposed goal. Self-compassion is closely related to happiness, wisdom, and emotional resilience, so it is a useful resource for eliminating self-sabotage from a student's life.
2. *Practice acceptance* – acceptance takes practice to become a skill in situations where the student is faced with failure of any kind. Learning to use expressions like "I can't change what happened in the past, BUT I can change how I react now" can help reduce self-sabotage.
3. *Changing the perception of workload* – self-sabotage is common at any age as a result of certain parts of the brain trying to avoid danger. Replacing the phrase "This task terrifies me" with expressions more oriented toward self-compassion and curiosity, such as "It would be

worth seeing what I can do to solve this task" or "I am curious to see what this task entails," causes training the brain in the sense of eliminating actions that lead to self-sabotage and becoming an "ally" for the student's success and not an "enemy."

4. *Developing a more comfortable attitude toward failure* – self-sabotage also arises from the fear of failure or rejection, which is why the student chooses not to attempt difficult tasks. This avoidance of learning by trial and error, of taking risks in order to achieve success, signifies unconscious self-sabotage. For example, in a learning situation where the student continues to perform, if they are used to self-sabotage, they may consider that this is only a temporary improvement and things will soon get worse, so they start to avoid learning tasks on time or to solve them with the same conscientiousness as at the beginning.

Field (2023) presents a series of recommendations for reducing and subsequently eliminating self-sabotage among students:

1. *Stop procrastinating*. Task procrastination is specific to self-sabotaging students. They find it easier to put off something important to them, experiencing emotional comfort, than to take the initiative to achieve a goal for which they feel they do not have the necessary resources or according to which they have been told they will never achieve it. This mismatch between the context in which students finds themselves and the misconceptions about their abilities causes self-sabotage. In the case of procrastination, the factors that contribute to its adoption refer to the students' high degree of freedom, the temptations that surround them, and the long deadlines for the assignments. In this context, creating a systematic work schedule, understanding the usefulness of school tasks, and recording the progress in solving the tasks are strategies that contribute to the reduction and subsequent cessation of procrastination.
2. *Avoid focusing only on the overall goal*. When students set themselves or are set goals that are difficult to achieve or the goal is far too general in scope, they tend to lose themselves in the whole, which is a first step toward self-sabotage. Thus they are determined to avoid engaging in tasks that lead to the achievement of that goal. A solution, in this case, involves crafting more specific objectives, with progressive levels of difficulty, which will motivate the student to start taking the necessary actions to achieve them and subsequently achieve success. Another way in which students can avoid getting lost in the big picture of an objective, thus reducing the risk of self-sabotage, is refraining from making decisions

of the "all or nothing" type and replacing this habit with consistent actions that show progress to give the student the satisfaction of their accomplishment and the motivation to move forward to achieve success.

3. *Stop perfectionistic thinking.* The student's focus on every detail, believing success can be achieved only if everything is done correctly, should be replaced with striving for excellence rather than perfectionism. In this case, it is recommended that students make small improvements in reducing perfectionist thinking and to have a clear record of their progress in the form of a graph or table. A clear picture of their progress toward the goal will encourage them to continue to gradually improve their thinking and lessen the risk of self-sabotage.

Martin (2002), cited in Martin and Marsh (2003), describes four factors that underlie success orientation and at the same time reduce self-sabotage:

1. *Self-confidence* – this refers to students' belief that they can understand how to act in different contexts, make the best decisions according to the situation they face, to face everyday challenges both in school tasks as well as personal life. Self-confidence gives students a better chance to perform in different fields of interest.

   There are three reasons why self-confidence becomes important in orienting students to success: it represents a generative capacity so that students who demonstrate a high level of self-confidence tend to try alternative courses of action when success is delayed; students respond better to tasks under the influence of a high level of self-esteem because it is associated with an increased potential for effort and persistence during a task. A third reason why self-confidence guides students to achieve success is that it helps them to effectively manage a problematic situation by being able to influence the cognitive and emotional processes related to that situation (Bandura, 1986; Bandura, 1997, as cited in Martin & Marsh, 2003). Students who are not characterized by a high level of self-confidence tend to focus on their limits at the expense of strengths and evaluate tasks at a higher level of difficulty than they are, while high levels of self-confidence were correlated with several positive outcomes for student development such as self-regulation and achievement.

2. *The value of the school* – this is a factor that contributes to the orientation of students toward success as it reflects how much they believe what they learn in school is relevant both to them and to the society they

belong to. When they understand the usefulness of school assignments, it increases the likelihood that students will be more involved in completing them. Also, when students believe in the value of school for their development, they become more resilient in the face of adversity, and this ability to withstand school failure and learn by trial and error differentiates students into two categories: those who prematurely drop out of schoolwork and, later, school, and those who systematically learn to deal effectively with difficult situations. Martin and Debus (1998), cited in Martin and Marsh (2003), believe that it is useful for the value of the school to be reinforced among students from their early developmental periods to ensure their willingness to continue their studies in the future, even if they face uncertain times that may affect the vocational training decision through personal studies.

3. *Focus on the learning activity* – it is operationalized by focusing students on solving problems and developing skills. When concentration in learning intervenes, students show the willingness to increase the effort to reach the proposed objective, while developing their intrinsic motivation, with the rewards not being the primary goal. Focusing on the act of learning is associated mostly with one's improvement in a certain field and less with the desire to surpass others, thus stimulating competition with oneself. Middleton and Midgley (1997), cited in Martin and Marsh (2003), argue that students who focus during learning perceive the results obtained from school tasks as a representation of their effort and not their ability or failure. By emphasizing the quality of the process that led to the outcome, the focus on learning is associated with reduced odds of failure although expected outcomes may not be met. Duda (1992), cited in Martin and Marsh (2003), find that students who focus on learning do not avoid challenging school tasks and show a reduced tendency to worry about performance. More important for these students is the process that led to their achievement and the skills that were formed during that process.
4. *Control* – in the context of school learning, it refers to the extent to which students believe they are capable of achieving success and reducing the risk of failure. As students face a low level of control over school results, they cannot predict with certainty the situations in which they will register success or failure at school, and as a result adopt counterproductive behaviors in learning such as self-imposing barriers that make learning difficult, which can eventually result in the abandonment of the respective task or, in extreme cases, the abandonment of school (Martin, 2002, as cited in Martin & Marsh, 2003).

Students who are characterized as having a high level of control over learning develop persistence in the task, have high attention capacity, show effort to achieve the objectives, and exhibit willingness to engage in the task to achieve the anticipated result. Students who have uncertain control over learning and are unable to anticipate school success or failure face reduced possibilities for self-realization and evaluation of their competences (Harter & Connell, 1984, as cited in Martin & Marsh, 2003).

Student resilience

A student's responsibilities often involve challenging situations, which can be demotivating and may cause them to self-sabotage as a way to justify potential failure. In this context, the challenge encountered by the student requires the adoption of a resilient attitude to achieve the objective.

In a systematic review on the development of a model of individual resilience, Llistosella et al. (2022) inventoried a series of definitions of this concept, as shown in Table 5.3.

Table 5.3 Development of the model of individual resilience – concept inventory

Definitions of Resilience	
The ability to generate positive emotions and return to a better mental state following stressful experiences (Zhang et al., 2020)	Resilience is associated with personal competence, and self-acceptance, and with the acceptance of life experiences (Cénat et al., 2018)
A transitory phenomenon influenced by the student's capabilities, and by the social, cultural, and historical context in which they reside, which takes into account the importance of sharing and redefining experiences (Hildebrand et al., 2019).	Resilience aims to prepare students to deal with prejudice, aiming to raise children's awareness of prejudice that can occur throughout life and to provide the necessary advice and tools to deal with the manifestations resulting from prejudice (Burt & Simons, 2015).
The ability of the student to overcome the harsh conditions to which they are exposed and to function normally despite being exposed to risk (Forres-Bank et al., 2015).	Phenomenon or mechanism by which the student shows a good adaptation in the face of stressful situations although their difficulty would normally be associated with negative consequences on mental health (Pérez-González et al., 2017).

Resilience refers to a class of phenomena that involves the adaptation of the student in the face of adversity or risk. Several factors contribute to development of resilience since childhood, such as high-level cognitive skills, including problem-solving skills, easily adaptable personality, positive self-perceptions, self-efficacy, and good self-regulation of emotional impulses (Masten & Reed, 2002).

Along with the previously mentioned factors, there is a model that includes some characteristics for a successful adaptation in the face of adversity. It considers commitment, dynamism, a sense of humor in the context of challenging life experiences, patience, optimism, faith, and altruism (Connor & Zhang, 2006). For students to integrate this model, behavioral models are needed both from the family or reference persons for them and from the teaching staff.

The usefulness of students' resilience in learning is also associated with emotional regulation, impulse control, causal analysis to reflect on problems and identify causes accurately, self-efficacy, and the search for development opportunities (The Education Hub, 2019).

In the context of school learning, students' resilience takes into account metacognitive adaptation, sociability, optimism, perseverance, and efficiency in communication, allowing them, especially in the early stages of learning or in situations where learning becomes difficult, to continue learning despite adversities encountered (Martin, 2002, as cited in Kim et al., 2018).

An increased level of resilience contributes to reducing low motivation as a result of the student's lack of self-confidence and an unsupportive learning environment. In this context, to stimulate the level of resilience, students need to be determined to persevere and be encouraged to interact with peers (Kim et al., 2018).

Factors that contribute to the development of resilience

Herrman et al. (2011) described the factors that represent sources of resilience in the case of students:

1. *Personal factors* – refers to personality traits (extraversion, openness), the level of self-esteem, the interpretation of events in a positive way, and the level of optimism.
2. *Biological factors* – research in the field of biology has indicated that students exposed to harsh environments from early developmental periods exhibit changes in brain size, neural networks, receptor sensitivity,

and neurotransmitter synthesis. These alterations reduce the brain's capacity to regulate negative emotions and resilience in the face of adversity (McEwen & Gianaros, 2010; Teicher & Samson, 2016; Smith & Pollak, 2020).

3. *Environmental factors* – at the microsystem level, the factors that contribute to the development of resilience in students include social support, including family members and teachers, colleagues, or other important people for students; secure maternal attachment; stable family dynamics; and parental competence. At the macrosystem level, the environmental factors that stimulate the development of resilience include access to high-quality educational services, community services that students can access according to their needs, opportunities to pursue sports or arts, education to improve cultural awareness, and, most importantly, avoiding exposure to violence.

Masten et al. (2021), cited in Mesman et al. (2021), inventoried a list of factors that determine a high level of resilience. Only the factors that are valid for students were taken from that list (see Table 5.4).

Table 5.4 Factors that determine a high level of resilience

Sensitivity to self-care (physical, mental, emotional)	Encouraging and constantly experiencing a sense of belonging to the group
The existence of family management	Problem-solving and follow-up planning skills
Motivation to meet high standards (mastery motivation)	Motivation to adapt to varied situations
The existence of a purpose and meaning in life	Positive opinions about oneself

Raghunathan et al. (2022) mention three factors that contribute to the development of resilience, namely individual factors, interpersonal factors, and factors related to the institution to which the individual belongs. At the level of individual factors, the authors mention positivism, motivation, self-confidence, emotional capacity, perseverance, and self-reflection. Interpersonal factors consider social support, the organization of a support system for students, and peer-to-peer relationships, while institutional factors refer to the organizational climate and leadership skills. All these present in a school institution determine the improvement of the level of resilience.

Strategies for developing resilience in learning

In the context of promoting resilience among students, it is recommended to pay attention to the prevention of their abuse or neglect, the development of self-efficacy, and the learning of effective coping strategies for challenging or stressful situations from the perspective of school learning (Masten & Reed, 2002), such as imbibing a large volume of information within a short time or the uncertainty caused by the evaluation.

At school, students can acquire resilience when they experience relationships of trust, based on respect, help, and care between adults and students, and in situations where learning contexts are created that promote autonomy and the development of self-regulation skills. The approach to educational practices based on the previously noted elements contributes to the development of students' resilience regardless of their social and economic status (Doll & Song, 2023).

How can teachers and parents detect low levels of student resilience early?

The Payne Resilience Training & Consulting platform features the following factors:

1. Episodes of anger and irritability occur frequently even in situations that do not warrant these behaviors.
2. Chronic illness resulting from a weakened immune system due to the release of a large number of stress hormones.
3. Lack of a consistent sleep schedule and decrease in quality sleep.
4. The choice to isolate oneself from the group and family, or on the opposite pole, to become much too dependent on socializing. It is important to find a balance in this perspective for the student to form his autonomy and to be aware that there is a support group comprising family members, friends, and teachers who can offer them support.
5. The presence of unjustified mood swings. Along with the hormonal changes and fluctuations in the student's body as a result of low resilience, frequent mood swings occur throughout the day.
6. The presence of an excessive reaction to a normal stressor. In this case, challenging situations that can usually be approached with calm, assertive communication are met with exaggerated reactions, disproportionate to the seriousness of the problem, and even anger.
7. Frequent sadness and extreme sensitivity are often manifested by crying.

8. Lack of vision for the future that can spiral into despair, diminishing planning and problem-solving skills, but contributing to cynicism or lack of concern. As a result, students with a low level of resilience risk engaging in dangerous activities, unaware of the existing dangers.

According to The Education Hub (2019), teachers can help improve student resilience in several ways, such as:

1. Providing opportunities for self-determination because resilience is also related to the student's belief that they have the ability and the necessary tools to face the environment in which they live and to positively influence it. As resilience develops, the student becomes autonomous and experiences self-efficacy, thus forming a sense of confidence in solving problems. The student's feeling that they have self-control facilitates adaptation in difficult situations.
2. Implementation of activities based on challenges – learning experiences that make the student feel confident and competent allows them to adapt to different situations, thus building their resilience. The teacher's role in this situation is to provide challenges appropriate to the student's level of development because otherwise, the presence of an inadequate and overwhelming challenge increases the risk of psychological distress.
3. Allowing the student to reflect on past experiences and seek feedback to develop resilience, reflection, information, and learning from the experiences lived by the student is necessary. Seeking feedback from teachers or reference persons for the student helps the latter to adapt their course of action according to the difficulty of the situation and make the necessary adjustments to perform.
4. Training the skills of asking for help and self-disclosure through the following methods:
   4.1. The initiation by the teaching staff of discussions that can determine whether the student knows who to turn to when faced with a problem.
   4.2. The implementation of didactic activities through which the student learns how to recognize and manage his emotions, and how to respond with empathy to the emotions of others.
   4.3. Guiding the student in identifying situations in which they feel stressed, anxious, or angry and ways to manage them.

Resilience takes time and perseverance to develop and subsequently to perfect. Harvard Health Publishing (2017) recommends some strategies that determine its development:

1. *Meditation*: students can be guided by specialists in meditation activities that can counteract the stress they feel every day. In this way, relaxation responses will be triggered that contribute to the lowering of blood pressure and heart and respiratory rates, decreasing the release of stress hormones. In this regard, there are many applications to facilitate meditation, but it is recommended to guide students in choosing the most suitable application.
2. *Rethinking the situation in which the student finds themself*: paying more attention to the positive side of a situation contributes to the development of resilience. Instead of experiencing the disappointment of receiving a low grade, a student could reflect on the effort they put in and the skills they developed, even if the result was not up to expectations.
3. *Paying attention to the social network*: in this context, the social network is not associated with social platforms, but with family and friends who can cushion the stress felt by the student when they feel safe to share experiences.
4. *Practice positive thinking*: stress causes the student to easily pay attention to wrong things. Positive thinking can also be formed by practicing exercises, such as "Write down three things that are going well/for which you are grateful," and by experiencing the joy of small things: a bike ride, an exchange of pleasant messages from a friend/colleague, helping a person in need, etc.
5. *Increasing the frequency of laughing episodes in a day*: laughter contributes to the reduction of stress hormones, thus leading to the strengthening of the immune system. Funny movies/videos and humorous books encourage this practice which facilitates the development of resilience.
6. *Dealing with situations with optimism*: although the student may tend to anticipate the negative aspects of a situation, specialists recommend emphasizing the positives and possible adjustments that can be made. For example, a student may worry about how disappointed their friend will be with the gift they give, but instead fixating on this concern, they can focus on discovering the friend's passions and buying a gift that better aligns with the friend's needs, thereby reducing the risk of them not liking it.

School learning is a prerequisite for the student's multilateral development. As a long-term process with beneficial effects on the learner, learning is not without obstacles. This chapter outlined the effects of self-sabotage and low and high levels of resilience on learning, so that students, parents, and professors can be aware of the negative effects and work toward diminishing them. The lack of resilience, or low levels of resilience, and the constant presence of self-sabotage diminishes the student's ability to learn, increases the risk of avoiding opportunities for personal and professional growth, and leads to poor development of self-efficacy and low self-esteem. In this context, adults can guide the student in learning activities, provide the necessary independence in learning over time, and, more importantly, offer emotional support during challenging times, thereby contributing to the student's optimal development. Thus, it is recommended that parents and teachers pay more attention to strategies for reducing self-sabotage and developing resilience to achieve optimal student development.

References

Andrews, B. (1998). Shame and childhood abuse. In P. Gilbert, & B. Andrews (Eds.), *Shame: Interpersonal behavior, psychopathology and culture series in affective science* (pp. 176–190). Oxford University Press.

Bandura, A. (1986). *Social foundations of thought and action: A social cognitive theory*. Prentice Hall.

Bandura, A. (1997). *Self-Efficacy: The exercise of control*. Freeman & Co.

Bartels, J., & Herman, W. (2011, May 28). Fear of failure, self-handicapping, and negative emotions in response to failure. *Annual Convention of the Association for Psychological Science*, 1–11.

Bartels, J. M., & Herman, W. E. (2011). Fear of failure, self-handicapping, and negative emotions in response to failure. *Journal of Student Leadership*, 1(2), 3–7. Retrieved from https://journals.uvu.edu/jsl/article/view/19

Besser, A., Flett, G., L., & Hewitt, P. L. (2004). Perfectionism, cognition, and affect in response to performance failure versus success. *Journal of Rational-Emotive and Cognitive Behavior*, 22(4), 301–328. <https://doi.org/10.1023/B:JORE.0000047313.35872.5c>

Birney, R. C., Burdick, H. A., & Teevan, R. C. (1969). *Fear of failure motivation*. Van Nostrand.

Blankstein, K. R., & Winkworth, G. R. (2004). Dimensions of perfectionism and levels of attributions for grades: Relations with dysphoria and academic performance. *Journal of Rational Emotive & Cognitive-Behavior Therapy, 22*(4), 271–299. <https://doi.org/10.1023/B:JORE.0000047312.20212.30>

Burt, C. H., & Simons, R. L. (2015). Interpersonal racial discrimination, ethnic-racial socialization, and offending: Risk and resilience among African American females. *Justice Quarterly*, *32*(3), 532– 570. <https://doi.org/10.1080/07418825.2013.781205>

Cénat, J. M., Derivois, D., Hébert, M., Amédée, L. M., & Karray, A. (2018). Multiple traumas and resilience among street children in Haiti: Psychopathology of survival. *Child Abuse & Neglect*, *79*, 85– 97. <https://doi.org/10.1016/j.chiabu.2018.01.024>

Connor, K., & Zhang, W. (2006). Resilience: Determinants, measurement, and treatment responsiveness. *CNS Spectrums*, *11*(10), 5–12. <https://doi.org/10.1017/S1092852900025797>

Conroy, D. E., Kaye, M. P., & Fifer, A. M. (2007). Cognitive links between fear of failure and perfectionism. *Journal of Rational-Emotive & Cognitive- Behavior Therapy*, *25*(4), 237–253. <https://doi.org/10.1007/s10942-007-0052-7>

Davis, T. (2023a). Self-sabotage. *Psychology Today*, <https://www.psychologytoday.com/us/basics/self-sabotage>

Davis, T. (2023b). 6 Ways to stop sabotaging yourself. *Psychology Today*. <https://www.psychologytoday.com/intl/blog/click-here-for-happiness/202209/6-ways-to-stop-self-sabotage>

Doll, B., & Song, S. Y. (2023). Enhancing resilience in classrooms. In A. Thapa & J. Cohen (Eds.), *Handbook of resilience in children*. Springer Publishing. < https://doi.org/10.1007/978-3-031-14728-9_29>

Duda, J. L. (1992). Motivation in sport settings: A goal perspective approach. In G. C. Roberts (Ed.), *Motivation in sport and exercise* (pp. 57–91). Champaign, IL: Human Kinetics Publishers.

Elliot, A. J., & Thrash, T. M. (2002). Approach-avoidance motivation in personality: Approach and avoidance temperaments and goals. *Journal of Personality & Social Psychology*, *82*(5), 804–818. <https://doi.org/10.1037/0022-3514.82.5.804>

Field, B. (2023). Self-sabotaging: Why does it happen. *Very Well Mind*. <https://www.verywellmind.com/why-people-self-sabotage-and-how-to-stop-it-5207635>

Forres-Bank, S. S., Nicotera, N., Anthony, E. K., & Jenson, J. M. (2015). Finding their way: Perceptions of risk, resilience, and positive youth development among adolescents and young adults from public housing neighborhoods. *Children and Youth Services Review, 55*, 147–158. <https://doi.org/10.1016/j.childyouth.2015.05.015>

Gould, D., Tuffey, S., Udry, E., & Loehr, J. (1997). Burnout in competitive junior tennis players: Individual differences in the burnout experience. *The Sports Psychologist, 11*(3), 257–276. < https://doi.org/10.1123/tsp.11.3.257>

Harter, S., & Connell, J. P. (1984). A model of children's achievement and related self-perceptions of competence, control, and motivational orientation. In J. G. Nicholls (Ed.), *Advances in motivation and achievement* (Vol. 3, pp. 219–250). Greenwich, CT: JAI Press.

Harvard Health Publishing. Harvard Medical School. (2017). Ramp up your resilience. <https://www.health.harvard.edu/mind-and-mood/ramp-up-your-resilience>.

Herrman, H., Stewart, D. E., Diaz-Granados, N., Berger, E. L., Jackson, B., & Yuen, T. (2011). What is resilience? *The Canadian Journal of Psychiatry, 56*(5), 258–265.

Hewitt, P. L., & Flett, G. L. (1991). Perfectionism in the self and social contexts: Conceptualization, assessment, and association with psychopathology. *Journal of Personality and Social Psychology, 60*(3), 456–470. <https://doi.org/10.1037//0022-3514.60.3.456>

Hildebrand, N. A., Celeri, E., Morcillo, A. M., & Zanolli, M. L. (2019). Resilience and mental health problems in children and adolescents who have been victims of violence. *Revista de Saude Publica, 53*, 17. <https://doi.org/10.11606/S1518-8787.2019053000391>

Ho, J. (2020). What are your self-sabotage triggers? *Psychology Today*. https://www.psychologytoday.com/us/blog/unlock-your-true-motivation/202003/what-are-your-self-sabotage-triggers.

Jacob, B. (2017). Fear of failure and student achievement. National Bureau of Economic Research (NBER) Working Paper No. 23780. https://doi.org/10.3386/w23780.

Kelly, J. D. (2015). Your best life: Perfectionism – The bane of happiness. *Clinical Orthopaedics and Related Research, 473*(10), 3108–3111. <https://doi.org/10.1007/s11999-015-4279-9>

Kim, T. Y., Kim, Y., & Kim, J. Y. (2018). Role of resilience in (de)motivation and second language proficiency: Cases of Korean elementary school students. *Journal of Psycholinguistic Research, 48*, 371–389. <https://doi.org/10.1007/s10936-018-9609-0>

Langens, T. (2002). Tantalizing fantasies: Positive imagery induces negative mood in individuals high in fear of failure. *Imagination Cognition and Personality, 21*(4), 281–282. <https://doi.org/10.2190/HGH6-3RM6-2VCG-YCQH>

Llistosella, M., Castellvi, P., Limonero, J. T., Ortiz, C. P. V., Velasco, C. B., & Rosado, T. G. (2022). Development of the individual and environmental resilience model among children, adolescents and young adults using the empirical evidence: An integrative systematic review. *Health and Social Care in the Community*, *30*(6), 3277–3299. <https://doi.org/10.1111/hsc.13899>

Martin, A. J., & Debus, R. L. (1998). Self-reports of mathematics self-concept and educational outcomes: The roles of ego-dimensions and self-consciousness. *British Journal of Educational Psychology*, *68*(4), 517–535. <https://doi.org/10.1111/j.2044-8279.1998.tb01309.x>

Martin, A. J. (2002). Motivation and academic resilience: Developing a model for student enhancement. *Australian Journal of Education*, 46(1), 34–49. https://doi.org/10.1177/000494410204600104.

Martin, A. J., & Marsh, H. W. (2003). Fear of failure: Friend or foe? *Australian Psychologist*, *38*(1), 31–38. https://doi.org/10.1080/00050060310001706997

Masten, A. S., & Reed, M. G. J. (2002). Resilience in development. In C. R. Snyder & S. J. Lopez (Eds.), *Handbook of positive psychology* (pp. 74–88). London, England: Oxford University Press.

Masten, A. S., Lucke, C. M., Nelson, K. M., & Stallworthy, I. C. (2021). Resilience in development and psychopathology: Multisystem perspectives. *Annual Review of Clinical Psychology*, *17*, 521–549. https://doi.org/10.1146/annurev-clinpsy-081219-120307

McEwen, B. S., & Gianaros, P. J. (2010). Central role of the brain in stress and adaptation: links to socioeconomic status, health, and disease. *Annals of the New York Academy of Sciences*, 1186(1), 190–222. https://doi.org/10.1111/j.1749-6632.2009.05331.x.

Smith, K. E., & Pollak, S. D. (2020). Early life stress and development: potential mechanisms for adverse outcomes. Journal of Neurodevelopmental Disorders, 12, 34. https://doi.org/10.1186/s11689-020-09337-y. McGregor, H. A. (2003). The shame of failure: Exploring the relationship between fear of failure and shame. Doctoral dissertation, University of Rochester. *Dissertation Abstracts International*, *64*(1), 1942–1950.

xTeicher, M. H., & Samson, J. A. (2016). Annual Research Review: Enduring neurobiological effects of childhood abuse and neglect. Journal of Child Psychology and Psychiatry, 57(3), 241–266. https://doi.org/10.1111/jcpp.12507.

Smith, K. E., & Pollak, S. D. (2020). Early life stress and development: potential mechanisms for adverse outcomes. Journal of Neurodevelopmental Disorders, 12, 34. https://doi.org/10.1186/s11689-020-09337-y.

Mesman, E., Vreeker, A., & Hillegers, M. (2021). Resilience and mental health in children and adolescents: An update of the recent literature and future directions. *Current Opinion in Psychiatry*, *34*(6), 586–592. <https://doi.org/10.1097/YCO.0000000000000741>

Middleton, M. J., & Midgley, C. (1997). Avoiding the demonstration of lack of ability: An unexplored aspect of goal theory. *Journal of Educational Psychology*, *89*, 710–718. <https://doi.org/10.1037/0022-0663.89.4.710>

MindTools (n.d.). Overcoming fear of failure. https://www.mindtools.com/ajg1x98/overcoming-fear-of-failure.

Nakhla, M. A. (2019). *The relationship between fear of failure, academic motivation and student engagement in higher education: A general linear model*. Department of Educational Research, Lancaster University, UK.

Nelson, K. L., & McDaniel, J. R. (2023). Fear of failure: Why is pursuing success so scary? *Scholarly Journal of Psychology and Behavioral Sciences*, 7(1), 799–804. <https://doi.org/10.32474/SJPBS.2023.07.000254>

Neumeister, K. L. S. (2004). Understanding the relationship between perfectionism and achievement motivation in gifted college students. *Gifted Child Quarterly*, *48*(3), 219–231. <https://doi.org/10.1177/001698620404800306>

Payne Resilience Training & Consulting (2020). How to know when your resilience is low. https://payneresilience.com/blog/low-resilience.

Pérez-González, A., Guilera, G., Pereda, N., & Jarne, A. (2017). Protective factors promoting resilience in the relation between child sexual victimization and internalizing and externalizing symptoms. *Child Abuse & Neglect*, 72, 393–403. <https://doi.org/10.1016/j.chiabu.2017.09.006>

Raghunathan, S., Singh, A. D., & Sharma, B. (2022). Study of resilience in learning environments during the Covid-19 pandemic. *Frontiers in Education*, 6, 677625. <https://doi.org/10.3389/feduc.2021.677625>

Smith, C. P. (1969). *Achievement-related motives in children*. Russell Sage.

Teicher, M. H., & Samson, J. A. (2016). Annual Research Review: Enduring neurobiological effects of childhood abuse and neglect. *Journal of Child Psychology and Psychiatry*, 57(3), 241–266. https://doi.org/10.1111/jcpp.12507.

Tipton, S. (2018). 4 ways you are self-sabotaging your learning efforts. *Litmos*. <https://www.litmos.com/blog/articles/4-ways-you-are-self-sabotaging-your-learning-efforts>

The Education Hub (2019). How to help students improve their resilience. <https://theeducationhub.org.nz/wp-content/uploads/2019/08/How-to-help-students-improve-their-resilience.pdf>

Voge, J. (2007). Classroom resources for addressing procrastination. *Research and Teaching in Developmental Education*, *23*(2), 88–96. <https://www.jstor.org/stable/42802292>

Zhang, F. (2022). A theoretical review on the impact of EFL/ESL students' self-sabotaging behaviors on their self-esteem and academic engagement. *Frontiers in Psychology*, *13*, 873734. <https://doi.org/10.3389/fpsyg.2022.8737>

Zhang, Q., Zhou, L., & Xia, J. (2020). Impact of COVID-19 on emotional resilience and learning Management of Middle School Students. *Medical Science Monitor: International Medical Journal of Experimental and Clinical Research*, *26*, e924994. <https://doi.org/10.12659/MSM.924994>

Literacy Competence Strategies in Training Primary School Teachers

Elena Lucia Mara

Abstract: Literacy skills reflect a person's ability to relate to a text. The competent reader understands and interprets the text – even on first close reading – in detail and nuance, uses the information in it, evaluates its ideational content and form, reflects on it, and interacts with it to achieve their goals, enrich their knowledge and enhance their potential, and participate in the society (OECD, 2018). Beyond the important differences between artificial intelligence systems and the complex reality of "natural" human intelligence, the meta-knowledge paradigm has unquestionable heuristic values: locating information, understanding, and reflection. Preparation for a teaching career involves the assimilation of a volume of theoretical knowledge in the specialist and psycho-pedagogical fields in conjunction with the training and development of psycho-pedagogical skills, which is achieved mainly through pedagogical practice of understanding the reading and writing process. The pedagogical practice placement involves a set of activities involving observation, analysis, and lesson support, all under the guidance of a pedagogical practice mentor. The role of the lityeracy skills in the relationship with the beginner teacher should be approached, in a broad sense, from at least three perspectives: before, during, and after writing some texts. This is accompanied by reflections on the design and implementation of personalized, induction programs for beginner teachers, with the goals of initiating the beginner teacher in the interactive design of teaching activities, training their skills, and supporting their professional development.

Keywords: literacy, pedagogical practice, initial training, mentoring.

Literacy skills, as defined by the OECD (2018), reflect a person's ability to relate to a text. Competent readers are able to interpret and evaluate texts, use information for their goals, enrich their knowledge, and actively participate in society. Beyond the important differences between artificial intelligence systems and the complex reality of "natural" human intelligence, the meta-knowledge paradigm has unquestionable heuristic values:

a. *locating information* is the ability to find information in the text that is directly expressed so that the student does not have to make assumptions or inferences to answer correctly.

b. *comprehension*, which involves the ability to make sense of words, sentences, or strings of events in the reading material. Thus, the dimension covers, on the one hand, specific vocabulary knowledge, and on the other hand, meaningful integration of disparate pieces of information in the material and the ability to follow the temporal sequence of events presented.
c. *reflection* is the ability to reflect on a particular part of a piece of material, in order either to get the central idea or to critically evaluate the information accessed.

Similar to the cognitive typology of knowledge (declarative, procedural, conditional), the concept and paradigm of meta-knowledge and meta-cognition have established themselves in the field of cognitive (cognitivist) approaches in psychology and artificial (computational) intelligence studies. Thus, in an expert system – that is, a knowledge-based system designed to model the reasoning of a human expert in a particular domain – meta-knowledge is responsible for managing the knowledge base, to access, select, and structure the knowledge in the knowledge base and ensure the appropriateness of the knowledge to the requirements of the task to be solved. In the same sense, meta-knowledge is responsible for deciding the subsets of knowledge needed to solve a specific problem and for choosing the best strategy to solve a particular problem. At the same time, meta-knowledge is used to control and monitor the use of the knowledge base and to assess its possibilities and limitations.

BRIO is a standardized testing system designed to meet the most rigorous global standards set by psychometric specialists. Together with civil society partners, BRIO launched its literacy test in January 2021. Through BRIO school tests, Romanian students in grades I–XII can objectively assess their knowledge in the main school subjects and improve their performance in exams. These tests measure a person's literacy skills, and more specifically, these skills relate to the ability to read and understand a text and to form an opinion about the information presented. Literacy skills also consist of the ability to express opinion, both orally and in writing, and to use new knowledge in a practical context. The reader has a number of traits relevant to the text and the task: he/she is of a certain age, has a set of general knowledge and life experiences, and a certain level of reading proficiency (decoding, reading speed, and the ability to comprehend, process, and interpret what is being read as well as the task).

The reader's relationship with the text is influenced by several factors related to the text, the reader, and the task. For example, each text has a certain level of complexity (e.g., length, ideational content and related language, structure, text type, and form of presentation) that is familiar to the reader.

The task we are reading for will influence how we read: the mode of reading (fast or deep) we use, the attention we pay to the whole text or parts of it, the context in which we read, the digital or print medium on which we access the text, the difficulty we attribute to the task (including comprehension of the task), and our own perception of the complexity of the text. The BRIO literacy test is accessible free of charge to both students (grades I–VIII) and teachers, based on an account registered on the BRIO platform (www.brio.ro), where the test generation and administration process is carried out, active and completed sessions of students are managed, their results and evaluation reports are centralized, and the progress of tested students can be identified and monitored.

We assume that the students being tested can independently read and manage not only their relationship to the texts offered in the test, but also the requirements of each item. The items were constructed based on the approach of the international tests PIRLS (Progress in International Reading Literacy Study) and PISA (Programme for International Student Assessment), respectively, but do not cover the full range of literacy skills assessed in these tests. In summary, the BRIO literacy test is based on an item bank of approximately 8,000 literacy items, grouped into 3 assessment units (Locating Information, Understanding Text, Reflecting). Each test is custom-generated based on a sample of the items in the item bank, so that two students taking the test at the same time do not receive identical tests. However, based on the item parameters in the system, equivalent tests are always generated in terms of difficulty level.

The BRIO literacy test has a duration of 60–90 minutes, automatically allocated by the system according to the selected test grade level and gives the student access to a set of problems. Each problem consists of a statement (presenting the test context), a text (measuring literacy level) and up to 12 items to solve (measuring each of the three literacy skills). For grade 1, a literacy test contains 3 problems, with a maximum of 30 items and about

60 minutes to solve. For grades 2 to 4, a literacy test contains 4 problems, with approximately 35–50 items, to be completed within 60 minutes. For grades 5 to 8, a test contains 5 problems, based on 40–60 items, to be solved within 90 minutes.

The curriculum for the preparatory classes to second grade proposes a flexible offer that allows the teacher to modify, complete, or replace learning activities. The aim is thus to achieve a personalized teaching approach, which ensures the development of the competences set out in the curriculum in the specific context of each class and each pupil. The inclusion of the preparatory class in general and compulsory education implies a nuanced view of the curriculum at this age level. A specific approach to early education is needed, based essentially on stimulating learning through play, while at the same time offering a wide range of differentiation in the teaching approach, depending on the pupils' varying levels of acquisition. The curriculum of the subject is based on the communicative-functional model, focusing on communication as a complex field that encompasses the processes of receiving oral and written messages as well as oral and written expression. The current curriculum places active, learner-centered learning at its heart. Learning is not a passive process that happens to pupils, but a personal experience in which they must participate. The study of the subject of Communication in Romanian, which begins in the preparatory class, continues until the second grade and ensures a progressive development of competences, by using age-specific experiences of the students and emphasizing the affective-attitudinal and actional dimensions of the formation of the students' personality, as described in the Curricula for Communication in Romanian language, approved in 2013. All these competencies of understanding are continued in the subsequent grades. Developing the ability to receive and write messages in any communication context are the main competencies prioritized in the third and fourth grades, and especially in secondary school. Based on these tasks, we can measure the key competencies. During schooling, children make significant progress in physical and intellectual development, and organized learning becomes the fundamental type of learning activity. In school, they acquire knowledge and learn new skills, including those that cannot be acquired on their own. On advancing to primary school classes, the children experience a change in their social status, assuming greater importance within the family and in the peer group. The list of key competencies are presented, alongside the primary-level competencies, which are more related to literacy:

- *Communication competence in Romanian language*, and in the mother tongue in the case of national minorities, focuses on using a variety of verbal and nonverbal messages to receive and transmit ideas and experiences and monitoring of their own communication and adapting it to different audience categories; the correct and effective use of languages acquired in different disciplines or by informal and non-formal ways. This is the start of the literacy process.
- *Foreign Language Communication* begins formally in the preparatory class, but there are pupils who have acquired this competence at an early stage of oral communication formed in the family and in kindergarten.
- *Learning to learn* is aimed at self-motivation in terms of their own potential of success, the application of intellectual work techniques that valorize the autonomy in the learning process, the assumption of responsibility for their own learning, and so on, including literacy.

To develop key competences in primary school pupils, it is important to consider some of their psychological peculiarities. In primary grades, children are at a higher level of generalization than those in kindergarten, and they can more easily group objects according to common and essential features. In their actions, they remain tied to the concrete and link action to word. Continuing the process of forming the inner language, the student experiences emotions and feelings, is attracted to characters, and tries to imitate them. Learning to learn it can be measured by the school by the end of compulsory education, through PISA evaluation tests (reading, writing, mathematics, and sciences).

For students to be equipped with skills and competences that will help them in lifelong learning, model strategies can be provided in school; Literacy skills belong to the category of strategies that support lifelong learning, becoming an indispensable intellectual tool in adapting to the demands of society. Literacy has recently entered the vocabulary of the Romanian language but has yet to find a translation in the Explanatory Dictionary. Thus, to define the meaning of the notion, the English meaning has been taken as the ability to read, write, use numbers, and understand and use the information encountered in everyday life. The most widely known definition of literacy is the ability to write and read about one subject in everyday life. Romania's case is not a success in terms of literacy – according to the 2022 PISA report, more than 41% of children aged 15 years are functional linguistic illiterates. While reading skills are commonly divided into two categories: decoding of writing, also known as basic reading skill, and reading comprehension, which in turn comprises two categories – word comprehension (semantic analysis of words) and text comprehension (syntactic and semantic analysis of sentences, phrases, or discourse) – we still measure the following skills:

a. *fluency*, which consists of the ability to recognize words spontaneously and to read the text quickly, correctly, and expressively. Fluency is practiced from the development of phonological awareness and the alphabetic principle by the pupil reading simple texts or books on familiar topics and containing mostly common and repetitive vocabulary, without words unknown to the child. As the child's reading becomes more fluent, he/she will read silently or expressively aloud, respecting the meaning of punctuation marks, which also enables him/her to better understand the meaning of the text read.
b. *comprehension*, which is the ability to easily make connections between ideas, extract the message from a text, reflect on it, and draw conclusions. Building an adequate skill in reading requires prior knowledge, language skills, and higher-order thinking skills.
c. *motivation to read*, which is a key factor in engaging the learner in reading. Engaging books with attractive iconography (relevant pictures) should be recommended, considering the chronological and mental age of the pupil.

Creative imagination is the most important form of human imagination – it represents the human capacity to combine old images in our consciousness, or rather in our subconscious, into new forms. Once they have been combined to form a new image, this image becomes objective and takes the form of a work (of art, technology, etc.). Inventions, innovations in various fields, rationalizations, and works of science fiction literature are, to a large extent, the fruits of the creative imagination. Imagination is valued for its originality and for being different from what exists and what has been perceived. As it is used, creative capacity develops and increases in effectiveness. This line of research conceives of creativity as a characteristic of personality, the most exploited understanding of creativity in the current literature. Based on these conceptions, numerous creativity tests have been developed, allocated from a series of appropriate samples, such as simulations of various creative situations, prompting to use intellectual functions. Following what has been presented, we can say that the defining elements of the creative act are: originality – expression of novelty; flexibility – adaptation of thinking to new situations; ingenuity – inventive spirit; sensitivity – ability to feel and to be sensitive; fluency – flow and flexibility in expression; expressiveness – expresses size, shape, color, rhythm, dynamics, productivity (includes solutions, ideas, and materials); and efficiency – usefulness of the creative product. Baseline literacy, which is not related only to reading and writing, involves knowledge of letters, words, and text structure, and involves the following:

a. functional literacy is concerned with the ability to read, write, and understand, which enables a person to function in school and in society.
b. multiple literacy is the ability to use the skills of reading, writing, comprehension, and making connections to produce, interpret, and critically evaluate information that is read or written.
c. in primary school, pupils should reach literacy levels 1 and 2, developing basic literacy and functional literacy skills, and from secondary school onwards, they should reach multiple literacy, developing lexical skills.

Literacy is the concept that refers to the set of skills and abilities that enable a person to collect and process information in each context by reading and transforming it into knowledge, which can be manifested orally or in writing. However, the concept of literacy is characterized by an emphasis on the sociocultural view of learning. This means that it goes beyond cognitive skills. In literacy, not only recognition and understanding through language, but also the influence of the social context and the roles and dynamics of the reader and writer, as well as possible interlocutors, are considered. Concepts used include metacognition, interaction, engagement, literacy, subject literacy, cognitive apprenticeship model, text structure, text diversity, strategies for academic vocabulary development, reading strategy, reading method, reading skills, and reading skills inventory in the subject area.

Some of the strategies used to promote literacy include:

1. Presenting teaching methods based on theories of consistent learning, like Frayer Model, which consists of a type of graphic organizer to construct and develop vocabulary. This model was created by Dorothy Frayer during the late 1970s in the US to fulfill academic vocabulary requirements and help students to learn more efficiently. Being a visual support, it help students to learn abstract concepts by the use of simple and concrete words, usually familiar, in order to apply in everyday life. Basically, it consists of four squares that represent a word's characteristics, definition, examples, and non-examples. This tool allows learners to gain a better understanding of difficult words through clarification and analysis. If teachers use the instructional methods involving the Frayer Model appropriately, they might be able to add the elements of vocabulary teaching described earlier in this chapter (i.e., word selection, clearly contextualizing and defining the vocabulary term, helping pupils actively participate in the word processing, and offering current understanding through several exposures to phrases). The benefits of the Frayer Model extend beyond vocabulary development, serving as an all-encompassing instructional tool that fosters a deeper understanding of subject-specific terminology. Its efficacy in propelling student learning makes the Frayer Model an indispensable resource for teachers, enhancing the educational experience across a wide array of disciplines (see Figure 6.1).

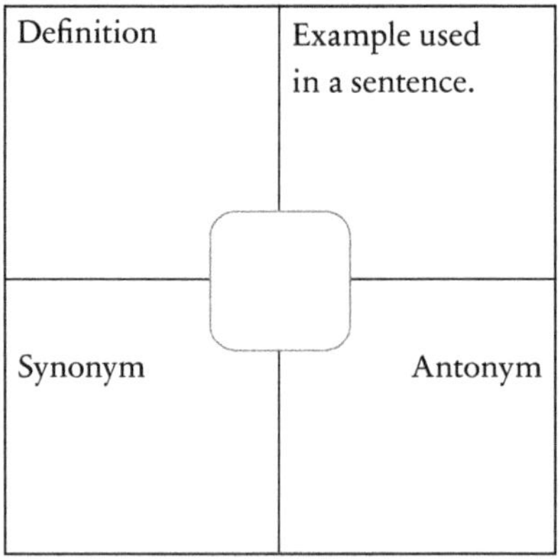

Figure 6.1 Frayer Model

2. Open, collegial, collaborative relationships among students to facilitate the sharing of ideas, in a *Definition Map*, which is a combination of words and visual designs/images that could help students to understand the meaning of the word by categories, properties, and illustrations (Figure 6.2).

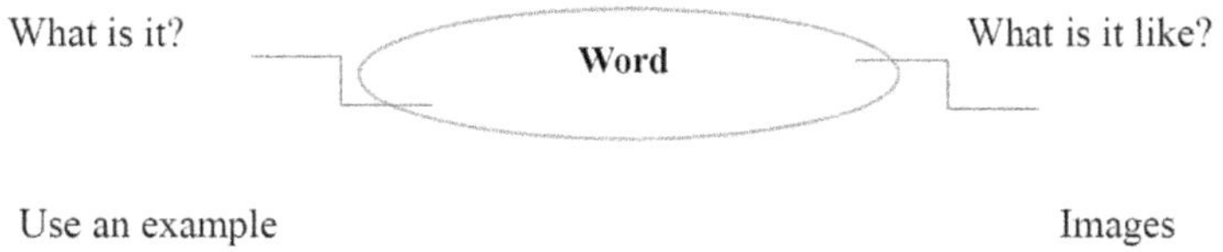

Figure 6.2. Definition map

3. Support teachers in their efforts to develop students' ability to think critically, engage in critical reflection, and take responsibility for their learning, form their own opinions, and respect the opinions of others, through a *Mind Map*, an important tool to help students to visualize thoughts and communicate them to the others, the steps of which are listed below.
   a. Enter the main topic. Start by entering the main subject in the center of the mind map,[1] for instance "Capitals of the world."
   b. Brainstorming topics. Create main branches to enter your topics such as "London," "Paris," "New York," and "Beijing." Do not worry about the order of the topics.
   c. Create sub-topics. Elaborate on your topics by creating sub-topics. Make sure to use very short phrases or even single words.
   d. Rearrange the topics. If you need to rearrange the topics in your mind map, most software tools allow you to drag-and-drop branches. This will enable you to structure the topics that you brainstormed.
   e. Add images and formatting. According to the mind mapping theory,[2] images and colors improve memory retention. You can use different colors and fonts and place images on branches.
   f. Notes and research. Take notes to your topics and attached research files – if your mind mapping software allows you to.

---

1 https://www.mindmapping.com/mind-map
2 https://www.mindmapping.com/mind-map#mindmap-theory

At the end of the initialization in studying courses regarding literacy, students should be able to plan and develop lessons that contribute to the development of critical thinking, use strategies to develop modern learning skills leading to interdisciplinary and cross-curricular extensions, and foster the training of individuals for whom information is more the point of rather than the end goal of learning. If during the Romanian language and literature class hours, active-participatory methods are used, centered on the student, these will determine the development, activation, and enrichment of the active vocabulary of the students; the development of oral and written expression; the education of creative and original skills in finding solutions to a given task; engagement in free, open, creative discussions; as well as development of superior cognitive mechanisms: thinking, memory, and imagination. The independent variable involves using modern methods specific to stimulate creativity and development and to enrich the vocabulary in Romanian language and literature in the third grade. The dependent variable consists of the active involvement of the students in the learning process, the changes that take place at the level of the vocabulary as well as the way of expression, the development of confidence in their own forces, but especially in the results obtained from the activities carried out.

Literacy skills are important for the following reasons:

- Improves school results: A child who can use a textbook without difficulty will learn much faster, irrespective of the subject. He is likely to understand tasks easily and solve them correctly. Children can achieve learning objectives and learn the skills required by the curriculum and syllabus. School results will be commensurate, so in the long run, the children have a chance to reach prestigious educational centers.
- Helps improve future career prospects: We may live in a world of images, but written text is essential for professional development. Literacy skills ensure quick learning on the job, adaptation to different situations, and effective communication with colleagues and clients. In a competitive job market, being able to relate to text quickly and effectively is very important.
- Helps prevent manipulation: A person who can interpret a text and make judgments based on information, tone, or style is less vulnerable to manipulation and fraud. In the digital world, people are safe targets for manipulation if they cannot understand a text in depth.

Reading is a good tool for practicing and improving literacy skills. Books should be appropriate to a person's level of mental and intellectual development. Books with quoestions or games at the end are also useful because they stimulate active reading. It is recommended to read texts in print, whether books or magazines. When reading digitally, the temptation to glance at other apps or software is great. Literacy strategies in general – and those presented here in particular as important steps in learning and in the formation of functional literacy – have several advantages in school practice, ensuring an understanding of specialized texts facilitating learning and fixation of knowledge through associations with previously assimilated information, ensuring durability of information and applicability of knowledge, and facilitating motivation, involvement, and activation of students in learning. Literacy strategies should be an area familiar to teachers across all specialties to help shape students' well-rounded literacy skills in order to prepare them to become functionally literate citizens.

References

Iliescu, D., & Airinei, M. (2022). *Raport privind nivelul de literație al elevilor din România* [Report on the literacy level of students in Romania]. București, Romania: Editura BRIO.

OECD. (2018). PISA 2018 Results (Volume I): The State of Learning and Equity in Education. OECD Publishing.

Rizescu, I., Filipescu, V., & Serdean, I. (2011). *Diferentierea activității cu elevii în ciclul primar* [Differentiation of teaching activities with primary school pupils]. București, Romania: Editura Didactică și Pedagogică.

Stanciu, M. (1999). *Reforma conținuturilor învățământului* [The reform of school curricula]. Iași, Romania: Editura Polirom.

Stoica-Constantin, A. (2004). *Creativitatea pentru studenți și profesori* [Creativity for students and teachers]. Iași, Romania: Editura Institutul European.

Wolf, M. (2008). *Proust and the squid: The story and science of the reading brain*. Icon Books.

Online resources

www.brio.ro
https://stats.oecd.org/glossary/detail.asp?ID=5420
https://en.unesco.org/themes/literacy

http://uil.unesco.org/literacy/global-alliance
https://www.theliteracybug.com/stages
https://dictionary.cambridge.org/dictionary/english/literacy
https://www.sedl.org/.../teaching_content_area_literacy_and_disciplinary_literacy.pdf
www.sedl.org
https://community.articulate.com/discussions/building-better-courses/free-mind-map-template
https://www.nchsoftware.com/

School Management in the New Context

Marius Claudiu Langa

Abstract: In the fast-paced world of education, school management faces both unprecedented challenges and opportunities. Rapid technological advancements, shifting demographics, and changing societal expectations have given rise to a new context for school management. In this chapter, we will explore the multifaceted aspects of school management in this evolving landscape, delving into the key areas that demand attention and innovation. From embracing technology to future trends and challenges in education, this chapter provides a comprehensive guide to navigating the complexities of school management in the new context.

Keywords: school management, learning, teacher empowerment, well-being.

Introduction

The role of technology in education cannot be overstated. In the new context, schools must integrate technology seamlessly into their operations. This involves investing in robust IT infrastructure, providing digital resources, and equipping educators with the skills needed for effective technology integration. Moreover, schools must address issues such as digital equity, data security, and the evolving role of digital citizenship in education.

1. Embracing Technology

In light of the swift and ongoing digitalization of our economy, it is crucial for educators to lead the way in terms of curriculum and practical resources, ensuring that our students develop the essential skills of critical thinking, creativity, and inquiry. These skills are vital for them to contribute effectively in a future where machines will collaborate with human professionals. By embracing digitalization to enrich the learning process and offer engaging, interactive activities and experiences, educators can proactively address the technological advancements on the horizon (Crittenden et al., 2018)

1.1 Benefits of Technology Integration

Technology enriches the learning process by providing interactive, multimedia-rich content. It caters to different learning styles and allows students to explore concepts through simulations, videos, and online resources. Technology enables adaptive learning platforms that can tailor content to individual student needs. This personalization fosters greater engagement and better learning outcomes.

Educational technology can streamline administrative tasks, allowing teachers to focus more on instruction and personalized support for students.

1.2 Strategies for Successful Technology Integration

Vision and Leadership: School leaders should create a clear vision for technology integration and provide strong leadership to drive the initiative forward.

Infrastructure Development: Schools need reliable Wi-Fi, hardware, and software to support technology integration. Investment in infrastructure is essential.

Professional Development: Comprehensive training programs should be offered to teachers and staff to ensure they are comfortable and proficient in the technology they use.

Curriculum Alignment: Technology integration should align with the curriculum to enhance learning outcomes. Teachers should incorporate technology seamlessly into their lessons.

Continuous Evaluation: Regular assessment of the effectiveness of technology integration is essential. Schools should collect feedback from students, teachers, and parents to make necessary adjustments.

Embracing technology in schools is not merely an option but a necessity in the 21st century. It enhances learning experiences, personalizes education, and prepares students for a digital world. While challenges exist, with careful planning, leadership, and investment, schools can harness the power of technology to provide students with a more engaging and effective education.

2. Data-Driven Decision Making

Data has become an invaluable asset in school management. The utilization of data to guide educational practices has gained prominence in the last decade (Mandinach & Jackson, 2012). This approach encompasses not only the collection and reporting of data but, more significantly, the analysis of data and the exploration of explanatory or predictive models. These endeavors are aimed at acquiring valuable insights for informed decision-making in addressing intricate educational matters (Bichsel, 2012)

2.1 The Significance of Data-Driven Decision Making

Data-driven decision making (DDDM) enables schools to identify at-risk students, assess their progress, and tailor interventions to meet their needs, ultimately leading to improved academic performance. Schools must allocate resources more efficiently based on data, ensuring that funding, personnel, and time are directed where they will have the greatest impact. Data-driven practices enhance accountability by providing evidence of progress and outcomes, fostering transparency in school management.

2.2 Challenges in Implementing DDDM

Data Quality and Availability: Ensuring that data is accurate, complete, and accessible can be challenging. Schools must invest in data infrastructure and data management systems.

Privacy and Security: The collection and storage of student data must adhere to strict privacy and security regulations. Schools need robust data protection policies.

Professional Development: Teachers and staff require training to effectively collect, analyze, and use data in their decision-making processes.

Resistance to Change: Implementing DDDM may face resistance from stakeholders who are uncomfortable with data-driven approaches or fear the misuse of data. Resistance to DDDM often stems from fear of the unknown. Stakeholders may be comfortable with traditional decision-making processes they have used for years, and the introduction of data-driven approaches can be perceived as disruptive or threatening.

2.3 Strategies for Successful DDDM Implementation

Establish Data Culture

Creating a culture that values data as a driver of improvement is foundational. Schools should communicate the importance of data and provide training. Organizations that embrace a data culture are better equipped to thrive in a data-driven world. By fostering a culture that values data, prioritizes data literacy, and upholds ethical data practices, organizations can make more informed decisions, drive innovation, and remain agile in the face of uncertainty.

Align Data with Goals

Data should align with the school's educational goals and priorities. Aligning data with goals empowers school leaders to make informed decisions based on evidence, rather than intuition or tradition. This leads to more effective resource allocation and strategic planning. Data alignment allows schools to track progress toward their goals, identifying areas of success and areas that need improvement.

Continuous Improvement

DDDM is not a static process; rather, it is an ongoing journey of improvement and refinement. Organizations that embrace DDDM must continuously adapt, learn, and evolve to maximize its benefits. Implement data quality assurance measures to ensure that the data being used for decision-making is accurate, complete, and reliable.

DDDM has the power to transform education by improving student outcomes and enhancing school management. While challenges exist, with the right strategies, a commitment to data culture, and investments in data infrastructure, schools can harness the potential of data to make informed decisions that benefit students and the entire educational community.

3. Flexible Learning Environments in Modern Education

The concept of a flexible learning environment has gained significant traction in recent years, reshaping the way education is delivered and experienced.

Educational experiences can occur through various modalities, commonly categorized into face-to-face classroom instruction, virtual learning, and further divided into asynchronous and synchronous formats (Chaeruman et al., 2018). Presently, online technologies are predominantly employed for virtual and asynchronous learning, while the combination of these technologies with traditional classroom instruction is known as blended learning. Personalized adaptive learning can be developed based on four key components, which include learner profiles, competency-based progression, individualized learning, and adaptable learning environments (Peng et al., 2019).

There are various models of flexible learning environments, such as blended learning, flipped classrooms, and self-paced learning.

Blended learning, often referred to as hybrid learning, is an educational approach that combines traditional in-person classroom instruction with online or digital components. This approach seeks to leverage the strengths of both face-to-face and online learning to create a more flexible and effective learning experience.

In a blended learning environment, students typically engage in a variety of learning activities, including:

1. *In-Person Instruction:* This aspect involves students physically attending classes with teachers or instructors. These in-person sessions often include interactive discussions, hands-on activities, group work, and lectures.
2. *Online Learning:* In addition to in-person instruction, students use online resources such as video lectures, discussion forums, interactive simulations, and digital assessments. These resources can be accessed both inside and outside the classroom.
3. *Self-Paced Components:* Blended learning often incorporates self-paced learning modules, allowing students to progress through materials at their own speed. These modules can include quizzes, readings, and multimedia content.
4. *Assessment and Feedback:* Assessment may occur through both traditional methods (e.g., in-class exams or presentations) and digital assessments (e.g., online quizzes or assignments). Feedback is often provided electronically.

5. *Collaborative Activities:* Blended learning encourages collaborative activities both in person and online. Students may collaborate on projects, engage in online discussions, or work together on group assignments.

A “flipped classroom” reverses the traditional teaching model. In a flipped classroom, students are introduced to new content or concepts outside of class through digital resources like videos, readings, or online tutorials. Class time is then used for active engagement, such as discussions, problem-solving, and collaborative projects, allowing students to apply what they have learned. This approach promotes deeper understanding and active participation.

On the other hand, “self-paced learning” places students in control of their learning pace and path. Students can progress through course materials independently, choosing when and how they engage with the content. This approach accommodates diverse learning styles and allows students to focus on areas where they need more time or exploration.

Both flipped classrooms and self-paced learning leverage technology to enhance education. They provide flexibility, foster student independence, and can lead to more personalized learning experiences. These pedagogical approaches reflect the evolving landscape of education, adapting to the needs and preferences of today’s students.

3.1. Benefits of Flexible Learning Environments

Personalization: Flexible learning environments allow for personalized learning experiences tailored to individual student needs and preferences.

Increased Engagement: Students are more engaged when they have agency over their learning, leading to improved retention and motivation.

Accessibility and Inclusivity: Flexible learning environments can accommodate diverse learning styles and needs, making education more accessible and inclusive.

Preparedness for the Future: These environments better prepare students for the changing demands of the modern workforce, where adaptability and self-directed learning are essential skills.

3.2 Strategies for Successful Implementation

Vision and Leadership

Visionary leaders in education are not content with the status quo. They envision a future where learning is not bound by the constraints of time, place, or pace. A well-defined vision serves as a compass, guiding the development and transformation of learning environments to meet the needs of diverse learners. A compelling vision for flexible learning environments aligns with broader educational goals. Leaders must ensure that the pursuit of flexibility supports key educational objectives, such as personalized learning, improved student outcomes, and equity in education.

Leaders in flexible learning environments must be adaptive. They understand that change is constant and embrace it as an opportunity for growth. Adaptive leaders inspire their teams to innovate and evolve, creating dynamic and responsive learning environments. Effective leadership empowers educators to explore new teaching methods, leverage technology, and design learning experiences that cater to individual student needs. Leaders foster a culture of collaboration and experimentation that fuels innovation.

Inclusive leadership is vital in ensuring that flexible learning environments benefit all students, regardless of their backgrounds or abilities. Leaders prioritize diversity, equity, and inclusion, taking deliberate actions to bridge achievement gaps and remove barriers to learning.

In the ever-changing landscape of education, visionary leadership is the compass that guides the transformation of learning environments into flexible, adaptive spaces that empower learners. A well-crafted vision, aligned with educational goals, and adaptive leadership that empowers educators and promotes inclusivity are the cornerstones of success. Through real-world case studies, we gain insights into how visionary leaders are shaping the future of education, ensuring that all students have the opportunity to thrive in flexible learning environments.

Infrastructure and Resources

High-speed and reliable internet access is the backbone of modern flexible learning. Schools and institutions must invest in robust connectivity to ensure seamless online interactions. They must curate a diverse collection of digital learning resources, including e-books, interactive simulations, videos, and online assessments, to support various learning styles and preferences. Educational institutions should also explore the use of Open Educational Resources (OER), which are freely available educational materials, to reduce costs and enhance access to high-quality learning content.

Flexible learning environments have the potential to revolutionize education by providing personalized, engaging, and adaptable learning experiences. While challenges exist, with thoughtful planning, strong leadership, and investments in technology and teacher training, schools can harness the benefits of flexible learning to prepare students for a rapidly changing world.

4. Community Engagement

Schools are recognizing the vital role of community engagement in the current educational landscape shaped by digital transformation, post-pandemic changes, and the emphasis on flexibility and lifelong learning. Community engagement in the context of education emphasizes the collaborative nature and focus on shared goals. Identifying the various stakeholders in community engagement, including parents, local businesses, nonprofit organizations, government agencies, and community members, is essential for a quality education.

Teachers, school staff, and administrators at various educational levels, including schools, districts, and states, must not only acknowledge the significance of these partnerships but also allocate resources toward programs that foster professional growth and the effective execution of these approaches. The perspective regarding the families and communities served by schools should transition from a focus on deficiencies to one that emphasizes their strengths (Molina, 2013)

4.1 The Importance of Community Engagement

Resource Enrichment: Engaging with the local community can provide educational institutions with valuable resources. This can include financial support, donations of materials, access to facilities, and even expertise from community members. These resources can enhance the learning environment and provide opportunities for students that may not have been possible otherwise.

Real-World Learning: Community engagement often involves students in practical, real-world learning experiences. For example, internships, service-learning projects, and collaborations with local businesses or organizations expose students to authentic problems and challenges. This hands-on learning approach can deepen their understanding of academic subjects and boost their problem-solving skills.

Support Systems: Community engagement can help establish strong support networks for students. Community members, such as mentors or volunteers, can provide guidance, tutoring, and mentorship, which can be particularly beneficial for students facing academic challenges.

Career Readiness: Many community engagement activities, such as internships or apprenticeships, provide students with practical skills and experiences that are directly relevant to their future careers. This can increase their employability and success in the job market after graduation.

Positive School Culture: Community engagement can contribute to the development of a positive school culture. When schools are seen as integral parts of the community, there is often a sense of pride and ownership among students, parents, and community members. This positive culture can boost students' confidence and well-being, which in turn can lead to academic success.

Research Opportunities: Collaboration with the community can open up research opportunities for academic institutions. Research projects that address community needs can provide students with valuable research experience while also benefiting the community.

Community engagement is a cornerstone of effective education. By fostering collaboration between schools and their communities, educators can enhance student success, mobilize resources, and promote a sense of civic responsibility. While challenges exist, with careful planning, inclusive practices, and a commitment to open communication, schools can create strong partnerships that benefit both students and the broader community.

5. Teacher Empowerment and Well-being

Empowered teachers are not only more effective in the classroom but also lead healthier and more fulfilling lives. Teacher empowerment refers to the process of equipping educators with the knowledge, skills, resources, and authority to make meaningful decisions about their work and environment. It involves granting teachers a sense of autonomy, trust, and ownership in their professional roles. Empowered teachers feel that they have the capacity to influence change, both in their classrooms and within the broader education system.

Numerous research studies and academic literature have consistently concluded that empowerment exerts a substantial and favorable influence on the organizational behaviors of teachers (Calibayan, 2015; Shah & Abualrob, 2012; Somech & Bogler, 2002). Organizational behaviors of teachers encompass their actions and attitudes in relation to both their peers and the educational institution itself (Babu & Venkatesh, 2016; Thurlings et al., 2015). Encouraging and embracing positive organizational behavior among teachers should be a priority across all educational institutions, as its primary objective is to foster an environment that is dedicated to the sustainability and advancement of the organization (Cartwright & Cooper, 2014; Demir, 2015).

5.1. The Relationship Between Empowerment and Well-being

Enhanced Job Satisfaction: Empowered teachers are more satisfied with their jobs. They feel valued, respected, and trusted, which positively impacts their overall job satisfaction. When teachers are content in their roles, it naturally contributes to their overall well-being. According to Hoy and Miskel (2013), many factors that contribute to increased job satisfaction also serve to empower teachers. Interestingly, one way to identify empowered teachers is by evaluating their capacity to make independent decisions (Jiang et al., 2019). Harper (2018) find a significant correlation between empowerment levels and job satisfaction. However, while Ceminsky (2018) demonstrates that job satisfaction and teacher empowerment are not identical, a meta-analysis conducted by Chamberlin et al. (2018) reveal a substantial association between these two concepts, indicating that higher empowerment tends to be closely linked with increased job satisfaction.

Reduced Stress: Empowerment can reduce stress levels among educators. When teachers have control over decisions related to their teaching methods,

Artificial Intelligence and Machine Learning

The integration of artificial intelligence (AI) and machine learning is revolutionizing education. These technologies are being harnessed to provide adaptive learning experiences, automate administrative tasks, and enhance educational outcomes. AI-powered chatbots can provide immediate support to students, while machine learning algorithms can analyze data to identify areas where students may struggle and recommend personalized resources or interventions. In addition, AI-driven assessment tools are capable of providing real-time feedback, allowing educators to tailor instruction to individual student needs.

Virtual and Augmented Reality

Virtual reality (VR) and augmented reality (AR) are transforming the way we learn by creating immersive educational experiences and simulations. VR can transport students to historical events, distant planets, or even inside the human body, providing a level of engagement and understanding that traditional textbooks cannot match. AR overlays digital information onto the physical world, allowing students to interact with 3D models or access additional context and resources in real-time. These technologies have the potential to make learning more engaging and interactive.

Lifelong Learning

The concept of lifelong learning is gaining prominence in an era where the skills needed for the workforce are constantly evolving. Lifelong learning emphasizes the importance of ongoing education and skill development throughout one's life. As automation and AI continue to reshape industries, individuals must be prepared to adapt and acquire new skills. Educational institutions and employers are increasingly offering flexible, online, and micro-credentialing options to support individuals in their pursuit of lifelong learning. This trend reflects a shift away from traditional education pathways and toward a more dynamic and continuous approach to learning.

The future of education is marked by a commitment to personalized learning, the integration of AI and machine learning, the use of virtual and augmented reality, and the promotion of lifelong learning. These trends hold the potential to transform education, making it more accessible, engaging, and responsive to the needs of learners in a rapidly changing world. As educators, administrators, and policymakers embrace these trends, they have the opportunity to shape a brighter future for education and prepare students for success in the present time.

6.2. Future Challenges in Education

While the future of education holds promise, it also presents a set of challenges that educators, policymakers, and stakeholders must address to ensure equitable, effective, and future-ready learning environments.

Digital Divide

The digital divide remains a significant challenge, potentially exacerbating educational inequalities. Disparities in access to technology and the internet can limit students' opportunities for online learning and digital literacy development. Bridging this divide is essential to ensure that all students, regardless of their socio-economic background, have equal access to educational resources and opportunities.

Data Privacy and Security

As education increasingly relies on data collection and analysis to personalize learning experiences and improve outcomes, concerns about data privacy and security continue to grow. Schools and institutions must navigate the complexities of data governance, protecting student privacy while leveraging data for educational purposes. Robust policies, ethical data practices, and cybersecurity measures are essential to address these challenges.

Teacher Training and Professional Development

The rapid evolution of educational technologies and teaching methodologies requires ongoing teacher training and professional development. Educators must acquire the skills and knowledge necessary to effectively integrate technology into their classrooms and adapt to changing pedagogical approaches. Ensuring that teachers have access to quality training opportunities is crucial for maintaining educational excellence.

Curriculum Relevance

The challenge of keeping curricula relevant in a fast-paced, ever-changing world is a pressing concern. Educational institutions must continually update and adapt their curricula to align with the skills and knowledge needed for the future workforce. Ensuring that education remains relevant and responsive to societal and economic shifts is vital to preparing students for success.

Data Governance and Ethics

Developing robust data governance policies is essential. Schools and institutions should establish clear guidelines for data collection, storage, and usage. Ethical data practices, including informed consent and data anonymization, should be prioritized to protect student privacy.

Curriculum Flexibility

Creating flexible and adaptable curricula is crucial for addressing changing educational needs. Curriculum development should involve collaboration between educators, industry experts, and policymakers to ensure alignment with workforce demands. Integrating interdisciplinary and project-based learning can foster adaptability.

While future challenges in education are significant, they also present opportunities for positive change and growth. By addressing the digital divide, prioritizing data governance and ethics, investing in teacher training, and ensuring curriculum relevance, education can adapt to the evolving needs of students and society, ultimately preparing learners for a dynamic and uncertain future.

Conclusions

School management in the new context is a multifaceted endeavor that demands adaptability, innovation, and a commitment to excellence. By embracing technology, fostering inclusivity, engaging the community, empowering teachers, and addressing financial sustainability, schools can navigate these challenges successfully and provide students with a high-quality education that prepares them for the dynamic world of the 21st century.

The field of education stands at a pivotal juncture, poised for transformation in the face of rapid societal, technological, and pedagogical changes. We underscore the importance of collaboration and adaptability. Schools must recognize that the challenges and opportunities discussed in this book are not isolated; they are interconnected facets of modern education. Effective school management in the new context requires holistic approaches that consider all these elements simultaneously.

As schools strive to embrace these changes, they must also be vigilant about addressing potential challenges. Bridging the digital divide, protecting data privacy, providing ongoing professional development, and ensuring curriculum relevance are vital endeavors. These challenges are not obstacles but opportunities for growth and improvement.

References

Babu, M. R., & Venkatesh, K. (2016). Organizational climate among primary school teachers with respect to gender and management. *The International Journal of Indian Psychology*, *3*(3), 6–9.

Bichsel, J. (2012). *Analytics in higher education: Benefits, barriers, progress, and recommendations*. EDUCAUSE Center for Applied Research. <http://net.educause.edu/ir/library/pdf/ERS1207/ers1207.Pdf>

Calibayan, M. L. (2015, December). Teacher empowerment and organizational commitment in state colleges and universities of region XII. *Paper presented at the 3rd International Conference on Higher Education*, Olongapo City, Philippines.

Cartwright, S., & Cooper, C. L. (2014). Towards organizational health stress, positive organizational behavior, and employee well-being. In G. F. Bauer & O. Hammig (Eds.), *Bridging occupational, organizational, and public health* (pp. 29–42). Springer.

Ceminsky, S. (2018). *Principal leadership behaviors that influence teacher job satisfaction* (Doctoral dissertation). University of La Verne.

Chaeruman, U. A., Wibawa, B., & Syahrial, Z. (2018). Determining the appropriate blend of blended learning: A formative research in the context of Spada-Indonesia. *American Journal of Educational Research*, *6*(3), 188–195.

Chamberlin, M., Newton, D. W., & LePine, J. A. (2018). A meta-analysis of empowerment and voice as transmitters of high-performance managerial practices to job performance. *Journal of Organizational Behavior*, *39*(10), 1296–1313. <https://doi.org/10.1002/job.2295>

Crittenden, W. F., Biel, I. K., & Lovely, W. A. (2019). Embracing digitalization: Student learning and new technologies. *Journal of Marketing Education*, 41(1), 5–14. https://doi.org/10.1177/0273475318820895.

Demir, K. (2015). The effect of organizational trust on the culture of teacher leadership in primary schools. *Educational Sciences: Theory and Practice*, 15(3), 621–634.

Hoy, W. K., & Miskel, C. G. (2013). *Educational administration: Theory research and practice* (9th ed.). McGraw Hill.

Jiang, Y., Li, P., Wang, J., & Li, H. (2019). Relationships between kindergarten teachers' empowerment, job satisfaction, and organizational climate: A Chinese model. *Journal of Research in Childhood Education*, 33(2), 257–270. <https://doi.org/10.1080/02568543. 2019.1577773>

Harper, K. L.-I. (2018). *Shared decision making and its relationship to job satisfaction and organizational climate* (Doctoral dissertation). University of Alabama.

Mandinach, E. B., & Jackson, S. S. (2012). *Transforming teaching and learning through data-driven decision making*. Corwin Press.

Molina, S. C. (2013). Family, school, community engagement, and partnerships: An area of continued inquiry and growth. *Teaching Education*, *24*(2), 235–238. <https://doi.org 10.1080/10476210.2013.786894>

Peng, H., Ma, S. & Spector, J. M. (2019), Personalized adaptive learning: An emerging pedagogical approach enabled by a smart learning environment. *Smart Learning Environments*, *6*, 9. <https://doi.org/10.1186/s40561-019-0089-y>

Shah, M., & Abualrob, M. M. (2012). Teacher collegiality and teacher professional commitment in public secondary schools in Islamabad, Pakistan. *Procedia – Social and Behavioral Sciences*, *46*, 950–954. <https://doi.org/10.1016/j.sbspro.2012.05.229>

Somech, A., & Bogler, R. (2002). Antecedents and consequences of teachers' organizational and professional commitment. *Educational Administration Quarterly*, *38*(4), *555–577*.

Thurlings, M., Evers, A. T., & Vermeulen, M. (2015). Toward a model of explaining teachers' innovative behavior: A literature review. *Review of Educational Research*, *85*(3), 430–471. <https://doi.org/10.3102/0034654314557949>

Reflections on Students' Teaching Practice

Letiţia Simona Muntean Trif and Maria Iulia Felea

Abstract: Training future teachers involves both theoretical (in university) and practical (before and after graduation) learning within the classroom that regards the translation of teaching theory into practice as a natural development. This translation takes place within a process that involves sequences of acquiring theoretical knowledge on fundamental subjects, applied disciplines specific to primary and preschool education, and specialized didactics, combined with practical and reflective activity, thereby ensuring the efficiency of the teaching activity. Learning teaching skills means not only that students know the subject and the didactical methodology of their area of specialization, but also that they learn a wide array of processes and activities taking place in the classroom. Students need skills, tools, and procedures that can help them continue their lifelong professional learning and constantly reflect on their own professional/didactic practices. Nowadays, the transition from theory to practice must authentically take place in schools, and mentors should be able to help practicing students apply reflective didactic practice. In this regard, this chapter presents a quality analysis of practicing students' teaching activities enrolled in the Primary and Preschool Education Pedagogy Bachelor's Program by identifying their specific behaviors based on reflections supported by the mentor teacher.

Keywords: pedagogical practice, didactic competence, learning how to teach, reflection.

Introduction

From the perspective of students undergoing their initial teacher training, *the pedagogical practice* they underwent during their studies, followed by the beginner stage in school, often highlights the crucial role played by the mentor in the training and development of didactic skills. Students take the road from merely knowing about the teaching process to applying that knowledge in a realistic context under the supervision of their mentor. Showcasing teacher-like behavior in a schooling context must be complemented by a trial of analytical skills development, by which the soon-to-be teacher in training creates meaning and establishes the significance of their efforts channeled toward developing their practical experience. It allows the student, as a novice teacher, and the mentor to decide during the planning and teaching stages and subsequently act autonomously in different contexts, increasingly aware of their potential.

Theoretical framework

During the initial training as teachers, students focus on forming their fundamental teaching competencies. These competencies are practiced and demonstrated in pedagogical practice. The formation of competence depends on a fair balance between the isolated activity carried out by each of its various elements and their integration in operationalizing situations (Şerbănescu et al., 2020).

The didactic competencies specific to the teachers' initial training include transferring the procedures specific to the subject studied at an undergraduate level to a didactic methodology that is relevant to that subject; identifying learning/teaching/assessment problems at classroom/group level; conducting research projects relevant to classroom/school level in order to optimize the didactic process and the development of meta-cognitive competencies; and promoting activities based on certain practices and didactic experiences with a social and ethical impact, in both mono-and trans-disciplinary views (OMEC nr. 4524/2020).

The development of teaching competencies is described from the perspective of two approaches to learning the didactic profession, in the form of two conceptual models:

- the initial training model, which is based on acquired competencies that view the didactic profession as a pragmatic, executive occupation, wherein practice is the key element. During initial training, this model prioritizes the development of specific skills, which become competencies and are used as means of achieving validation within the workplace.
- the initial training model which is based on reflective practice. There are many arguments in favor of adopting such a model, as superior to the aforementioned one. First, not only do the current socio-economic dynamics demand professionals to continuously develop their skills and competencies, but they also require them to improve their attitudes and professional personality. Moreover, teachers must decide on the go, adapt to the new digital technologies, to the trends and mentalities in education, and improvise and learn to properly react to the unknown.

Moreover, the teacher's activity carries moral and social values. Developing a critical conscience through reflection facilitates the transformation and constant improvement of teachers' practical actions and enhances their possibility to adapt to unique situations (Bernat, 2009).

A contrast analysis of the two perspectives, the *technical* teacher and the *artistic*, *reflective* one, has initiated numerous discussions on the necessary elements that must be a part of any training program for future teachers.

In the context of the pedagogical practice analysis, the mentor, through discussion and detailed analysis of the experiences and challenges encountered in the teaching activity, completes the structure of the teaching paradigm with pedagogical reflection as a fundamental component of teaching practices and professional behavior (Olsen et al., 2020).

The characteristics of initial training based on reflection are (Pavelescu & Mara, 2011, p. 38):

- Accepting the complexity of the relationship between practice and personal and formal theory;
- Accepting a holistic conception of practice;
- Problem-solving as a method of approaching practice;
- Acknowledging the trainee's need to investigate their practical activity;
- Seeking the meaning of the experience by reflecting on it;
- Attempting to discover what lies behind the practice – hypotheses, values, beliefs, and personal theories;
- Collaborating with coworkers – the framework to reflect, deliberate, and better understand the practice.

It is currently considered that the transition from theory to practice must authentically take place in schools and that mentors can help practicing students cultivate reflective didactic practice (Hattie, 2014; Marzano, 2015; Pop-Păcurar, 2021; Quinn et al., 2014; Stolovitch & Keeps, 2017).

Therefore, we can affirm that teaching is learned experientially, reflectively, and subsequently, as per the typology of the *learning teaching cycle*, through which reflection is a process transcending all sequences of learning teaching skills and consists of the following stages:

- *planning and reflection*, which begins with accepting the need to plan and project the lesson, and the didactic activity;

- *action and reflection*, as the stage in which the teaching activity in the classroom takes place;
- *supervision and reflection of results,* which is the stage meeting the need to establish how the quality of the performed activity, as the stage of verification, appreciation, including measurement (evaluation) of the results;
- *the reverse connection* from the perspective of two dimensions: the initial feedback for the final result; secondary feedback, a reflective one, aimed at correcting, optimizing and improving a future activity of another teaching approach.

The process is cyclical and spiraling, having a developmental nature in acquiring the competencies specific to the didactic profession (Pavelescu & Mara, 2011, p. 39).

At the same time, students need to be provided with explanations and to understand this cycle, still through reflection, under the guidance of a mentor, and by practicing it with their support. During the process of developing teaching competencies, again, reflection is fundamental because it highlights the need for offering and receiving feedback.

Scope and study objectives

In this context, we set out, as a general scope, to analyze the quality of the teaching activities carried out by Primary and Preschool Pedagogy Education students, by identifying their specific behavior, based on some reflection and self-reflection activities conducted in collaboration with their mentor teacher.

The present study aims to achieve the following important objectives:

- Analyzing adaptation particularities and flexible approach of teaching behaviors explicitly concerning outcomes related to competencies/behavioral dimensions and learning situations projection in connection with the operational objectives;
- Identifying students' attitudes toward improving their lesson content selection and processing skills (systematized knowledge, formulations; clear and grammatically correct expressions) and adaptation to the classroom's psycho-pedagogical particularities;
- Identifying indicators for selecting learning-centered and pupil-centered didactic strategies (the teacher valorizes prior knowledge,

promptly corrects and offers correct models, organizes lesson contents in smaller units, facilitates the transition toward learning the new contents, and enables direct interaction between students and the reality they are learning about).

Sample population

The sample population is 55 full-time and distance-learning students enrolled in the Preschool and Primary Education Pedagogy Bachelor's Program. The respondents are primarily women (96.4%), of age 20 years (16.4%), 33 years (7.3%), 35 years (9.1%), and a long-distance student aged 54 years. The majority of the surveyed respondents have some level of seniority in education as follows: 45.2% have up to one-year seniority in education, 16.1% have seniority of 1–2 years, and 19.2% have up to 10 years seniority, the rest of the respondents having no seniority (see Figure 8.1).

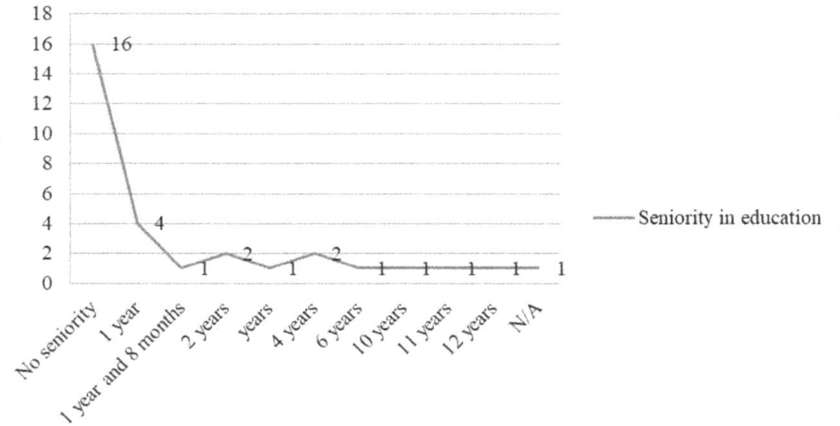

Figure 8.1. Seniority in education

Methodology

The research tool used is an opinion questionnaire, structured around three dimensions: outcomes, contents, and didactic strategies. For each question, students select the degree of achievement registered in their teaching activity, on a scale of five points (1–5), one being the minimum value and five representing the maximum value.

All answers were summarized within every question group.

Findings

The obtained results are grouped around the three followed objectives with the scope to answer the question of the present research:

From the point of view of the first objective, the answers provided by practicing students reveal that they are to a very large extent (47.3%) and to a large extent (36.4%) preoccupied with the specific mode in which outcomes are competence-based/behavioral dimension-based, whereas operational objectives are clearly and correctly formulated, with a focus on learning results (56%). At the same time, the learning contexts are planned in relation to the established operational objectives (54.5%) (see Figure 8.2).

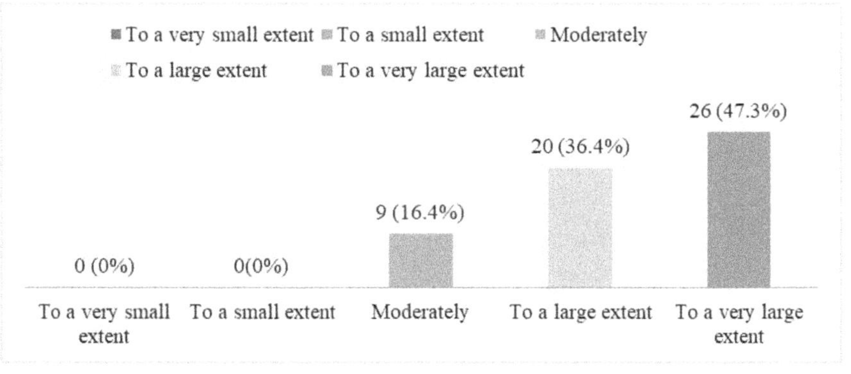

Figure 8.2 Competence-based outcomes are explicitly targeted

Regarding the second objective, 76.4% of respondents find it highly important to improve their lesson content selection and processing skills, to focus on systematized knowledge, to formulate more clearly, and to use grammatically correct expressions. Moreover, 61.8% of them admitted that they were able to adapt to a large extent to the psycho-pedagogical particularities of the classroom.

We appreciate these students' answers and highlight the importance offered to other factors, such as scientific correctness, connection to reality, and content contextualization.

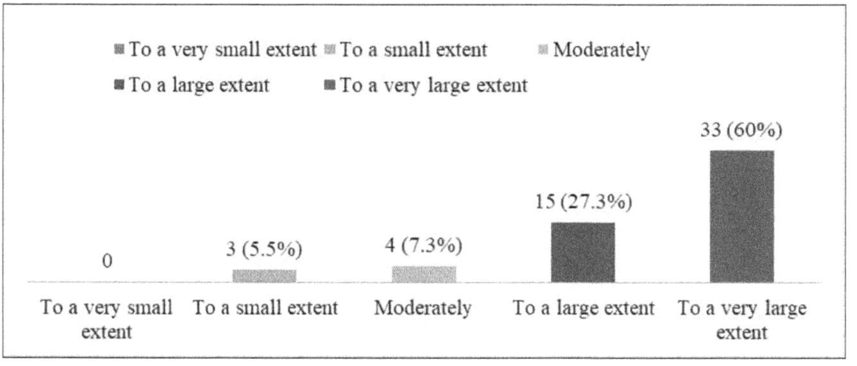

Figure 8.3 The selected and processed content is expressed in a variety of forms (text, image, sketches, theorization and examples)

At the same time, students face the need to learn from examples of good practices, required in the elaboration of declarative (40%), procedural (49%), attitude-value based (49.1%), and strategic contents (47.3%). Of all respondents, 52.7% demonstrate the ability to approach the curriculum with courage and boldness.

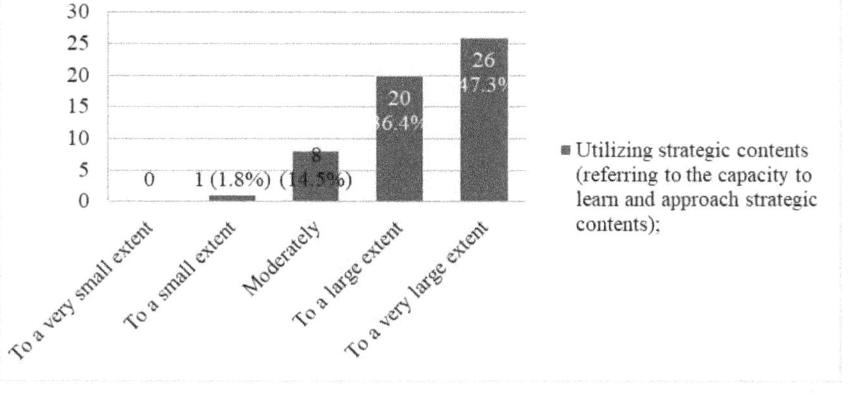

Figure 8.4 Utilizing strategic contents (referring to the capacity to learn and approach strategic contents)

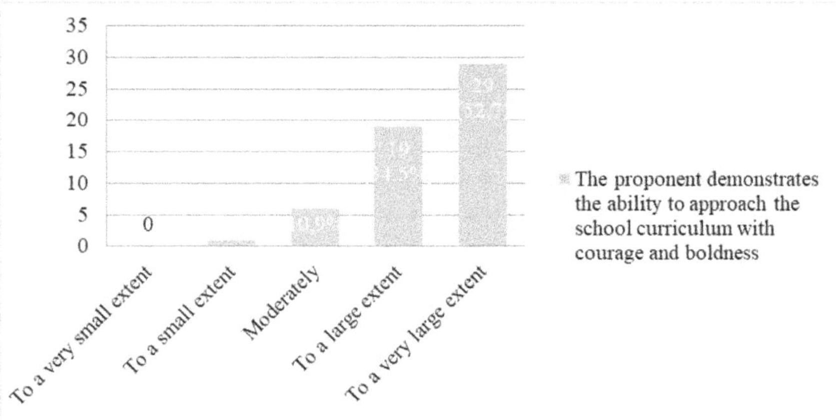

Figure 8.5 The proponent demonstrates the ability to approach the school curriculum with courage and boldness

As far as the third objective is concerned, 50.9% of respondents choose learning-centered and pupil-centered strategies, capitalize on previously acquired knowledge, promptly correct and offer correct models, organize the contents into smaller units, facilitate the transition toward understanding the new content, enable the direct interaction between pupils and the reality they are learning about, respectively.

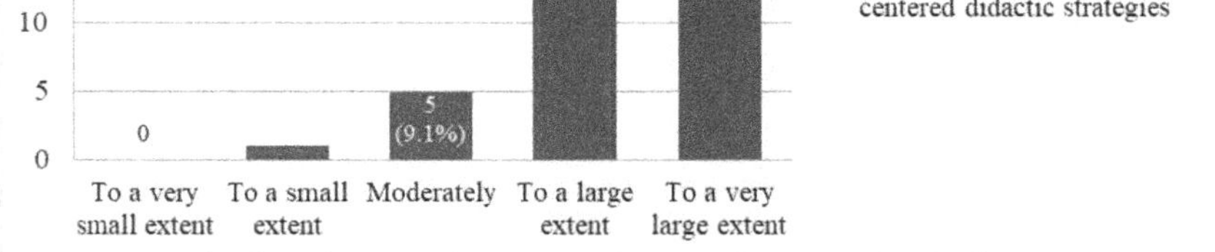

Figure 8.6 Learning-centered and pupil-centered didactic strategies

The structural component of teaching strategies comprises multiple interconnected elements, which we can analyze within a teaching activity. The answers provided by the surveyed students highlight the following ratios for each demonstrated behavior: the student demonstrates an argumentative-persuasive attitude while presenting the content; the practicing student demonstrates enthusiasm during the presentation of the contents in a proportion of 76%, the didactic strategy chose by the student is diverse, wherein they use both direct and indirect instruction, the didactic methodology is varied (54%), the concern for approaching a creative and flexible way of teaching is visible, the teaching manner is creative (54.5%), the didactic strategy enables the activation and mobilization of the classroom (58.2%), and the student facilitates the organization of new knowledge, through questions, examples, practice, graphic organizers (63.6%).

Conclusions and reflections

The evidence-based professional learning cycle can be a proper tool in training didactic competencies, underlining the fact that the students' needs relating to professional learning are tightly connected to the learning needs of their pupils, allowing them to recognize what pupils know and can do, identify what students need to know and do in the upcoming learning stage, and reflect and develop their professional capacity to meet pupils' needs, thereby finding out what they must still learn.

The professional learning cycle consists of five dimensions and is designed to facilitate answering two of the benchmark questions regarding how professional competence in teaching can be achieved, as stated by Raymond et al. (2016): "Given the needs of my pupils, what do I need to know and do differently in teaching to ensure their learning progress?" and "Considering students' learning needs, what do I need to know and, perhaps, do differently to support their learning?"

The previously mentioned authors affirm that there are five dimensions of the Professional Learning Cycle, which can be adapted to support the work carried out by mentor teachers with students, offering a series of reflective questions that can guide the mentoring process, such as: "What does the student need to know and be able to do to meet the pupils' needs?", "What does the mentor need to know and be able to do to support and identify students' learning needs?", "How can the mentor support students in deepening their knowledge and refining their teaching skills and practices?", "What happens in the classroom when students are supported to learn?", "What was the impact of the professional support offered during the learning process?", and "How did the mentor's professional learning impact their students' learning process and skills?"

The analysis tool entitled "The evidence-based Professional Learning Cycle" and the previously mentioned reflection questions can be considered subjects to analyses whose primary purpose is to improve and capitalize on pedagogical practice, during the training of students' competencies, as future teachers.

References

Bernat, D. H., & Resnick, M. D. (2009). Connectedness in the lives of adolescents. In R. J. DiClemente, J. S. Santelli, & R. A. Crosby (Eds.), *Adolescent health: Understanding and preventing risk behaviors* (pp. 375–389). San Francisco, CA: Jossey-Bass.

Hattie, J. (2014). *Învățarea vizibilă. Ghid pentru profesori* [Visible learning. A guide for teachers]. București: Editura Trei.

Marzano, R. J. (2015). *Arta și știința predării. Un cadru cuprinzător pentru o instruire eficientă* [The art and science of teaching. A comprehensive framework for effective instruction]. București: Editura Trei.

Ministerul Educației și Cercetării (2020, June 12). *ORDIN Nr. 4524/2020 privind înființarea și organizarea programelor universitare de master didactic* [Order No. 4524/2020 on the establishment and organization of didactic master's degree programs]. Monitorul Oficial [Official Gazette], No. 528.

Olsen, K. R., Bjerkholt, E. M., & Heikkinen, H. L. T. (2020). *New teachers in Nordic countries: Ecologies of mentoring and induction*. Cappelen Damm Akademisk.

Pavelescu, L. M., & Mara, D. (Eds./coord.). (2011). *Formarea profesorilor mentori din învățământul gimnazial* [The training of mentor teachers in lower secondary education]. ULB Sibiu.

Pop-Păcurar, I. (2021). *Managementul curriculum-ului și al programelor de formare (mentorat/stagiatură). Elemente de management și* leadership strategic, suport de curs [Curriculum management and training programs (mentoring/internship). Elements of management and strategic leadership, course support]. Master Management Curricular IFR.

Quinn, R. E., Heynosky, K., Thomas, M., & Spreitzer, G. M. (2014). *The best teacher in you: How to accelerate learning and change lives*. Berrett-Koehler Publishers Inc.

Raymond, L., Flack, J., & Burrows, P. (2016). *A reflective guide to mentoring and being a teacher-mentor*. State of Victoria, Department of Education and Training. Retrieved from https://www.education.vic.gov.au/Documents/school/teachers/profdev/Reflectiveguidetomentoringschools.pdf

Şerbănescu, L., Bocoş, M. D., & Ioja, I. (2020). *Managementul programelor de formare continuă a cadrelor didactice* [Management of continuing teacher training programs]. Iaşi: Polirom.

Stolovitch, H. D., & Keeps, E. J. (2017). *Formarea prin transformare. Dincolo de prelegeri* [Training by transformation: Beyond lectures]. Bucureşti: Editura Trei.

Approaches to the Operationalization of Transversal Competencies: Entrepreneurial Competence and Learning to Learn Competence

Sofia Loredana Tudor, Maria Magdalena Stan, and Adriana Nicoleta Lazăr

Abstract: Curricular innovation involves change, novelty, restructuring, and invention applied in the field of the university curriculum, with the aim of improving it, solving problems, and thus contributing to increasing the efficiency of the educational process. The new paradigm of education, focusing on skills, develops new directions in terms of the design and implementation of the educational process, with the introduction of skills as the goal of the school curriculum representing an opportunity for curricular innovation. The development of the graduate's competence profile is based on the description in operational terms of two essential competences for social and professional integration: the entrepreneurial competence, and the competence of learning to learn.

Keywords: transversal competences, the entrepreneurial competence, learning to learn competence.

Introduction

The transition from objective-centered pedagogy to competency-centered pedagogy, and the transition from content-centered teaching to interactive approaches to teaching represent some of the challenges developed in this context of the evolution of competency-centered theory. These challenges are built around two poles: what difficulties must be overcome in relation to the operationalization of competencies in the design of the educational approach, and how will these curricular practices be reflected in the holistic development of students, ensuring the state of well-being, beyond the development of some competencies (Ulrich, 2016).

For practitioners, the projective curricular milestones will focus on relating disciplinary knowledge, promoting the idea of organizing interdisciplinary and transdisciplinary educational activities, and introducing integrated teaching-learning approaches, thus achieving a move away from the strict separation of school subjects.

Pedagogy through competences must give meaning to learning, facilitating real learning contexts through which the students are motivated by their belief that everything they learn is useful. Competences should not be seen as a sum of knowledge, skills, and other acquisitions, but as the result of their combined application to solve concrete situations.

The necessity for complementarity in shaping the skills profile of university graduates.

The ultimate goal of education is to form *interdependent learners* who have the skills, dispositions, and experiences to meet the challenges of the extraordinary world of information, ideas, creativity, and connectivity created by open access. In this context of a diverse conceptualization of goals, in the analysis of a skills profile, we start from derived concepts, such as the well-being of the student, general/specific skills, key skills, and transversal skills, where the challenges emerge from the labor market.

The *student's well-being* is a fundamental indicator in assessing the quality of school life, although it is not a dimension of the skills profile. The school must ensure the well-being of students, and teachers must be sensitive to their cognitive, social, and emotional needs. The idea of well-being reflects new curricular approaches and interactive practices between teachers and learners. Physical, intellectual, and emotional well-being are interdependent. People who experience such well-being are able to learn, have healthy and prosocial behaviors, show more willingness to invest not only in their own well-being, but also that of others, and responsibly assume social, school and family roles (Ulrich, 2016).

A consistent and authentic approach to the well-being of school members fosters the positive development of school climate and culture, facilitating the development of students' academic performance as well as the professional performance of teachers (Tudor et al., 2023).

The *integration of transversal competences* in the curriculum is the requirement of a curriculum that provides each learner with that "survival kit" in terms of knowledge, skills, and values/attitudes (OECD, 1994).

The Conference Board report *Are They Really Ready to Work?, 2006* highlights the need for new skills, not specific to the technological age, for the workplace, such as understanding complex problems, collaboration, self-motivation and community-oriented ability, creativity, innovation, critical thinking, and problem-solving capability. As Gordon Brown, cited in Senge et al. (2016), states, "In order to be a teacher, you have to be a prophet – because you are trying to prepare people for a world that will be thirty or fifty years in the future." Other studies (e.g., Stan et al., 2023) highlight the importance of developing the research competence of future graduates by practicing various cognitive, reflective, and motivational skills, which can be defined either from the perspective of a specific academic discipline or through interdisciplinary approaches. On the other hand, it is necessary to have students who learn on their own initiative, with access to independent and personalized learning, and who reflect on what they learn and cultivate a positive attitude toward training (Roman & Balaş, 2015).

Alzahrani et al. (2022) define six transversal competencies necessary for a graduate in favor of a good socio-professional integration:

- creative thinking (possessing revolutionary ways of thinking, relating isolated ideas, finding alternative solutions and valuable perspectives),
- critical thinking (solving problems, making decisions, asking questions, and building new knowledge based on past experience),
- collaboration (asking questions, offering support, negotiating ideas, sharing resources, taking advantage of the skill and ingenuity of others and social responsibilities),
- communication (using verbal and nonverbal language appropriately and taking into account different perspectives of a problem),
- learning to learn (to develop capacities to regulate and control one's learning process),
- social responsibilities (collaborate with social factors and participate in community services).

Transversal competences are explained in terms of transferable acquisitions that are not strictly disciplinary ones (Bocoş, 2008). They are skills that have been learned in a certain context or to master a certain situation/problem, but which can be transferred to another context (CEDEFOP, 2008). They outline capacities that each person must develop in order to adapt to concrete life situations. They are fundamental components for integration into the professional workplace and can be acquired through both formal activities and informal or leisure contexts.

These competences are required in the social environment and constitute integration norms, proposed to be acquired through education. Transversal competences have their origin in primary socialization, comprising social, civic, and moral competences. The educational models built at the intersection of the family environment with informal environments and social, cultural, and economic resources contribute to shaping transversal skills.

Transversal competences represent "value and attitudinal acquisitions" that transcend a certain field and are expressed through descriptors such as autonomy and responsibility, social interaction, and personal and professional development (Guide for the application of the methodology for the construction of the National Framework of Qualifications in Higher Education, 2012). Transversal competences are integrative, transferable, interdependent, and multifunctional (Asegui & Galiana, 2023). They provide "learning transfer," that is, the transfer of acquired knowledge and metacognitive skills of the graduate to solve real-life situations. The development of transversal competences also contributes to building subject competences and orients students toward lifelong learning (Liubarets et al., 2022).

Operationalization of transversal competences – open and multidimensional approaches

In the development of the competence-centered approach, we can talk about compatibilities and incompatibilities between the approaches and practices recommended in the specialized literature. The approach to education from the perspective of competence-centered training has some essential coordinates (Ardelean & Mândruț, 2012): it emphasizes the pursuit of the way to achieve the goals assumed at the end of the study program, gives new meaning to the learning process, develops a balanced report between competences and curricular contents, and certifies the results of the training by multiplying the ways of assessing competences.

A competence is manifested through a set of attitudes toward the associated task and engages a set of skills and knowledge (cognitive, emotional, and physical) in order to successfully solve a situation.

The focus is on the learner's ability to structure and integrate knowledge to respond to a new situation (Rey et al., 2012). The analysis of the concept highlights the structural components of the competence, although in the theoretical approaches we find different nuances:

- knowledge (to know that),
- attitudes and behaviors (being aware of how you act, in context and why),
- dispositions (being open to change, feeling the motivation),
- procedural skills (knowing how to do),
- cognitive skills (processing information, critical thinking and critical analysis),
- skills based on experience (knowing how).

A model for the operationalization of transversal competences is the model of the nine transversal competences grouped into four intellectual competences (exploring information, solving problems, practicing critical thinking, implementing creative thinking), two methodological competences (effective learning methods, exploring information and communication technologies), two personal and social skills, and one communication skill (communicate properly) (Crețu, 2019).

For the academic programs, the focus has shifted toward the integration of transversal skills in the curriculum, as a premise for the optimal social and professional integration of the future graduate (Senge et al., 2016). The need to develop transversal skills is determined especially by the labor market (OECD, 2018). They designate capacities that each person must develop through formal activities, but also in nonformal contexts, in order to be able to adapt to concrete life situations. The acquisition of transversal skills is especially favored by collaborative learning through developing cooperation skills, favoring interactions between group members, improved reflective processes, involvement and assuming responsibility, efficient time management, and recognition of different roles (Borzea, 2017).

Taking as a benchmark the functional organization of the curriculum (Minder, 2011), which represents the integrated way of operationalizing the didactic approach, we identify approaches to operationalize competences. This can be realized over longer time intervals, which requires that its operationalization be achieved by specifying the targeted capabilities or learning outcomes.

We propose two operationalization models for reflection: the SOLO taxonomy and Marzano's taxonomy.

The SOLO taxonomy is a systematic way of describing how comprehension progresses from easy to difficult. It is a tool to assess the depth of knowledge that students demonstrate at a given point in the learning process. The SOLO taxonomy of organizing observable learning outcomes highlights learning outcomes for different levels of thought development (Boulton-Lewis, 1995; Borzea, 2017):

- Surface learning: pre-structural level (lack of ideas or superficial ideas, based on memory processes), unistructural (one idea), multistructural (several ideas),
- Deep learning: relational level (association of ideas), conceptual development (development of ideas, extrapolation of ideas, skills transferred to new contexts).

Marzano's taxonomy brings an improved approach, which includes two interacting dimensions: three fields of knowledge (information, mental procedures, and psychomotor procedures) and three levels of processing (cognitive, metacognitive, and internal). The model considers the role of motivation in the training process. Learning outcomes are defined on several levels (Jeff, 2020):

- Auto system: emotions associated with knowledge, motivation for learning,
- Metacognitive system: reasoning and evaluation, goal setting and planning,
- Cognitive system: application, assimilation and understanding, to complete the task at hand.

The entrepreneurial competence: An operationalization model

The training or development of students' entrepreneurship skills, regardless of the study program completed, brings added value for the continuous development of professional skills. It is crucial that economic growth strategies are supported by a system of education and continuous professional training that ensures, on the labor market, professionals capable of adapting, developing, organizing, making decisions, etc.

Entrepreneurship is an activity placed at the service of the well-defined objectives of the organization, regardless of its type, with the main goal of maximizing profit for the benefit of the organization (therefore, also of the employees, and in our case, students and teaching staff). Entrepreneurial activities involve a range of skills and capabilities that can be learned and applied to any organizational context. The entrepreneurial talent and the ability to accumulate, adapt, and apply knowledge and technologies represent the essential element of global competitiveness.

The development of the entrepreneurial culture at the academic level largely depends on the entrepreneurial culture and the attitude of the teaching staff, expressed through the constructive analysis of their own teaching/professional activity (Tudor et al., 2020). Entrepreneurship education plays a key role in cultivating students' intentions, which entails the development of opportunities that universities must offer to students to train them as future entrepreneurs, such as entrepreneurship education courses in universities, extracurricular activities, and practicing experiential learning.

Entrepreneurial competence defines those features and skills of students that describe them as successful entrepreneurs. Ismail and Zulihar (2015) summarize 10 dimensions of entrepreneurial skills:

- the need for achievement (a successful entrepreneur scores high on the need for achievement in pursuit of adequate and competitive performance),
- the need for autonomy (independence in decision-making, the ability to overcome one's problems and bring all activities to a successful end with one's own efforts),
- the need for power (entrepreneurs know how to influence others to achieve their goals),
- social orientation (entrepreneurs value interactions with others to realize their ideas),
- self-efficacy (confidence in one's own ability and one's own strengths),
- resistance (to effort, to failure),
- the ability to take risks (to cope with uncertainty, the willingness to take risks to be losers),

- market awareness (the ability to sympathize with customer needs, to anticipate changes),
- creativity (the ability to identify new opportunities),
- flexibility (adaptability).

Entrepreneurial competence includes not only entrepreneurial knowledge and skills but also the entrepreneurial spirit. (Lv et al., 2021). Barrientos-Báez et al. (2022) define entrepreneurial competencies as a "set" of values, knowledge, motivations, traits, attitudes, and skills necessary to develop a successful organization and argue that they can be developed through experience and education.

The entrepreneurial competence of students is evidenced by a series of individual and contextual predictors: psychological factors and personality traits, such as propensity toward risk and place of control (internal or external), creativity, emotional intelligence, values, motivations, and attitudes (Ferreira et al., 2022).

Concerns about an individual profile development of the human resource relevant to entrepreneurship highlight several components, which can be operationalized of competence, based on which the levels of entrepreneurial competence development can be expressed, as follows:

- development of managerial competence;
- development of the ability to solve problems; planning, making decisions, assuming responsibility;
- development of social competence;
- development of cooperative skills, assuming roles in the team;
- development of personal autonomy and self-efficacy;
- increasing self-confidence and motivation to perform, to think critically and independently, to learn autonomously;
- development of proactivity and creativity, preparation for confronting the risks of the activity.

The description of entrepreneurial competence on the three components is presented as follows:

- knowledge: knowledge of different contexts and opportunities, ethical principles, and self-knowledge,

- skills: skills in the field of project development and management, social skills, communication skills, resource management skills, project initiation, etc.
- attitudes: creativity (imagination, critical thinking, problem solving), communication, mobilizing resources and dealing with uncertainty, ambiguity and risk, self-confidence, motivation and perseverance, and appreciating the ideas of others.

The didactic approach to *entrepreneurial* competence at the curriculum level assumes (Ardelean & Mândruţ, 2012):

- knowledge: identifying opportunities for activities with personal, academic, and professional goals, identifying professional development opportunities for the student, acknowledging of the student's status;
- skills: managing an anticipatory project (the ability to plan, organize, lead, analyze, communicate, evaluate, etc.); effective negotiation; ability to work individually and collaboratively; the ability to identify strengths and weaknesses, to assess and take risks;
- attitudes: willingness to take initiatives, willingness to be independent and innovative in personal and professional life, motivation and determination to achieve a proposed objective.

The competence of learning to learn: An operationalization model

Analyzed as a set of skills (the ability to use knowledge and information interactively, analytical and critical thinking, autonomous learning skills, problem solving) (European Commission, 2018), the competence of learning to learn expresses the ability to learn in an efficient and autonomous way, according to their own goals and needs. People who develop this competence become more efficient, flexible, and self-organized in a variety of contexts. The development of these skills in a school context requires a reorganization of strategic approaches in the sense of developing didactic approaches and motivating students to strive for autonomous study (Espada et al., 2020).

Learning to learn competence is a relevant engine for change, for promoting professional integration and competitiveness and can be analyzed by reporting to two fields (Sala et al., 2020).

Related to the cognitive field, the *learning to learn* competence involves three dimensions:

- a cognitive dimension (problem-solving skills and the use of different learning methods),
- a metacognitive dimension (self-awareness and self-evaluation),
- an affective-motivational dimension (the motivation to learn and the regulation of emotions triggered by the learning activity).

Related to the social field, the *learning to learn* competence involves social, historical, economic, and cultural aspects of the context in which learning takes place. The social dimension of the competence involves the relevance of the student's perception of the support received from others.

The importance of competence development during university studies is determined by the ever-changing demands of the labor market toward graduates, by the need to prepare graduates who demonstrate an active participation in the professional environment and in the civil society and, implicitly, as a way to cope with social and professional exclusion.

The ways in which students perceive themselves and cooperate with others are related to how they construct their learning style. Finnish schools, for example, emphasize recognizing students' personal learning methods, improving learning strategies, developing intrinsic motivation, and positively perceiving lifelong learning (Suwalska, 2021).

It is the competence that defines the student's awareness of individual learning needs, the identification of opportunities for development, and the ability to overcome obstacles that may arise in order to achieve successful learning (Tudor, 2019). *Learning to learn* is a competence that helps learners become more independent, monitor their learning by identifying their own strengths and weaknesses, think metacognitively, and reflect on their achievements (Alzahrani et al., 2022). The development of the *learning to learn* competence favors the students' abilities to follow and persist in learning, and to organize their own learning through the effective management of time and information, both individually and in groups (Asegui & Galiana, 2023).

Sala et al. (2020) describe three indicators to operationalize the *learning to learn* competence:

a. Growth mindset:
   - awareness and confidence in one's own abilities to learn;
   - understanding that learning is a lifelong process that requires openness, curiosity, and determination;
   - critical reflection on other people's feedback as well as on success or unsuccessful experiences;

b. Critical thinking:
   - awareness of potential, but also of personal limits;
   - comparing, analyzing, evaluating, and synthesizing information, in order to draw logical conclusions
   - developing creative ideas, synthesizing and combining information from different sources in order to solve problems;

c. Learning management
   - awareness of one's own learning interests, learning needs;
   - planning and implementing learning objectives, strategies, resources.

The operationalization of the competence can be achieved on the following dimensions:

- the ability to manage one's own learning process (effective management of time, information, resources used);
- the ability to identify own learning needs, available opportunities
- the ability to overcome obstacles in order to learn successfully;
- the ability to search, systematize, and effectively use new information
- the ability to identify learning support and counseling tools;
- the ability to transfer knowledge and skills in a variety of learning and training contexts.

The didactic approach to the competence to learn to learn at the level of the school curriculum assumes (Ardelean & Mândruţ, 2012):

- *knowledge*: the required knowledge, skills and qualifications (related to the specialization / study program), knowledge and understanding of one's own preferred learning strategies, knowledge and understanding of strengths and weaknesses regarding one's skills and abilities, and the ability to seek opportunities for academic development and professional;

- *skills*: acquiring the basic literacies necessary for lifelong learning (e.g., ICT skills), assimilation of new knowledge; effective self-management of learning, career and professional activity; perseverance in learning; concentration over extended periods of time; critical reflection on the final goals of one's own learning approach; sharing learning acquisitions; organizing the autonomous learning process.
- *attitude*: the motivation and confidence to continue and succeed in lifelong learning, solving problems to support one's own learning process, the individual's ability to overcome obstacles, showing the desire to exploit learning experiences and life experiences.

Conclusions

Even though it is not a topic of interest for students, skills training of students is a complex process that must be carefully designed and based on criteria of efficiency and effectiveness of the study program. Although the way of organizing the activities specific to the university program creates the guidelines for outlining transversal competencies, most transversal skills are acquired in a self-taught way, in a nonformal and informal environment, through the transfer of skills to various tasks. That is why it is extremely important to strengthen the collaborations of the university environment with the local community, in order to facilitate opportunities for the professional integration of students.

References

Alzahrani, S. M., Almalk, M. S., & Almossa, S. Y. (2022). Conceptualizing life competencies: EFL teachers' qualitative perspective. *Saudi Journal of Language Studies*, **2**(4), 189–204. <https://www.emerald.com/insight/2634-243X.htm>

Ardelean, A., & Mândruţ, O. (Eds.) (2012). *Didactica formării competenţelor. Cercetare-dezvoltare-inovare-formare* [Didactics of skills training. Research-development-innovation-training]. Vasile Goldis University Press.

Asegui, L., & Galiana, M. (2023). The challenge of developing and assessing transversal competences in higher education engineering courses. *International Journal of Engineering Education*, *39*(1), 2–13. <https://www.ijee.ie/1atestissues/Vol39-1/02_ijee4287.pdf>

Autoritatea Naţională pentru Calificări. (2012). Ghid de bune practici pentru implementarea Cadrului Naţional al Calificărilor din Învăţământul Superior [Good practice guide for implementing the National Qualifications Framework in Higher Education]. *Bucureşti: Autoritatea Naţională pentru Calificări*. https://nastasepavel.files.wordpress.com/2012/06/ghid-de-bune-practici-pentru-implementarea-cadrului-national-al-calificarilor-din-invatamantul-superior1.pdf

Balaş, E., & Roman, A. (2015). Transversal competences and interactive teaching strategies. *Agora–psycho-pragmatica*, *9*(1), 26–41. <https://www.uav.ro/jour/index.php/app/article/view/471>

Barrientos-Báez, A., Martínez-González, J. A., García-Rodríguez, F. J., & Gómez Galán, J. (2022). Entrepreneurial competence perceived by university students: Quantitative and descriptive analysis. *Journal of International Studies*, *15*(2), 40–49. <https://doi:10.14254/2071-8330.2022/15-2/3>

Bocoş, M. (2008). Didactica disciplinelor pedagogice. Un cadru constructivist [Didactics of pedagogical disciplines. A constructivist framework]. Piteşti, Romania: Editura Paralela 45.

Borzea, A. (2017). *Integrarea curriculară şi dezvoltarea capacităţilor cognitive* [Curricular integration and the development of cognitive capacities]. Polirom.

CEDEFOP (2008, 2009). Strengthening European cooperation in vocational education and training policy. https://www.cedefop.europa.eu/files/9010_en.pdf

Comisia Europeană (2018). RECOMANDARE A CONSILIULUI privind competenţele-cheie pentru învăţarea pe tot parcursul vieţii.<https://eur-lex.europa.eu/resource.html?uri=cellar:395443f6-fb6d-11e7-b8f5-01aa75ed71a1.0019.02/DOC_1&format=PDF >

Creţu, D. M. (Ed.). (2019). *Predarea şi învăţarea în învăţământul superior. Aspecte teoretice şi practice* [Teaching and learning in higher education: Theoretical and practical aspects]. Bucureşti, Romania: Editura Universitară.

Espada, M., Navia, J. A., Rocu, P., & Gómez-López, M. (2020). Development of the learning to learn competence in the university context: Flipped classroom or traditional method? *Research in Learning Technology*, *28*.<https://eric.ed.gov/?id=EJ1244355>

European Commission. (2018). Proposal for a Council recommendation on key competences for lifelong learning. Brussels: European Commission. https://eur-lex.europa.eu/legal-content/EN/TXT/?uri=CELEX:52018DC0024.

Ferreira, A. da S. M., Loiola, E., Gondim, S. M. G., & Pereira, C. R. (2022). Effects of entrepreneurial competence and planning guidance on the relation between university students' attitude and entrepreneurial intention. *The Journal of Entrepreneurship*, *31*(1), 7–29.<https://doi.org/10.1177/09713557211069261>

Gillian Boulton-Lewis, M. (1995). The SOLO taxonomy as a means of shaping and assessing learning in higher education. *Higher Education Research & Development*, *14*(2), 143–154.<https://doi.org/10.1080/0729436950140201>

Ismail, V. Y., & Zulihar, E. Z. (2015).The portrait of entrepreneurial competence on student entrepreneurs. *Procedia - Social and Behavioral Sciences*, *169*, 178–188. <https://doi.org/10.1016/j.sbspro.2015.01.300>

Jeff, I. (2020). Marzano's new taxonomy as a framework for investigating student affect. *Journal of Instructional Pedagogies*, *24*, 1–31. <https://eric.ed.gov/?id=EJ1263740>

Liubarets, V., Bakhmat, N., Kurylo, L., Spitsyna, A., & Biriukova, O. (2022). Formation of transversal competences of future economists in the conditions of digital space.*Journal of Higher Education Theory and Practice*, *22*(14), 67–80. <https://ekmair.ukma.edu.ua/server/api/core/bitstreams/b76de910-d367-4c0d-9912-33722d668526/content>

Lv, Y., Chen, Y., Sha, Y., Wang, J., An, L., Chen, T., Huang, X., Huang, Y., & Huang, L. (2021). How entrepreneurship education at universities influences entrepreneurial intention: Mediating effect based on entrepreneurial competence. *Frontiers in Psychology*. https://doi.org/10.3389/fpsyg.2021.655868

Minder, M. (2011). Didactica funcţională. Obiective, strategii, evaluare. Cognitivismul operant. [Functional didactics. Objectives, strategies, evaluation. Operant cognitivism]. ASCR.

OECD (1994). *OECD Economic Outlook*, 1994(1), OECD Publishing, Paris. <https://doi.org/10.1787/eco_outlook-v1994-1-en>

OECD. (2018). *The future of education and skills: Education 2030*. OECD Publishing.

Rey, B., Carette, V., Defrance, A., Pacearcă, Ş., & Kahn, S. (2012). *Competenţele în şcoală. Formare şi evaluare* [Competences in school: Training and assessment]. Bucureşti, Romania: Editura Aramis.

Sala, A., Punie, Y., Garkov, V., & Cabrera Giraldez, M. (2020). LifeComp: The European Framework for Personal, Social and Learning to Learn Key Competence, EUR 30246 EN, Publications Office of the European Union. <https://edudoc.ch/record/212410/files/lcreport_290620.pdf>

Stan, M. M., Dumitru, C., Dicu, M. M., Tudor, S. L., Langa, C., & Lazăr, A. N. (2023). Modelling research competence in social and engineering sciences at master's level programs: A scoping review. *Sustainability*, 15(1), 574. <https://doi.org/10.3390/su15010574>

Suwalska, A. (2021). Transversal competencies in physical education in the Finnish National Core Curriculum 2014 for Basic Education. Annales Universitatis Mariae Curie- -Skłodowska. *Sectio J, Paedagogia-Psychologia*, *34*(2), 83–94. <https://doi.org/10.17951/j.2021.34.2.83-94>

Senge, P., Cambron-McCabe, N., & Lucas, T. (2016). *Şcoli care învaţă: a cincea disciplină aplicată în educaţie*. [Learning schools: The fifth applied discipline in education]. Trei.

The Conference Board, Corporate Voices for Working Families, Partnership for 21st Century Skills, & Society for Human Resource Management. (2006). *Are they really ready to work? Employers' perspectives on the basic knowledge and applied skills of new entrants to the 21st century U.S. workforce*. The Conference Board. https://files.eric.ed.gov/fulltext/ED519465.pdf

Tudor, S. L. (2019). The competence of learning to learn–An indicator of employability in the labor market. *Paper presented at the 11th International Conference on Electronics, Computers and Artificial Intelligence (ECAI)*, Pitesti, Romania. <https://doi.org/10.1109/ECAI46879.2019.9041978>

Tudor, S. L., Langa, C., Bulgaru, I., & Lazăr, A. N. (2020). Study on the development of entrepreneurial culture in the university environment. *Paper presented at the 12th International Conference on Electronics, Computers and Artificial Intelligence (ECAI)*, IEEE. <https://doi.org/10.1109/ECAI50035.2020.9223153>

Tudor, S. L., Langa, C., Stan, M. M., & Lazăr, A. N. (2023). Teacher's well-being: A premise for the development of the professional community. In E. Soare & C. Langa (Eds.), *Education Facing Contemporary World Issues – EDU WORLD 2022* (Vol. 5, pp. 1382–1390). European Proceedings of Educational Sciences. <https://doi.org/10.15405/epes.23045.141>

Ulrich, C. (2016). *Învăţarea prin proiecte. Ghid pentru profesori* [Learning through projects. Guide for teachers]. Polirom.

Educational Resources for Valuing Learning Contexts at the University Level

Carmen Maria Țîru

Abstract: University teachers must create educational contexts with specific characteristics to develop student-centered teaching and in-depth learning. These contexts are related to the students' needs to solve problems, capitalize on reflective experiences, and maximize their potential. Whether teachers use context-based learning (learning based on context, or learning in context), the goal is to choose the appropriate context to produce students' learning. So, this approach uses students' engagement in solving issues that the context induces. Teachers must use problem-based learning, reflective learning, interactions carried out by it, and concrete actions that the context requires to ensure the personal and professional development of the student. To provide real value to these educational contexts, university teachers must develop teaching and learning resources that sustain their impact. This chapter describes some of the resources and gives tips to transform the learning materials or other types of resources related to this approach, such as resources for interactive teaching and learning, autonomous learning, and formative assessment at the university level. The focus will be on adapting and transforming traditional materials/resources to create a valuable learning context. In addition, this chapter suggests methods that could be useful in producing situational interest and in-depth learning for students. In conclusion, didactic materials and resources are considered a resource in the student's learning, allowing personalization of the learning process through the provided teacher support and the student's continuous involvement.

Keywords: learning context, curricular materials, educational resources.

What is a learning context in the university educational process?

The shift from a process centered on the teacher's activity to one centered on the student (Postareff et al., 2007) in the university educational process is a fact and a necessity. University students must be challenged and engaged in an educational context that sustains their involvement and personal and professional development. Students will experience activities requiring them to solve problems, capitalize on reflective experiences, and maximize their potential. So, the student's learning will focus on aspects contributing to solving important problems and assimilating meaningful results. In this respect, the university teacher is less focused on their knowledge and beliefs and more open to listening to the learners and their needs, feelings, and opinions on the taught content. It is an in-depth learning of the students focusing on relationships between different content issues and formulating hypotheses or beliefs with an intrinsic interest in learning (Smith & Colby, 2007).

A certain dynamic exists in the teaching process between theoretical thoughts and practical approaches to scientific content. The dynamic of educational situations ensures their vitality, grounded in structuring and coherence, while also reflecting flexibility and adaptability to change that accompanies several teaching and learning contexts (Ionel, 2002; 2015). A good learning context is student-centered, relevant to the learning results, stimulates critical thinking and the desire to research, and supports the application of learning competencies in social and professional contexts. The students' situational interest arises in response to the characteristics of the context (interventions brought to an instructional context) (Linnenbrink-Garcia et al., 2010).

Therefore, university teachers must be veritable exponents of the educational challenges that support the student's transformation, creating meaningful learning contexts for their students. Adapting the approach of Gilbert (2006), we state that four models of context can be used in the university educational process:

a) The first model presents the context as the direct application of the concepts in an attempt to give meaning to a concept after it has been learned.
b) The second model approaches the context as reciprocity between the concepts and applications (subtopics of discussion within a larger topic).
c) The third model provides contexts by the student's activity and uses the ideas of constructivist pedagogy.
d) The fourth model situates the context as a cultural entity in society (a problem determined by social trends).

Choosing the appropriate context to produce students' learning is a complex process related to many factors: the specificity of the discipline (more theoretical or more practical), the competencies developed through the chosen context, the experience gained in the field by the students, the student's learning needs, the teaching strategies, the methods of evaluation, and the existing relevant researches for the context.

Context-based learning (i.e., learning based on context or creating context) analyzes context as a way to make sense of an experience, distinguishing between what is relevant and irrelevant (Sharples et al., 2015). *Learning based on context* focuses more on the situational involvement of the student, and their presence in the created learning context. Therefore, the educational content structure must be adapted to the pre-instructional conceptions and its relevance in the student learning (Duit et al., 2012). *Learning in context* involves student learning through their engagement in solving issues that the context induces and comprises problem-based learning, reflective learning, interactions carried out within the learning context, and concrete actions that the context requires from the student. This type of learning supposes situational involvement of the student in the created learning context, connected to the real-world and workplace problems in learning activities, and creation of work-integrated learning experiences (Osika et al., 2022).

Nowadays, the context of learning extends to blended learning contexts, including online activities. In blended learning contexts, when the focus is on the student, learning technologies improve and support the student learning experiences (Crawford, 2017) and offer experiences impossible to create in face-to-face interactions (Adams Becker et al., 2017). Teachers with more sophisticated conceptions of teaching present advanced methods of e-teaching and approaches that focus on communication and knowledge building (Roberts, 2003), which assures veritable contexts for learning.

The previously mentioned characteristics of a learning context are based on efficiency by following some guidelines (Parchmann et al., 2006; Gräsel et al., 2005). All learning units created for context-based learning are based on topics, authentic questions, and problems involving daily-life situations and interpersonal relationships, important issues for the society or community, and scientific and technological issues specific to particular communities.

- The investigation of relevant topics leads to the assimilation of basic concepts and the development of different skills.
- A "context" should enable the learner to identify the relevance and possible application of their learning outcomes, relating to the student's interests. In this way, it will ensure success in the learning process, attending to the proposed objectives.
- The curricular content used in context-based learning must possess the following characteristics: be relevant, raise questions, provoke

critical thinking, stimulate the desire to research, and encourage sharing of the student's personal research.
- The context as a way to stimulate learning involves fostering an environment that encourages personal cognitive engagement to enable the success of the learning processes.
- As a framework for situational development and application of knowledge and competencies, the context ensures the consolidation and social support in the training and development of competencies. It is about the important transfer of learning outcomes from one content unit to another learning context.

As we can see, unlike traditional approaches which start with scientific ideas that determine applications, context-based learning is the starting point for the development of students' scientific ideas, abilities, and attitudes (Bennet et al., 2007).

Learning materials or learning resources?

The use of the expression "teaching and learning materials" is based on the assumption that teaching and learning are considered separate activities. Mincu and Desire (2015) propose a movement from the concept of "materials" to "resources," indicating the necessity for teaching that is centered on student's learning and not on the instructor who prepares the materials. When using teaching and learning material that is focused on presenting only theoretical or theoretical-pragmatic curricular content, the teacher does not provide a sufficient foundation for students to gain skills, abilities, and attitudes. Even if some didactic materials offer contexts for practicing models, theorems, and skills, the competence is not always achieved. Students are stuck at the stage of rote learning and are not involved in discovering, solving, researching, innovating, and proposing solutions.

The concept of "educational resources" overcome this rigid framework of teaching and tilt the balance toward the importance of the learning process. The didactic material must be considered a resource in the student's learning, giving the chance to personalize the learning process, through his permanent involvement and capitalizing on his experience and situational interest. Educational resources propose a comprehensive approach to university didactic materials, comprising all the resources that support both the entire educational process and each individual step in the process, with the goal of developing students' competencies.

Educational resources for student-centered learning

Context-based learning is student-centered, supporting the efforts of students to be actively engaged in the learning process with teacher support and facilitation in this way. The literature has presented, over time, many strategies to sustain and improve the shift from a theoretical approach to a practical approach in university classes. Teachers have many resources to develop a student-centered approach to teaching and engage students in a context of learning. They should determine modalities to teach better and optimize student learning (Sawyer, 2005).

Building an efficient context for sustaining student-centered learning requires passing the power and decision onto students and giving them opportunities to manifest this power. In this respect, teachers must ensure educational resources that facilitate skills acquisition rather than just memorizing concepts. Active learning resources develop students' responsibility for learning, becoming independent, self-motivated, and open to improving their learning outcomes based on the teacher's feedback. It is about assuring a learning environment centered on students' needs using appropriate techniques and resources (Adebisi & Oyeleke, 2018). It is not a very difficult goal if teachers prepare all the educational resources such as different learning environments, such as classes for formal, informal, and social activities; different design approaches and teaching strategies that support students' access to learning; accommodation for various tasks and critical thinking of the student; and the use of institutional resources and staff support (Strange & Banning, 2015). The key to creating a student-centered context is to assure a correlation between all institutional and class resources and to be flexible and dynamic in the teaching process. This process starts with a student-centered design that is very important to student achievement along with classroom instruction and climate (Schneider & Preckel, 2017), and its ends with a student-centered assessment.

Also, it is very important to design teaching and learning elements that ensure student engagement through content and high-level achievement of learning outcomes (Hoidn & Hoidn, 2017) and to implement learning contexts based on a student-centered approach. Teachers can choose different teaching contents, teaching and learning methods, curricular materials, and modalities to foster students' interaction and assess their learning outcomes in a constructive way.

The following section describes some tools for student learning which could act as effective educational resources and gives tips to transform curricular materials and other types of resources into instruments for sustaining students learning. All the proposed resources share the following characteristics: they promote student activity and independence, ensure the teacher adopts a coaching role, and demonstrate that knowledge is a tool rather than an aim to enhance competencies (Dochy et al., 2002).

Educational resources to ensure an interactive student-centered learning

Omerović (2016), cited in Čirić (2016), states that interactive classes are scientifically based and follow systematically organized teaching plans and programs using dominant methods for interactive learning. The active curricular material transforms into an educational resource when the teachers select content that is relevant, up-to-date, and related to the actual research in the field. The chosen teaching and learning material can have different levels of interaction, depending on the modality in which the assigned task to the student is structured, and vice versa (Northcott, 2001). In this sense, reading materials and the bibliography suggestions for reading should be accompanied by teaching aids that facilitate individualized or group learning of the students and the achievement of the educational objectives set by the teacher through an activity. To achieve these objectives, university teachers must design and use different tools in the didactic process (Weimer, 2002), transforming the content material into a learning resource for the students. It is where the pedagogical mastery of the teacher comes into evidence to support the student's learning. An active content material meets a series of characteristics that assures its use as a learning resource, including highly scientific character, specialized language, structuring and systematization of knowledge, examples of good practice, models, practical reflections, and specific learning activities for students. Using such resources, the teacher creates a motivational learning context and assures in-depth learning. The teaching patterns in these cases refer to how the teaching content is presented and used for lecturing, developing note-taking skills, and meta-talk (Hoidn, 2017). The content will not only scientifically inform students but also train them to gain practical abilities related to discipline competencies.

Table 10.1 presents a few examples of the tools that can be used to encourage active learning in university classes, depending on the student needs and discipline objectives:

Table 10.1 Active learning tools

Tools for active Learning	How to use it to become an educational resource for Learning (a possible structure of the tool)
Active lecturing sheet (based on recommendations of Nilson (2016, pp. 113–126).	The content of the reading: text, link, or any additional materials. Key concepts identified in the reading: will be stated and explained by the students. Key questions from reading content: students' questions regarding curiosities, issues, and misunderstandings that need to be clarified by the teacher. Difficult text: paragraph/s that raised difficulties to understand and solutions identified for its understanding. The usefulness of the lecture content: students will respond to the question: What did you learn from lecturing this material? Reflection on the lecture: A concrete method could be proposed by a teacher that will ensure the possibility to reflect on different issues learned by the student lecturing – e.g., a mind map.
Active learning journal	Connections with previous knowledge: students will specify the concepts (from the actual or other disciplines of study) and explain the possible relations and implications. Questions on the topic: students will note questions raised during the learning process. Personal observations/remarks on the learning contents. Visual representations: drawings, graphs, and schemes representing possible connections between concepts, or important thoughts. "I wonder if…": students will imagine some practical situations to use the learning content, other than those exemplified in the learning support. Knowledge transfer: students will mention how the new knowledge can be used in other learning, professional, and life contexts. "What changes did the new knowledge cause me?" For example, at the level of understanding a concept, learning a new skill, having a different attitude on an issue, etc.

(Continued)

Table 10.1 Continued

Tools for active Learning	How to use it to become an educational resource for Learning (a possible structure of the tool)
Interactive group worksheet	Students' workload: issue to solve, exercises, text, tables, and links to the issue. The objectives of the task: will be mentioned and related to the specific objectives of the discipline. Solving directions and different types of solutions: are offered by the teacher or other resources. Group reflection on the task: the effective solution of the group, reflective remarks or questions about the issue, strategies, and difficulties to work together, modalities to solve the issues, etc. Group self-assessment on the task: related to the mentioned objectives and the assessment criteria; modalities to improve in the future group work.
Critical observation sheet of a presentation	The students will complete this sheet during a college or group presentation. Organization of the activity: e.g., if the presenter(s) specified the objectives of the presentation, the time management was efficient, etc. Method of the presentation: e.g., the PowerPoint presentation complied with the scientific quality and design criteria. Presented content: e.g., if the presenter chose the most current and relevant scientific content. Application of theory in practice: e.g., if the presenter chose the most relevant examples or practical applications. Presentation skills: e.g., if the presenter conveys emotion, if the diction is clear, if the tonality of the communication is appropriate, etc. Interaction with the audience: e.g., what modality of interaction uses the presenter, and how to manage the interaction with the group. Creativity: e.g., originality in the construction of the materials used, in assuring the interaction with the audience, etc.

(Continued)

Table 10.1 Continued

Tools for active Learning	How to use it to become an educational resource for Learning (a possible structure of the tool)
The reflexive scale of a problem (based on recommendations of Ryan (2013, pp. 144–155)	*Reporting and response* What key factors were involved? Explain their interaction in the situational context. *Create the link* Have we encountered such a problem before? Were the conditions the same or different? Do I have the necessary skills and knowledge to solve such a situation? Motivate. *Argue* Explain which significant factors are important to solving the problem. Consider different perspectives as a study/ an expert who already studied this problem. For example, is a specialized study/book that empirically supports the problem. What elements of professional ethics does the problem situation involve? *Rebuild* How would I fix the problem (provide optimization solutions)? Who will be the beneficiaries of the proposed optimization solutions? What might not work and why?
Useful wall displays	Literature-based displays: keywords, connectors, sentence starters, etc. Data-driven displays: relevant to the topic/theme or a specific topic. Rule-based displays: highlight the rules in solving problems or certain types of tasks. Displays for models or examples for students' activity. Success criteria display: what students need to do to complete successful learning and assessment.
The reference space for the classroom	This space could have: Informative materials on the theme/subject: books, dictionaries, collections, encyclopedias, etc. Laptops/ computers: with internet access to use online resources. Flipcharts sheets: on which students can suggest to peers how they could use the reference corner, or even write down suggestions for their future work.

Educational resources for autonomous learning

As an adult, the student feels the need for autonomy and control over his learning activity. In a formal university context, the teacher guides the student's autonomy in a situational self-directed learning context.

By learning autonomously, the student assumes a form of study in which he takes the responsibility to plan, continue, and evaluate his learning experiences (Merriam et al., 2007), having control and active involvement in the learning process (Boyer & Usinger, 2015). It is a self-oriented learning process, and students assume responsibility for the various decisions associated with their learning efforts. Student learning becomes self-planned, self-directed, self-initiated, and often involves individually completed learning activities. This type of learning can take place in the formal university setting, under the guidance of a teacher, as well as in other environments or learning contexts. To be able to achieve these goals, the students must gain specific knowledge, abilities, and skills. Some activities support an educational context that assures a framework for optimizing the students' ability to manage their learning process and gain autonomy (Gargallo et al., 2015). Teachers should build and use didactic materials (reflective journals, learning performance evaluation scales, and different cognitive and creative thinking learning strategies) that support the formation and development of specific knowledge acquisitions (Tekkol & Demirel, 2018). The student should plan their learning activities and participate actively in the proposed learning contexts. Table 10.2 presents a few examples of the tools useful to sustain the planning of autonomous learning of university students:

Table 10.2 Autonomous learning tools

Planning tools for autonomous learning	How to use it to become an educational resource for Learning (a possible structure of the tool)
Learning plan	The actual level of knowledge: students' background in the field, knowledge, skills, attitude, and beliefs on learning, etc. Goals and specific objectives to attend: in the long and short term, regarding each component of a competence (knowledge, skills, attitude) Specific activities to attend to the goals and objectives: on-time unit, content unit, assessment tasks, etc. Resources to attend the planned activities: people, community of learning, informative resources, institutional resources, etc. Assessment of the activities: modalities of receiving feedback and optimizing the obtained results, self-assessment, progress reports, etc.
Learning objectives plan	Argue on the motivation for participation in the course. Long-term learning objectives. Medium-term learning objectives. Short-term learning objectives. Concrete activities for attending each objective. Deadlines for each activity. Expected results for each objective, related to the specific competencies of the course. Self-assessment scale for participative learning.
Learning time management plan	A to-do list for the discipline. A plan of the learning activities per semester for the discipline. A plan of the learning activities per week. A plan of the learning activities on a specific topic. Deadlines for an entire semester and each planned activity.

Educational resources for formative assessment

Formative assessment involves a systematic process that evaluates students' work and proposes solutions to maximize the effectiveness of the teaching and learning process by providing constant and timely feedback (Hamodi et al., 2017). Contextual learning is doubled by assessment tasks prioritizing quality over quantity. Teachers develop authentic tasks for their students in a formative manner. It is necessary to eliminate the separation between summative and formative assessment and to create an educational context in which the assessment process is part of the learning process. The context of learning within an exam-focused context must be pertinent to the local and professional context, which involves students and sustains their motivation to learn. In such a context, the evaluation and self-evaluation carried out by both the teacher and the student ensures the optimization of the educational process and student development. Feedback and self-reflection are parts of such formative assessment contexts in university classes.

Table 10.3 presents as a few examples of the tools that can be used for sustaining formative assessment in university classes:

Table 10.3 Formative assessment tools

Tools for formative assessment	How to use it to become an educational resource for Learning (a possible structure of the tool)
Teachers' Feedback Plan	Discipline: mentioned in the curricula. Modalities for offering feedback: oral, written, online. Terms for each feedback. Objectives of the feedback. Students' results after the offered feedback.
Teachers'Reflexive Journal (based on recommendations of Zulfikar & Mujiburrahman, 2018, pp. 1–13).	Discipline: mentioned in the curricula. Theme: mentioned in the syllabus. Objectives of the theme: formulated around the discipline's competencies. The teacher will complete the answers to the following questions. The answers must be argued. *The objectives of the activity:* Did the students understand what we did in this activity? Was what we did too easy or too difficult for the students? What problems did the students encounter (if any)? What were the outcomes of the activity for the student's learning? Was what they learned or practiced in this activity useful to them? *Activities and didactic materials:* What different materials and teaching methods did I use? How did the materials and activities keep students interested and engaged?

(Continued)

Table 10.3 Continued

Tools for formative assessment	How to use it to become an educational resource for Learning (a possible structure of the tool)
	• Could I have done a sequence in this activity differently? Justify your answer! • Were all students engaged in the tasks given (did they do what they were supposed to do)? • If not, when and why did this happen? • When did the students seem to be most excited? But least excited? Why do you think this happened? *Time management:* • Did the activities fit within the predetermined time? • Was the activity dynamic constant? • Did I work with the whole group of students, in groups, in pairs, or individually? • Why did we use these forms of organization? Did they work? • Did the students understand what to do during the activities? • Were the instructions I offered clear enough? • Have we provided opportunities for participation for all students? • Was I aware of the progress of all students? *A general retrospective activity:* What would I do differently if I were to teach the activity again?
Tools for students' feedback	*Student feedback questionnaire* (Rowley, 2003): A set of questions addressed to students regarding specific aspects of teaching–learning–evaluation carried out in a university didactic activity. *Student feedback journal*: A student's reflection on the teaching and learning of a taught topic. *Tools for students' quick feedback* (Domilescu, 2002, pp. 136–138): ✓ *The 5-minute essay*: Was structured to help students gather their ideas related to the topic taught and give the teacher a clearer idea of what happened intellectually in that activity. ✓ *Flashlight*: A brief written presentation of a point of view on the topic discussed. ✓ *Feedback on colored cards*: Written information by the students regarding how the didactic activity was carried out until then, on cards containing concrete tasks, differentiated by colors. ✓ *Exit tickets*: Feedback on cards at the end of the activity on various exit tickets corresponding to a requirement.

(Continued)

Table 10.3 Continued

Tools for formative assessment	How to use it to become an educational resource for Learning (a possible structure of the tool)
Reflexive learning journal of the student (based on recommendations of Langley & Brown, 2010).	The students will respond to the following question at the end of the semester: PROFESSIONAL DEVELOPMENT DIMENSION 1. How did the learning for this discipline support me in my professional training? 2. What aspects of my learning in this discipline will I be able to apply most effectively to other courses this semester? 3. Which of the good practice models offered by this discipline teacher will be most useful in my professional training? PERSONAL DEVELOPMENT DIMENSION 1. Which of my strengths did I capitalize on in the interactions in this discipline? 2. What weaknesses of mine have I corrected through the interactions in this discipline? 3. How can I use this learning experience for my training in the future? EMPOWERMENT 1. Did I use a particular learning style in learning this discipline? 2. What difficulties did I encounter in the learning process of this discipline? 3. What would I do if I could change anything about my motivation and implication in this discipline? FACILITATING THE LEARNING PROCESS 1. What helped me to perform the responsibilities better in this discipline? 2. How well did I relate to other colleagues and teachers? How could I have related otherwise? 3. Did I use my time efficiently in the learning activities? How could I use it better?

Because of the growing use of technologies in the university teaching process, teachers create a veritable student-centered ecosystems framework (Hoidn, 2020) that supports an interactive personalized learning. Resources such as digital tacking-notes tools, digital tools for facilitating academic reading and writing, learning platforms, online material courses, blended learning contents, mobile device applications, gaming and artificial intelligence tools, active learning spaces, and classroom response systems encourage and facilitate student learning. In addition, teachers use digital resources for assessment. Classroom response systems (CRSs) are considered "promising" for improving student learning (Beatty & Gerace, 2009), such as Clickers, Plickers, and Kahoot digital quizzes, Mentimeter, Socrative, RecaP, etc. The use of learning technology should be flexible, and in choosing an educational resource, one should determine if it delivers contexts that offer support for both students learning and assessment.

Conclusions

In the context of the didactical-methodical structure of higher education classes, the model of interactive teaching "does not discard completely the traditional model of the organization of teaching work, but represents particular innovation in the context of the methodical concept of organization of teaching work with students" (Ćirić, 2016, p. 79). Therefore, the existing didactic material created by a teacher for each discipline could be rearranged, reconsidered, or optimized for students' participation in a veritable context of deep learning. Teachers could develop their skills in this way if they are flexible, dynamic, open-minded, and informed about how to do it. At the same time, the teacher can build new materials and resources, starting from the previous experience of working with students and fieldwork professional development.

Some *guidelines* for assuring that each didactic material becomes an educational resource are useful for the university teacher:

- ✓ Connect each educational resource to the specificity of the discipline.
- ✓ Redesign the existing resources in the literature according to the discipline's competencies and objectives and the theme's objectives.
- ✓ Adapt the designed resources to the student's background, learning needs, and educational contexts.
- ✓ Choose resources that assure active and interactive learning, self-directed learning, and formative assessment.
- ✓ Design resources that permit individualized ways of solving and constructive feedback.
- ✓ Create resources connected to the field's professional requirements and social issues.
- ✓ Be creative in optimizing and developing new personal tools for assuring in-depth learning of your students.

The final result of applying these guidelines could be a *portfolio of educational resources* for each discipline. It grows for the benefit of the students and sustains their learning process. It speaks about how to design new resources or optimize the existing ones for making veritable contexts of learning. This dynamic portfolio and the entire teaching and evaluation strategy should facilitate and support the students' transformation in the university educational process. Teachers must continuously enhance their educational resources to help their students develop the capacity of axiological reporting while solving a problem (Sandin, 1992):

- The choice must be made freely, between several alternatives, and after the individual considers the consequences of all choices;
- Valuing the work done should lead to joy, the happiness in choosing, and to the public affirmation of the choice made;
- The action should be carried out such that, after the choice has been made, you can do what you have chosen and you can repeat the action in similar circumstances.

Any educational resource built on such educational values successfully becomes a useful learning tool and a development context in itself for the students.

Acknowledgments

Some of the tools presented in this chapter were created by the author and adapted from the 'Student Notebook – Development of Didactic Materials Specific to University Education,' (POCU/320/6/21/121030 project), and Student Notebook- Feedback and Reflective Teaching in the University Environment (POCU/ 379/6/21/124874 project).

References

Adams Becker, S., Cummins, M., Davis, A., Freeman, A., Hall Giesinger, C., & Ananthanarayanan, V. (2017). *NMC Horizon Report: 2017 Higher Education Edition*. The New Media Consortium <http://cdn.nmc.org/media/2017-nmc-horizon-report-he-EN.pdf>

Adebisi, T. A., & Oyeleke, O. (2018). Promoting effective teaching and learning in the online environment: A blend of pedagogical and andragogical models. *Bulgarian Journal of Science and Education Policy*, *12*(1), 153–172.

Beatty, I., & Gerace, W. (2009). Technology-enhanced formative assessment: A research-based pedagogy for teaching science with classroom response technology. *Journal of Science Education and Technology, 18*(2), 146–162.

Boyer, N. R., & Usinger, P. (2015). Tracking pathways to success: Triangulating learning success factors. *International Journal of Self-Directed Learning, 12*, 22–48.

Čirić, N. (2016). Interactive teaching as innovation in the quality of didactical methodical organization of academic teaching. *Metodički obzori: časopis za odgojno-obrazovnu teoriju i praksu, 11*(23), 76–91.

Crawford, R. (2017). Rethinking teaching and learning pedagogy for education in the twenty-first century: Blended learning in music education. *Music Education Research, 19*(2), 195–213. <https://doi.org/10.1080/14613808.2016.1202223>

Dochy, F., Segers, M., Bossche, P. V. D., & Struyven, K. (2005). Students' perceptions of a problem-based learning environment. *Learning Environments Research, 8*, 41–66.

Domilescu, G. (2002). *Profesorul facilitator sau cum să fii cu adevărat un profesor mai bun pentru elevii tăi!: Ghid metodologic şi cadre teoretice. Repere de concepere a strategiilor didactice în facilitarea educaţională* [The facilitating teacher or how to truly be a better teacher for your students!: Methodological guide and theoretical frameworks. Benchmarks for designing teaching strategies in educational facilitation]. Timişoara: Eikon.

Duit, R., Gropengießer, H., Kattmann, U., Komorek, M., & Parchmann, I. (2012). The model of educational reconstruction–A framework for improving teaching and learning science. In S. Vosniadou (Ed.), *Science education research and practice in Europe* (pp. 13–37). Brill.

Gargallo, B., Garfella, P., Sahuquillo, P., Verde, I., & Jiménez, M. A. (2015). Learning centered methods, learning strategies and learning approaches in university students. *Revista de Educación, 370*, 216–241.

Gilbert, J. K. (2006). On the nature of "context" in chemical education. *International Journal of Science Education, 28*(9), 957–976.

Gräsel, C. (2006). Chemie im Kontext–From situated learning in relevant con-texts to a systematic development of basic chemical concepts. In A. Gilbert & D. Boulter (Eds.), *Making it relevant: Context-based learning of science* (p. 155) Springer.

Hamodi, C., López-Pastor, V. M., & López-Pastor, A. T. (2017). If I experience formative assessment whilst studying at university, will I put it into practice later as a teacher? Formative and shared assessment in Initial Teacher Education (ITE). *European Journal of Teacher Education, 40*(2), 171–190.

Hoidn, S. (2017). *Student-centered learning environments in higher education classrooms*. Springer.
Hoidn, S. (2020). Beyond the student-centered higher education classroom: The student-centered ecosystems framework. *ETH Learning and Teaching Journal*, 2(2), 191–195.
Ionel, V. T. (2015). *Pedagogia situaţiilor educative* [The pedagogy of educational situations]. Craiova: Sitech.
Ionel, V. (2002). *Pedagogia situaţiilor educative* [The pedagogy of educational situations]. Iaşi: Polirom.
Langley, M. E., & Brown, S. T. (2010). Perceptions of the use of reflective learning journals in online graduate nursing education. *Nursing Education Perspectives*, 31(1), 12–17.
Linnenbrink-Garcia, L., Durik, A. M., Conley, A. M., Barron, K. E., Tauer, J. M., Karabenick, S. A., & Harackiewicz, J. M. (2010). Measuring situational interest in academic domains. *Educational and Psychological Measurement*, 70(4), 647–671.
Nilson, L. B. (2016). *Teaching at its best: A research-based resource for college instructors*. John Wiley & Sons.
Northcott, J. (2001). Towards an ethnography of the MBA classroom: A consideration of the role of interactive lecturing styles within the context of one MBA programme. *English for Specific Purposes*, 20(1), 15–37.
Merriam, S. B., Caffarella, R. S. & Baumgartner, L. M. (2007). *Learning in adulthood*. Jossey-Bass.
Mincu, M., & Desire, J. (2015). *Dezvoltarea de materiale didactice specifice pentru educaţia universitară* [Development of specific teaching materials for higher education]. Timişoara: Editura Waldpress.
Omerović, M. (2016). *Metodika nastavnog rada: pedagoška moć odlučivanja* [Methodology of teaching work: The pedagogical power of decision-making]. Tuzla: Off Set.
Osika, A., MacMahon, S., Jason M. Lodge, J.M., Carroll, A. (2022), Contextual learning: Linking learning to the real world. <https://www.timeshighereducation.com/campus/contextual-learning-linking-learning-real-world>
Parchmann, I., Gräsel, C., Baer, A., Nentwig, P., Demuth, R., & Ralle, B. (2006). "Chemie im Kontext": A symbiotic implementation of a context-based teaching and learning approach. *International Journal of Science Education*, *28*(9), 1041–1062.
Postareff, L., Lindblom-Ylänne, S., & Nevgi, A. (2007). The effect of pedagogical training on teaching in higher education. *Teaching and Teacher Education*, *23*(5), 557–571.

Roberts, G. (2003). Teaching using the web: Conceptions and approaches from a phenomenographic perspective. *Instructional Science*, *31*(1–2), 127–150.

Rowley, J. (2003). Designing student feedback questionnaires. *Quality Assurance in Education*, *11*(3), 142–149.

Ryan, M. (2013). The pedagogical balancing act: Teaching reflection in higher education. *Teaching in Higher Education*, *18*(2), 144–155.

Sandin, R. T. (1992). *The rehabilitation of virtue: Foundations of moral education*. Praeger Publishers.

Sawyer, R. K. (2005). *The Cambridge handbook of the learning sciences*. Cambridge University Press.

Schneider, M., & Preckel, F. (2017). Variables associated with achievement in higher education: A systematic review of meta-analyses. *Psychological Bulletin*, *143*(6), 565.

Sharples, M., Adams, A., Alozie, N., Ferguson, R., FitzGerald, E., Gaved, M., McAndrew, P.,

Means, B., Remold, J., Rienties, B., Roschelle, J., Vogt, K., Whitelock, D., Yarnall, L., (2015). *Innovating Pedagogy 2015. Exploring new forms of teaching, learning, and assessment, to guide educators and policymakers* (Open University Innovation Report 4). < https://oro.open.ac.uk/45319/1/ InnovatingPedagogy>

Smith, T. W., & Colby, S. A. (2007). Teaching for deep learning. *The Clearing House: A Journal of Educational Strategies, Issues, and Ideas*, *80*(5), 205–210.

Strange, C. C., & Banning, J. H. (2015). *Designing for learning: Creating campus environments for student success*. John Wiley & Sons.

Tekkol, İ. A., & Demirel, M. (2018). An investigation of self-directed learning skills of undergraduate students. *Frontiers in Psychology*, *9*, 2324.

Weimer, M. (2002). *Learner-centered teaching: Five key changes to practice*. John Wiley & Sons.

Zulfikar, T., & Mujiburrahman (2018). Understanding own teaching: Becoming reflective teachers through reflective journals. *Reflective Practice*, *19*(1), 1–13.

Pathways Toward Digital Pedagogy: Developing Digital Competencies of Teaching Staff

Evelina Balaş, Alina Felicia Roman, and Dana Rad

Abstract: The society of the second decade of the 21st century is one characterized by rapid transformations, a world in constant change, in which the rate of the development of technological progress has reached an unprecedented level in human history. The last twenty years in particular have been marked by the widespread digitization in all areas of life and society, directly or indirectly affecting every activity of the individual. From a timid beginning in the early 1990s, it has now reached a point where digitization is a component that is implicitly accepted in everyone's daily life, and its impact shows no signs of stagnating, on the contrary. This chapter aims to anticipate how the use of information technology will concretely affect the didactic activity, and how a teaching lesson will look in a few years or decades. In this context, what would be the role of the teacher in this teaching-learning activity? If such a role could be anticipated, what would be the digital skills necessary for the successful implementation of the didactic approach? After identifying these skills, at least at a theoretical level, what would be the optimal means for their development? And finally, what forms of support, both from a technical and pedagogical point of view, should be implemented at the institutional level to ensure effective and quality continuous training for teaching staff already in the workforce?

Keywords: digital pedagogy, digital competencies, DigComp framework, teaching staff.

Introduction

We live in a world where cars are autonomous and self-driving, doctors perform surgeries remotely through medical robots, industrial machines operate in production lines with minimal human intervention, administrative tasks and operation of machines require much less face-to-face interaction, multinational companies no longer face geographical barriers to communication within their organizations, and the information transfer and access takes place in real time.

We are currently witnessing an evolution of the vision on the integration of information technology in the educational process, for a more flexible adaptation of the educational system to the new realities of society. Digitization does not simply imply a use of technology in the classroom, but is also a means for adapting educational content. This change in perception, in which the teaching staff is one of the main actors for the creation and adaptation of content, also recognizes the fact that a simple theoretical training of the teacher in the use of technology is not enough. The introduction of the computer, the Internet, and other specific information technology tools in schools brought about a transformation in teaching methods and the gradual change in concepts mentioned earlier. Thus, the activity of teaching–learning–evaluation is no longer seen as the exclusive attribute of the teaching staff, but a result of the interaction, of the collaboration between teacher and student, mediated by the use of digitization. The final goals of this transition are to increase the efficiency of the learning process, enhance communication skills, and increase the availability of resources for personal study and self-improvement. Pedagogical preparation must be carried out taking into account a forecasting component, as long as it implies both a fairly consistent time interval for the initial training, as well as a considerable period during which a teaching staff will later be active on the labor market.

Of course, any initial pedagogical training cannot objectively anticipate all the social, technological, and geopolitical evolutions that will affect or influence the future activity of the teaching staff at the beginning of their career. Therefore, continuous training remains an indispensable component of any training system. Yet, one can easily see a tendency to minimize the effects of digitalization on the teaching profession, a conception according to which, unlike other fields of activity such as those exemplified above, in the field of pedagogy, digitalization only involves an alternative form for the transmission of information from the teacher to the receiver, i.e., to the student.

The present study aims to analyze the validity of these assumptions in the medium to long term and, if found invalid, how the psycho-pedagogical training of future teachers should be adapted to ensure it matches the existing educational needs at the level of society and the existing professional competences of the active teaching staff.

Digitization can be of real benefit to both teachers and students, but its use must be designed in such a way as to make the educational process more efficient, not inhibit it. The computer must be integrated in teaching in order to acquire new knowledge, but also to form and develop skills absolutely necessary for students in a modern society. The simple transition to digitalization, without being aware of the needs and possible difficulties of the students in adapting to these new methods, is not able to ensure this objective. Constant attention must be given to children, to the development of their own skills and abilities in the use of computer systems, increasing the degree of confidence in the use of these devices. They, in turn, must adapt, innovate, and improve.

The normative framework

National or international strategies aimed at the field of education will greatly influence the way in which the information technology will penetrate and influence the teaching–learning activity. The informational or digital age is no longer just a cliché applicable to a period in the near future, but is a reality recognized as such by international forums for some time. Thus, since 2006, the European Parliament and the European Council have adopted the Recommendation (2006/962/EC) on key competences for lifelong learning. This framework document encourages the member states of the European Union to include in their national strategies regarding education, eight key competences considered as fundamental for European citizens. One of these eight competences is the digital competence and the use of new technologies.

What this digital competence consists of is also explained by the European authorities in a subsequent document adopted in 2018 regarding the same key competences for continuing education (European Commission, 2019) in which it is stated that this involves "... the confident, critical and responsible use of, and engagement with, digital technologies for learning, at work, and for participation in society. It is defined as a combination of knowledge, skills and attitudes."

Also in 2010, at the request of the European Commission, the Joint Research Center started a project called DigComp, which aims to provide a common understanding of what digital competence is. DigComp identifies the key components of digital competence in the 5 domains and 21 specific skills summarized in Figure 11.1.

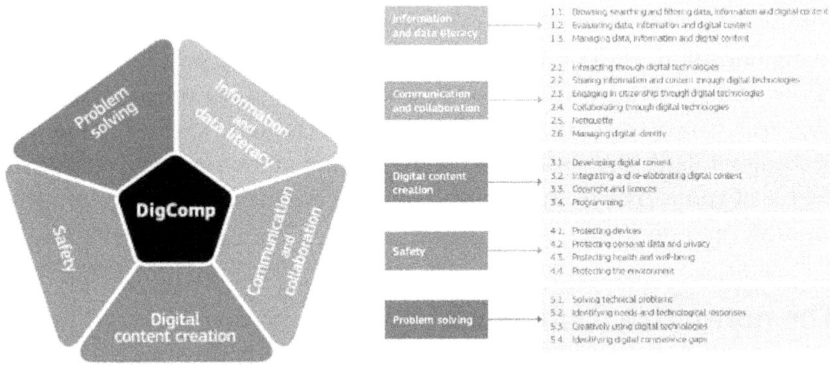

Figure 11.1 The DigComp framework
Source: https://joint-research-centre.ec.europa.eu/digcomp/digcomp-framework_en

The framework also describes eight proficiency levels, examples of knowledge, skills, and attitudes, and use cases in education and employment contexts. DigComp has remained central to EU objectives of enhancing digital skills of the whole population. DigComp is an important tool to support the EU's Digital Education Action Plan 2021–2027,[1] which in turn contributes to the Commission's priority 'A Europe fit for the Digital Age'[2] and to Next Generation EU.[3] DigComp is used for multiple purposes, such as designing competence assessment tools, creating training courses and materials, and identifying professional digital profiles, in the contexts of employment, education and training, and social inclusion (see DigComp Implementation Guides[4] for concrete examples).

At a global level, a reference document is the Qingdao Declaration adopted during the International Conference on Information Technology and Education Post 2015, from May 23–25, 2015, under the auspices of UNESCO (UNESCO, 2015). Related to the object of this study, the tenth paragraph of this Declaration, in the section dedicated to quality education, is relevant, and mentions the following:

Successful integration of ICT into teaching and learning requires rethinking the role of teachers and reforming their preparation and professional development. It calls for promoting a culture of quality in all its aspects: staff support, student support, curricula design, course design, course delivery, strategic planning and development. We will therefore ensure that teacher training institutions are equipped and prepared to use ICT adequately to expand the benefits of training and professional development programmes to all teachers, and to act as the vanguard for technology-supported innovations in education. We also commit to providing teachers with system-wide support for the pedagogical use of ICT, to incentivize teacher innovation, and to develop networks and platforms that allow teachers to share experiences and approaches that may be of use to peers and other stakeholders.

Education in the digital age

We previously stated that the informational or digital age has already begun and we are currently at a time when education is taking the first timid steps toward the implementation of information technology in the teaching-learning process. At the same time, perhaps even more timidly, steps are being taken to adapt the initial and continuous training programs for teachers to the new realities determined by the spread of digitization in all areas of social and professional life, although these steps mainly take the form of some theoretical studies.

The evolution of the technological progress in the information field, and the large-scale use of technology by both very young people and the elderly, has brought significant changes in terms of the professional training of personnel in most industries and occupational fields. Perhaps surprisingly, the training of future teachers did not seem to be influenced by these developments, either due to the fact that it was considered that the direct human interaction specific to the educational process would be able to "protect" the educational system from this interference, or simply due to a generalized conservatism related to the actual way of teaching in the classroom. However, a single, unforeseen element of novelty was enough for the entire system to be one step away from collapse, and the vulnerabilities of the classical teaching systems and the dangers for a field unable to adapt quickly enough became very clear. We are, of course, talking about the COVID-19 pandemic and its long-term effects on national educational systems due to the specific epidemiological measures implemented by governments to limit the spread of the disease.

Even if, at present, the need to adapt the training programs for teaching staff in the direction of developing digital skills is accepted by the vast majority of potential beneficiaries, the development of such programs is not an easy thing to achieve.

In our opinion, this difficulty is determined by two aspects. First of all, education involves an interaction between the teacher and the student. This interaction, which must remain in the future informational society, requires that the impact of technology be minimally invasive and not alter the quality of education, but on the contrary support, improve, and act as its catalyst. Starting from this reality, digital skills training programs must be intensively customized to the educational system. It would be difficult to conceive a way of adapting some training programs intended for workers in a technical field, for example, to teachers. Thus, this particular character of the implementation of digitization in education requires a longer duration of developing the curriculum for the programs of training, since they must begin "from scratch," but also a higher cost due to its uniqueness.

Second, the pedagogical training of teachers must take into account a forecast of the way in which the educational system will evolve for a considerably longer period of time than in most other professions. It is assumed that the teacher will be active in the labor market for several decades, during which technological developments can be rapid, even spectacular, as evidenced in the last two decades. It is not enough to develop training programs that prepare future teachers to implement and use the already existing technologies in the classroom, because it is very likely that those technologies will already become obsolete or morally worn out at the time when the teaching staff will actually begin their didactic work. It is thus necessary to prepare young educators for a future as distant as possible, anticipating or predicting how a lesson or a teaching–learning–assessment activity in the classroom would look like.

Although there is a widespread claim of an "explosion" of information technology use in schools post pandemic, this current use of technology in the educational process does not in reality represent a digitization of education. Technical equipment is used and perceived as an alternative way of remote communication to facilitate teacher–student interaction and ensure a virtual presence in the classroom. Or, the equipment is used as an alternative to the classic paper support on which school work or homework was done by students. In some cases, online platforms have been implemented to transmit assignments and tasks and facilitate communication between certain teachers and students or to maintain virtual catalogs where parents and students have real-time access to the school situation.

Teachers currently have at their disposal a considerable number of applications that can be and have been used in educational activities, and their numbers are constantly increasing. Examples include *World Wide Telescope* (focused on astronomy), *Microsoft Auto Collage* (to create collages), *Math Worksheet Generator* (to generate tests for grades I–VIII), *Songsmith* (to create background music for musical creations), *Storyjumper* (to create digital books with their own stories), *GoAnimate* (to create comics), *Padlet* (a wall where students can post comments on specific topics). Other online applications include *Blabberize* for creating talking "photos," ideal for games; *PhotoPeach* for creating interactive photo and video collages; *Animoto* for creating simple animated collages; *Genially* for creating interactive materials: infographics and presentations; *Animaker* for playful animations; the *Mailchimp* video editing tool; *Kizoa* for creating simple videos; *MakeBeliefsComix* for online comic creation; and *Renderforest* for creating animations.

There are several popular applications and programs widely used in online communication/teaching today. Some examples include:

Zoom, one of the most popular video conferencing platforms used in online teaching;

Google Meet, another widely used video conferencing platform that is integrated into the Google Workspace platform (formerly G Suite) and offers functions similar to *Zoom*;

Microsoft Teams, a communication and collaboration platform often used in the educational environment;

Moodle, a web-based distance learning platform that allows teachers to create interactive online courses and interact with students through forums, quizzes, and uploading course materials;

Google Classroom, a course management platform developed by Google;

Edmodo, a social learning platform that allows teachers to create and manage online courses, share materials, and communicate with students through messages and notifications;

Kahoot!, an educational gaming platform that allows teachers to create interactive quizzes, tests and games to assess students' knowledge in a fun way;

Nearpod, an interactive learning platform that allows teachers to create interactive presentations and engage students in real-time activities such as polls, questions, and assignments;

Canva, a versatile graphic design platform that allows students to express their creativity by designing a variety of content such as comics, infographics, and video presentations;

My Story Book, a digital tool that allows making simplistic books;

DroidCam app, with which teachers can easily connect their phone to their computer and share student content;

Wordwall, which educators can use to create customized teaching materials, interactive activities, and quizzes to enhance their lessons in a digital format; and

Twinkl, an online educational platform which offers a wide range of teaching materials and educational resources.

Of course, these achievements are beneficial and greatly facilitate communication and can be considered as a first step toward the transition to a digital pedagogy. However, digital pedagogy implies much more. While the earlier definitions of this concept offer only a basic, general explanation, such as "We define digital pedagogy as the study of how digital technologies can be used to the best effect in teaching and learning" (JISC, 2020/2021) or "In simple terms, a digital pedagogy is the study of how to teach using digital technologies" (Howell, 2013), in a 2022 study, Dr. Olimpius Istrate offers a much broader definition of this term that is closer to our vision:

> Digital pedagogy is the part of pedagogy that studies the design, implementation and evaluation of educational situations, which includes a significant component of digital technologies, as well as the necessary conditions for their implementation – synchronous and asynchronous interactions in virtual and mixed learning environments, learning management platforms and tools, digital educational

resources, educational use of various digital applications and tools, virtual assistants for learning and teaching, teachers' digital competences, educational policies and specific programs (Istrate, 2022).

The classroom lesson of the future presumes that information technology is an indispensable component of the educational content and not just a more attractive way of transmitting it. Thus, we are talking about computer-assisted teaching and not teaching through a computer. We can thus imagine a physics lesson in which the teacher's oral presentation about an optical or thermal phenomenon is accompanied in real time by a three-dimensional projection of these phenomena to which students have direct access through virtual reality or holography. Or a geography lesson that allows the student to fly by the landforms being discussed from the desired height, or graphically visualize the interaction of tectonic plates, or the explosion of a supernova. Or a chemistry lesson where interactions at the atomic or molecular level are visible in real time with the teacher's presentation. The simulation would of course be interactive, with the student being able to change an element of the chemical reaction in the last example and directly perceive the effects.

The use of interactive simulations through virtual reality opens almost unlimited possibilities. Limitations related to space, time, or costs become non-problems. For example, the student can virtually go back in time to the moment of the Big Bang and advance in time to the "first light" moment of the appearance of the first stars, then the first galaxies, or advance in time a few billion years from the present to observe the effect of the acceleration of the universe, all this from the comfort of a classroom and having the theoretical and practical support of the teaching staff and possibly of a digital assistant to provide answers to some possible questions. This virtual teaching assistant could provide substantial help in quickly searching for information in the online environment and making it available to the teacher for use in teaching. Similarly, it would be possible to search for and provide multimedia resources to support the oral presentation.

Unlike classic didactic materials, using these digital resources allows the teacher to personalize the contents and adapt them to each individual class. The specific needs related to the age of the students, their specialization, and the level of interest in the subject, according to their prospective careers, can be easily factored in through a modular design of these educational contents.

One could argue that, based on the examples described earlier on how we anticipate the lessons of the future will unfold, we have gone too far with our imagination, or perhaps too close, given that all the resources and applications described in these examples already exist and are used successfully in other fields. Examples include 3D projections in cinemas, to real-time speech-to-text converters, to virtual reality headsets and other gadgets with the same purpose already widely available on the market, or to the virtual assistants such as Amazon's *Alexa* or Apple's *Siri*[5] which runs on iOS and effectively uses voice queries and a natural language user interface to answer questions, make recommendations, and perform actions by delegating requests to a set of Internet services.

Thus, a teacher currently has at his disposal the necessary technological resources to carry out an example of a lesson from those presented above, and the costs of these digital devices are by no means prohibitive. Moreover, there are already cases in which some teachers who benefit from a higher technical training have implemented such technologies in their teaching activity. Possibly, the main factor that inhibits a greater spread of these alternative or additional teaching methods is insufficient training of the teacher's digital skills.

However, before carrying out a brief analysis of the digital skills necessary for teachers, it is important to try to anticipate the future role of the teacher in a digital classroom.

The role of the teacher in digital pedagogy

Of course, the possible implementation of virtual assistants could lead to the appearance of some questions regarding the possibility, in a short period of time, of even replacing the classroom teacher by artificial intelligence. It is thus important to determine what will be the role of the teacher in digital pedagogy and to what extent this role will undergo transformations compared to the current position.

From our point of view, the role of the teaching staff, far from being endangered, is rather empowered, because the creative potential of each educator could manifest itself more meaningfully. When part of the repetitive and time-consuming tasks of the didactic activity can be successfully taken over by a potential digital assistant, the teacher will have more freedom to focus his attention on the creation of educational content, adapting and personalizing them to the particularities of each student/each class, and constantly improving the way of presenting information.

The work involving prior preparation of a teaching activity could thus become an attractive part of the daily work for the teacher. With the support of technology, the teacher will be able to stay connected to the latest discoveries and developments in his field of specialization and will have the opportunity to incorporate these new achievements into the educational content that he designs. The possibilities for documentation are particularly vast in the digital age, but the role of the teacher remains fundamental, as he/she is the person who has the task, skills, and experience necessary to discern and select from the multitude of existing information, to filter this information and corroborate it with other sources in order to ensure the veracity of that information, and finally to transform and adapt the scientific information into didactic information in order to be accessible to the students to whom it is intended to be presented.

The content creator teacher will select the information from various spaces and sources both online and classical ones, of course in accordance with the standardized educational curriculum and will verify their veracity and analyze their relevance in relation to the topic of the classroom discussion. Then the information is to be integrated into a lesson plan and structure, which in turn needs to be personalized according to the age level or the abstraction capacity of the class of students to whom it is addressed to.

This predominantly creative role will become the main role of the teacher in the digital lesson. The development of the didactic content will be followed by the need to transpose it into an attractive form of presentation, also through or with the support of information technology. This stage of lesson preparation, which plays a secondary role to content generation, requires a different set of skills with a predominantly technical character.

However, it is more important that the teacher imagines, visualizes, and anticipates the concrete way in which he wants the information and the content to be presented (e.g., by using multimedia resources, interactive projections, etc.), so it is still a role of creation. The practical translation of this vision of the teacher does not need to be carried out – or at least not from the beginning or not entirely – by the very teacher who proposes this content, with the school institution being able to offer technical support in this regard through IT specialists. Of course, it would be preferable for the educator to benefit from or acquire the necessary skills for the technical realization of assisted teaching, knowledge that would allow him to save a significant amount of time in carrying out this part of the didactic approach. Anyway, the teacher should at least know the technological limitations that constrain the presentation as he imagines it, in order to be able to adapt his content to these realities.

A design of didactic contents by the teacher would be all the more effective if this design had a modular character. This character assumes that the information is organized and presented in the form of modules, which are interchangeable and can be complemented, modified, and improved, without affecting the integrity of the other modules. Similar to modular programming in IT, this type of lesson design would allow for the rapid introduction of a new module; it would allow the use of already developed modules to generate a new lesson, an aspect that would reduce time costs; it would allow several teachers to share their work and responsibilities in the generation of educational content; or it would enable the trans-disciplinary use of modules between teaching staff from different specializations.

From this brief exposition it can be easily observed that the role of the teacher in digital pedagogy is not an insignificant one. On the contrary, the role of the teaching staff will become even more important, acquiring increased and multiple responsibilities in the generation of contents compared to the present. Future teachers will have to be trained and encouraged to use their creative abilities on the one hand, to use the multiple possibilities of accessing information and filtering it, and on the other hand, to develop an efficient way of working, which allows for an easy collaboration both with other teaching staff and with existing IT specialists at the level of educational units.

The digital skills of teachers

In exercising the role described above, it can be observed that for a successful digital pedagogy, the teaching staff must have a set of appropriate skills. Although included under the title of digital competences, we are not talking about competences of an exclusively technical nature, but interdisciplinary competences, which, when they act in unison, lead to computer-assisted teaching, to which we referred previously.

Starting from the digital competence framework developed by the Institute for Prospective Technological Studies within the Joint Research Center of the European Commission and later the conceptual reference model for digital competences for citizens, which appeared under the auspices of the same institution (Vuorikari, 2016; Albulescu, 2021), we will try to enumerate the digital skills necessary for the teaching staff in the role within digital pedagogy explained earlier.

Information and data management

- ✓ Identifying, accessing, and selecting the data and information to be used to create the pedagogical content;
- ✓ Evaluation, verification, filtering, and comparison of the obtained data; it involves both an analysis of the credibility and reliability of the information sources and a critical evaluation of the information itself;
- ✓ Data management (storing, organizing, and processing raw information in a way that will be easy to access and later use).

Creating educational content

- ✓ Content programming (elaboration of a structured content plan, determination of lesson modules and final selection of information);
- ✓ Digital content development (integrating, refining, modifying, and improving data to create new, original, and relevant content);
- ✓ Analysis of the new educational resource from the perspective of the specifics of the learning objectives, the context and the pedagogical approach and the group of students.

Programming

- ✓ Developing a sequence of specific instructions for a computer system to perform a specific task in order to present the educational content;
- ✓ Generating lesson modules and verifying their compatibility in terms of interconnectivity and integration with the existing computer system in the educational institution.

Communication and collaboration with other teachers

- ✓ Ensuring access to data, information, and newly created digital content with other teaching staff in order to ensure a peer-review prior to actual use in teaching activity;
- ✓ Checking the compatibility of the digital content with those created by other collaborators or teaching staff and with the national educational curriculum.

Safety

Device protection (awareness of risks in digital environments, especially those related to the protection of personal data and implementation of security and safety measures);

- ✓ Verification of compliance with copyright and data licenses regarding the information selected to be part of the developed digital content.

Teaching

- ✓ The ability to implement digital devices and resources in the teaching process, to manage interventions in digital teaching, to experiment and develop new pedagogical formats and methods for training;
- ✓ Guidance, counseling, and monitoring of students in the use of alternative or interactive teaching methods;
- ✓ Collaborative learning (the use of digital technologies to encourage and enhance collaborative learning, enable learners to use digital technologies as part of collaborative tasks, as a means of enhancing communication and collaborative knowledge creation);
- ✓ Self-regulation of teaching (constant monitoring of the educational approach to support self-regulated learning).

Evaluation

- ✓ Feedback and planning regarding the use of new teaching–learning techniques;
- ✓ Analysis and selection of relevant information regarding the performance and progress achieved in the use of digital content;

- ✓ Development of common evaluation strategies at the level of an educational unit in order to select the most effective educational modules created by teaching staff.

Conclusions

The need to adapt the educational content to the needs and particularities of each group of students to whom it is addressed makes it impossible to develop a universal model for the use of information technology in the teaching-learning process.

Thus, students must be encouraged to use digital tools directly and not just passively attend a non-interactive lecture through technical means. Students can thus be directly involved even in the development of educational content, and not only representing its recipients. They will perceive that they have control over the possibilities offered by the technology and will be able to plan, select, explore, solve problems, monitor, and even self-evaluate or inter-evaluate.

Second, access to informational resources must aim to involve students in more realistic and authentic educational situations. Independent access to some databases can facilitate a better understanding of a phenomenon from different perspectives offered by other observers and the possibility to critically evaluate these opinions in relation to one's own perceptions or experiences.

Then, it is necessary to integrate and combine ICT with classic pedagogical strategies and not an attempt to remove or replace the latter. An informed and well-prepared teaching staff from a theoretical and technical point of view is able to be aware of the advantages and limitations of the two teaching methods and to try to take advantage of the strengths of each through a combined use, to achieve the proposed educational objectives.

Finally, a proactive approach is necessary in the sense of presenting the advantages of using technology in teaching to the teachers themselves, in order to facilitate their implementation at the level of each educational unit. A number of studies conclude that the formation and cultivation of a positive attitude of the teacher for the use of technology in the classroom is one of the factors that positively influence the degree of its effective use.

Change is always difficult – it requires effort and patience. The fears of the teachers in the adoption of digitization should neither be ignored nor minimized. On the contrary, concrete solutions must be found to overcome the impasse situations that will inevitably arise. The teacher's role becomes much more complex – it is not limited only to a transition from a teaching technique to a new one but involves an active involvement in the creation and adaptation of educational content using new technologies.

Under these conditions, just a good theoretical and practical training of teachers may appear insufficient for achieving the proposed objectives. Simply attending a technology use course will not guarantee that the teacher is willing to use it extensively in the classroom. It is necessary for him to have the mental comfort that he benefits from technical support at the level of the educational unit in which he works, to be sure that for technical reasons he will not end up in a situation where the lesson prepared with great efforts fails due to an error or deficiency in the equipment used, or that he has the possibility to quickly call on a consultant to guide him in the development of more difficult contents, by means of a technology with which he is not fully familiar.

Notes

1. Digital Education Action Plan 2021–2027.
2. A Europe Fit for the Digital Age.
3. Next Generation EU.
4. DigComp Implementation Guides.
5. Wikipedia contributors. (n.d.). Siri. In Wikipedia. Retrieved from https://ro.wikipedia.org/wiki/Siri

References

Albulescu, I. (2021). Competenţele digitale ale profesorilor [Teachers' digital competences]. In I. Albulescu & H. I. Catalano (Eds.), *e-Didactica. Procesul de instruire în mediul online* [e-Didactics: The online teaching process]. Didactica Publishing House.

European Commission. (2019). *Key competences for lifelong learning* (Directorate-General for Education, Youth, Sport and Culture). Publications Office. <https://data.europa.eu/doi/10.2766/569540>

Blewett, C. (2016). From traditional pedagogy to digital pedagogy: Paradoxes, affordances, and approaches. In M. A. Samuel, R. Dhunpath, & N. Amin

(Eds.), *Disrupting Higher Education Curriculum: Undoing Cognitive Damage* (pp. 265–287). Leiden, The Netherlands: Brill.

European Commission. (n.d.). *The Digital Competence Framework for Citizens (DigComp).* <https://joint-research-centre.ec.europa.eu/digcomp_en>

European Parliament and the Council of the European Union. (2006). *Recommendation on key competences for lifelong learning.* <https://eur-lex.europa.eu/legal-content/EN/TXT/PDF/?uri=CELEX:32006H0962&from=EN>

Howell, J. (2013). *Teaching with ICT. Digital pedagogies for collaboration and creativity.* Oxford University Press.

Istrate, O. (2022). Digital pedagogy. Definition and conceptual area. *Journal of Digital Pedagogy*, 1(1), 3–10. <https://doi.org/10.61071/JDP.0313>

JISC (2020/2021). *Digital Pedagogy Toolkit. Helping academics to make informed choices when embedding digital into the curriculum.* <https://www.jisc.ac.uk/guides/digital-pedagogy-toolkit>

UNESCO. (2015). *The Qingdao Declaration on Information and Communication Technologies (ICT) in education.* <https://en.unesco.org/icted/content/qingdao-declaration>

UNESCO. (2015). *Qingdao Declaration: Seize digital opportunities, lead education transformation. International Conference on ICT and Post-2015 Education*, Qingdao, People's Republic of China, 23–25 May 2015. UNESCO. https://unesdoc.unesco.org/ark:/48223/pf0000233352.

Vuorikari, R., Punie, Y., Carretero Gomez, S., & Van den Brande, G. (2016). *DigComp 2.0: The Digital Competence Frame-work for Citizens. Update Phase 1: The Conceptual Reference Model* (EUR 27948 EN). Publication Office of the European Union. <https://www.doi.org/10.2791/11517>

Digital Literacy and Beyond: Navigating Educational Landscapes in the Digital Age

Dana Rad

Abstract: In an era defined by rapid technological advancement, this chapter delves into the imperative role of digital literacy in modern education. The digital age has transformed how we access, process, and communicate information, necessitating a comprehensive understanding of digital tools and platforms. This chapter also explores the multifaceted nature of digital literacy, encompassing not only technical skills but also critical thinking, information evaluation, ethical considerations, and effective communication in digital spaces. It explores how educators can empower learners to navigate the complexities of the digital landscape. It highlights the significance of fostering digital literacy from an early age, ensuring that students are equipped to discern credible sources, protect their online privacy, and contribute positively to the digital realm. Moreover, this chapter also explores the integration of digital literacy across disciplines, emphasizing its role in promoting creativity, collaboration, and problem-solving. As technology continues to reshape educational paradigms, this chapter underscores the symbiotic relationship between digital literacy and broader educational goals. It advocates for an approach that extends beyond technical proficiency, encouraging educators to cultivate digital citizens who engage responsibly, critically, and ethically in the digital world. Ultimately, this chapter advocates for an education that equips learners with the skills to thrive in the digital age while nurturing their holistic development.

Keywords: digital literacy, education, technological advancement, digital age, critical thinking, information evaluation, ethical considerations, effective communication, digital tools, online privacy, digital citizenship, interdisciplinary integration, creativity, collaboration, problem-solving, holistic development.

Introduction

In an era characterized by exponential technological growth and digitalization, the educational landscape has undergone a profound transformation. The integration of digital technologies into various facets of modern life has necessitated a reevaluation of educational paradigms, prompting a critical examination of the competencies required to navigate this dynamic digital environment. As noted by Smith et al. (2009), "Digital literacy is no longer just a functional skill, it is a skill for success in a technologically advanced society." The current chapter delves into the nuanced dimensions of digital literacy within the context of contemporary education.

Digital Literacy Defined

Digital literacy transcends its technical connotations, emerging as a multidimensional construct that encompasses a far-reaching spectrum of cognitive, social, and ethical proficiencies required for navigating the intricacies of the digital age (Bawden, 2008; Eshet-Alkalai, 2004). Beyond a mere adeptness with digital tools, this multifaceted competency delves into the realms of cognitive acumen, fostering a cognitive agility that is pivotal for astute participation within the contemporary digital landscape. Evidently, digital literacy entails the astute discernment and critical assessment of digital information, enabling individuals to parse the veracity of content and discriminate trustworthy sources from the quagmire of misinformation (Ferrari, 2012; Martin, 2006).

Central to the encompassing umbrella of digital literacy is the cultivation of ethical comportment in digital realms. This involves navigating the labyrinth of ethical considerations, where individuals are equipped to engage responsibly, exhibiting digital behaviors that not only uphold moral standards but also contribute positively to the digital community. Indeed, this ethical facet is underscored by the works of Ferrari (2012) and Martin (2006), who illuminate the imperative of ethical digital behavior as a pivotal tenet of digital literacy.

Moreover, the symbiotic relationship between digital literacy and the cultivation of critical thinking and problem-solving competencies is irrefutable (Ertmer & Ottenbreit-Leftwich, 2010). Digital literacy serves as a catalyst for honing cognitive skills that are imperative for navigating the intricate digital milieu. Individuals adept in digital literacy exhibit the capacity to synthesize information, analyze complex digital landscapes, and deploy astute problem-solving strategies in response to novel challenges. Ertmer and Ottenbreit-Leftwich (2010) emphasize that the development of digital literacy is inherently intertwined with the augmentation of cognitive faculties, signifying its role as a cornerstone of modern education and societal participation.

In essence, digital literacy emerges as a dynamic amalgamation of cognitive, ethical, and social skills that surpass the boundaries of technical proficiency.

It is a catalyst for fostering discernment, ethical responsibility, critical thinking, and problem-solving abilities, collectively propelling individuals toward informed and empowered engagement within the digital epoch.

Multidimensional aspects of digital literacy

Digital literacy constitutes a multidimensional construct that permeates various facets of contemporary society, necessitating a comprehensive comprehension of technology's intricate roles and implications. This intricate competency transcends mere technical prowess, extending its domain to encompass the navigation of digital spaces, accompanied by the dual capacities of astute consumption and creative production of digital content (Hague & Payton, 2010). The evolution of digital literacy, as emphasized by Gilster (1997), encompasses a dynamic spectrum of proficiencies that equip individuals to adeptly comprehend and utilize information across a myriad of formats, originating from diverse sources, and presented through the medium of computers.

Central to this expansive paradigm of digital literacy is the multifaceted nature that comprises its foundation. Embracing the perspectives of Gilster (1997) and endorsed by contemporary scholars, digital literacy evolves as an intricate fusion of competencies spanning distinct domains, such as information literacy, media literacy, and social literacy. Information literacy equips individuals with the prowess to critically evaluate and judiciously discern the veracity of information within the digital domain, ensuring their adeptness in distinguishing reliable sources from the abundance of spurious content (Jenkins et al., 2006). Media literacy, on the other hand, augments individuals' capacity to decipher the nuanced languages and persuasive techniques embedded in multimedia platforms, allowing them to navigate the labyrinthine landscape of digital media with sagacity (Jenkins et al., 2006). In addition, social literacy underscores the ability to interact judiciously within digital social spaces, cultivating responsible, ethical, and meaningful engagements (Jenkins et al., 2006).

The synthesis of these diverse facets of digital literacy collectively furnishes individuals with a robust skillset, essential for flourishing in an increasingly technology-infused world. The holistic understanding of digital literacy, as heralded by Gilster (1997), serves as a beacon guiding individuals to comprehend, adapt, and harness the transformative potential of technology, thereby positioning them as adept participants within the digital milieu.

Digital literacy across education levels

In the ever-evolving landscape of our digitalized society, the resounding call for digital literacy resonates powerfully within the realm of education. This exploration delves into the intricate fabric of digital literacy, intricately threading its essence throughout the educational continuum. From the foundational realms of primary education to the intellectually sophisticated domain of tertiary institutions, this journey unravels a meticulous investigation, centering on the nuanced interplay between the developmental trajectories and cognitive acumen of learners at various educational strata. This approach stands as a firm foundation upon which educators can construct tailored strategies, artfully designed to bestow learners with the indispensable armor of digital literacy competencies (Hobbs, 2013; Ponton & Carrington, 2020).

At its core, this acknowledgment is essential: learners traverse a dynamic spectrum of developmental milestones, each accompanied by unique cognitive capacities. A harmonious fusion of scholarly insights, practical applications, and pedagogical wisdom empowers educators to adeptly navigate this multifaceted landscape, fostering digital literacy in a manner that harmonizes with the cognitive range of their learners. As emphasized by Hobbs (2013) and illuminated by Ponton and Carrington (2020), this strategic alignment of educational stages with digital literacy instruction creates a potent synergy, amplifying the cultivation of pivotal digital skills.

Embedded within the scholarly discourse is a fundamental cornerstone of digital literacy – an early introduction of its concepts within the educational journey. This strategic initiation does not merely sow the seeds of essential digital competencies but also constructs a robust scaffold for future learning endeavors (Pachler et al., 2010). The early exposure to digital literacy concepts acts as a catalyst, nurturing foundational skills that become the fertile ground from which advanced digital prowess can flourish.

Moreover, this exploration delves into the realm of higher education, unraveling the intricate process of seamlessly integrating digital literacy into the fabric of curricula. By strategically weaving digital literacy within the pedagogical tapestry of higher education, educators facilitate the harmonious fusion of academic pursuit and adaptive digital fluency, culminating in a culture of lifelong learning (Selwyn, 2016). This fusion not only equips learners for the intellectual challenges of the contemporary world but also ignites an insatiable thirst for continuous growth and exploration within the digital realm.

In summation, this journey navigates the variegated mosaic of digital literacy across educational stages, casting light on the essence of tailored strategies, early introductions, and seamless amalgamations. By adroitly acknowledging the developmental trajectories of learners and harmonizing with the cognitive nuances of each stage, educators wield the transformative potential to empower learners with the invaluable cloak of digital literacy, enabling them to navigate and excel within an increasingly digitalized era.

Interdisciplinary Integration

In the realm of education, the fusion of digital literacy extends beyond the confines of traditional academic silos, sparking profound shifts in learning experiences. Within this exploration, a critical spotlight shines upon the central role that interdisciplinary integration plays in amplifying the influence of digital literacy. It is crucial to recognize that digital literacy is more than a singular skill; it functions as a dynamic catalyst that fuels creativity, collaboration, and problem-solving capabilities (Friesen & Lowe, 2012).

This approach underscores the dynamic interplay between interdisciplinary integration and the potency of digital literacy. By embracing an interdisciplinary mindset, educators unlock the potential for digital literacy to intertwine seamlessly with various academic domains. This fusion fosters a rich tapestry of connections, where the interaction between digital literacy and diverse disciplines creates a synergistic effect that propels education forward.

The pivotal connection between digital literacy and interdisciplinary prowess is further illuminated. In this intricate dance, digital literacy emerges as a guiding force, equipping students with the agility to navigate the complex landscapes of different fields. The mastery of digital literacy tools empowers students to transcend disciplinary borders, enhancing both their cognitive flexibility and their capacity to tackle intricate challenges that span multiple domains (Roblyer & Doering, 2013).

In summary, this exploration delves into the profound resonance between digital literacy and the interdisciplinary landscape. By forging these connections, educators pave the way for learners to embrace a holistic educational journey that transcends boundaries, cultivates creativity, and hones problem-solving prowess, all while fostering a new generation of informed and adaptable thinkers.

Educator's role in fostering digital literacy

Educators, akin to luminous torchbearers, bear the responsibility of nurturing proficient and conscientious digital citizens. This exploration delves into the crucial and multifaceted role educators assume in cultivating the landscape of digital literacy competencies (Heitin, 2017a). The intricate dimensions of this role come to the forefront, as it entails not only guiding but also orchestrating meaningful interactions between learners and the vast array of digital tools, content, and platforms that populate the modern educational ecosystem.

At the heart of this responsibility lies the art of seamlessly integrating digital literacy instruction within the fabric of the curriculum. This integration, a tapestry woven with precision, grants educators the power to empower students with the discernment, evaluation, and ethical prowess necessary for navigating the labyrinthine expanse of digital information (Kajder, 2004b). By nurturing these competencies, educators equip students with the intellectual armor to not only navigate but also to thrive within the ever-evolving digital landscape.

In this symphony of guidance, the mentorship facet emerges with profound significance. Educators are not merely purveyors of knowledge but also custodians of values, ushering students through the complex terrain of the digital sphere with ethical sensibility (Gallagher, 2011b). This mentorship role is instrumental in fostering a deeper understanding of the ethical, social, and cognitive nuances embedded within the digital realm, thus empowering students to become discerning and responsible digital citizens.

In essence, this exploration magnifies the pivotal and transformative role educators embody in cultivating digital literacy competencies. Through seamless integration, mentorship, and ethical guidance, educators craft an educational experience that prepares students to navigate the digital sphere with acumen, integrity, and an unwavering commitment to responsible digital behavior.

Challenges and solutions

Embarking on the path of comprehensive digital literacy unveils a landscape marked by challenges that necessitate astute navigation. The focus squarely rests on identifying the common hurdles confronting both educators and learners throughout their transformative journey toward digital literacy (Gronlund, 2010).

Among the foremost challenges, the digital divide emerges as a formidable barrier to holistic digital literacy attainment. This divide, often rooted in socioeconomic disparities, defines access to digital tools and resources, shaping the contours of digital literacy achievement. Information overload stands as another hurdle, shrouding the digital landscape in complexity. The ceaseless influx of information can engender confusion, lack of focus, and an inability to discern credible sources amidst the sea of misinformation.

Compounding these challenges is the relentless pace of technological evolution, perpetually demanding adaptability. Swift changes in digital tools and platforms create an ongoing requirement for learners and educators to remain updated and proficient. In this context, the challenges become integral components of the narrative surrounding equitable digital literacy attainment.

Emerging as a beacon, this chapter illuminates pragmatic solutions and best practices poised to surmount these challenges. Inclusivity assumes center stage, bridging the digital divide by ensuring access and resources reach every learner. The clarion call for adaptive pedagogies resonates, advocating instructional approaches that cater to diverse learning styles and needs. Above all, the learner-centered ethos guides educators in nurturing digital literacy through engagement, relevance, and experiential learning. Aligned with West's (2012a) insights, this approach positions learners at the epicenter, facilitating a harmonious fusion between their educational journey and the dynamic digital realm.

In conclusion, this exploration navigates the landscape of challenges intersecting with the quest for comprehensive digital literacy. It underscores the duty to recognize these challenges and the responsibility to cultivate solutions that foster inclusivity, adaptive strategies, and learner-centric education. With strategic prowess and resolution, educators and learners can unlock the transformative potential of digital literacy, forging ahead toward a more informed, empowered, and digitally fluent future.

Digital literacy and holistic development

Amidst the educational landscape, a symbiotic relationship between digital literacy and broader educational objectives emerges, revealing a profound interplay. This exploration into the realm of digital literacy illuminates its capacity to nurture holistic development, encompassing adaptability, resilience, and lifelong learning (Rheingold, 2012).

At its core, this journey unveils a narrative that extends beyond technical prowess. It delves into the intricate fusion of cognitive growth and comprehensive attributes. As learners navigate digital terrains, they traverse a path of knowledge acquisition that not only equips them with information but also cultivates the art of critical thinking, transcending the digital arena to enhance their educational voyage.

In the digital domain, discernment becomes paramount. Effective communication is a linchpin skill. This chapter emphasizes that digital literacy does not merely create adept navigators but nurtures ethical sensibilities. The blend of digital literacy with ethical decision-making molds individuals who traverse both virtual and real-life scenarios with ethical aplomb.

A prevailing theme woven throughout this exploration is the resonance between digital literacy and ethical fabric, resulting in the shaping of responsible digital citizens. This synthesis is not confined to specific disciplines, rather it becomes the common ground where knowledge transcends siloed fields. This equips learners to grapple with intricate ethical challenges, both within digital spaces and the wider world.

In the pursuit of comprehending digital literacy's intricate dimensions within modern education, this chapter has traversed a multifaceted landscape. The insights gleaned resonate with an array of research endeavors that delve into diverse aspects of human behavior, development, and learning. Notably, Dughi et al. (2023) emphasize the importance of cognitive presence and support in fostering students' resilience and grit, aligning with the chapter's emphasis on nurturing holistic development through digital literacy. Marici et al. (2023a) explore the impacts of parental factors on adolescents' emotional experiences, mirroring the chapter's acknowledgment of educators' crucial role in guiding learners through the ethical and cognitive dimensions of digital realms.

Furthermore, the research by Runcan et al. (2023a) and Marici et al. (2023b) delves into anxiety, predictive factors, and the dynamics of interpersonal relationships, aligning with the chapter's consideration of challenges and solutions in cultivating digital literacy. Similarly, Runcan et al. (2023b) employ network analysis to illuminate the nuances of overt narcissism, reminiscent of the chapter's exploration of interdisciplinary integration and the synergistic potential of digital literacy. Marici et al. (2023c) examine attire attractiveness and perceptions, resonating with the chapter's emphasis on diverse academic domains and their intersections with digital skills.

The research by Marici et al. (2022) and Sârbu et al. (2022) underscores the importance of social predictors, transition from anomie to deviance, and the impact of parental factors on adolescents, aligning with the chapter's recognition of the educator's role in fostering responsible digital citizens. Finally, Iosim et al. (2022) investigate the effects of parental labor migration on social sustainability, mirroring the chapter's exploration of digital literacy's connection to broader educational objectives, such as adaptability and lifelong learning. Collectively, these research endeavors resonate with the chapter's insights, collectively illuminating the significance of digital literacy as a transformative educational tool and highlighting the pivotal role of educators in guiding learners through the intricate landscape of the digital age.

In essence, the synergy between digital literacy and holistic educational objectives becomes evident. This perspective portrays how digital literacy, far from being a mere technical skill, contributes to cognitive agility, ethical understanding, and the molding of socially responsible citizens adept at navigating the digital landscape and beyond.

Conclusion

As the journey through the intricacies of digital literacy culminates, this chapter encapsulates the insights and perspectives expounded in the preceding chapters. It succinctly summarizes the pivotal points discussed, reinforcing the pivotal role of digital literacy in nurturing informed and ethical digital citizens (McMahon, 2017). By reiterating the significance of continued exploration and implementation of digital literacy in education, the chapter accentuates its enduring relevance as a transformative force in contemporary education (Livingstone, 2012).

As educational institutions strive to prepare students for active participation in the digital society, the cultivation of digital literacy becomes an essential endeavor (Fraillon et al., 2013; OECD, 2019). The integration of digital literacy into curricula can enhance student' critical thinking abilities and their capacity to engage responsibly in digital environments (Fraillon et al., 2013; UNESCO, 2011). Moreover, the incorporation of digital literacy aligns with contemporary pedagogical approaches that emphasize active learning, collaborative problem-solving, and the development of lifelong learning skills (Prensky, 2001; Trilling & Fadel, 2009).

In conclusion, the emergence of the digital age has elevated the significance of digital literacy as a foundational skillset for informed citizenship and active participation in the digital landscape. This chapter delved into the intricacies of digital literacy within the context of modern education. It unraveled the multifaceted dimensions of this skill and underscored its pivotal role in equipping learners with the competencies required to thrive in an increasingly digitalized world.

References

Bawden, D. (2008). Origins and concepts of digital literacy. In *Digital literacies: Concepts, policies and practices*, Peter Lang Publishing, Editor: Colin Lankshear & Michele Knobel (pp. 17–32).

Dughi, T., Rad, D., Runcan, R., Chiş, R., Vancu, G., Maier, R., Costin, A., Rad, G., Chiş, S., Uleanya, C., & Mihaela M. C. (2023). A network analysis-driven sequential mediation analysis of students' perceived classroom comfort and perceived faculty support on the relationship between teachers' cognitive presence and students' grit – A holistic learning approach. *Behavioral Sciences*, 13(2), 147. <https://doi.org/10.3390/bs13020147>

Ertmer, P. A., & Ottenbreit-Leftwich, A. T. (2010). Teacher technology change: How knowledge, confidence, beliefs, and culture intersect. *Journal of Research on Technology in Education*, *42*(3), 255–284.

Eshet-Alkalai, Y. (2004). Digital literacy: A conceptual framework for survival skills in the digital era. *Journal of Educational Multimedia and Hypermedia*, *13*(1), 93–106.

Ferrari, A. (2012). *Digital competence in practice: An analysis of frameworks*. JRC-IPTS.
Fraillon, J., Ainley, J., Schulz, W., Friedman, T., & Gebhardt, E. (2013). *Preparing for life in a digital age: The IEA International Computer and Information Literacy Study International Report*. Springer.
Friesen, N., & Lowe, S. (2012). The questionable promise of social media for education: Connective learning and the commercial imperative. *Journal of Computer Assisted Learning, 28*(3), 183–194.
Gallagher, C. W. (2011a). Be a mentor, not a tormentor: Supporting students online. *Journal of Adolescent & Adult Literacy, 55*(1), 32–41.
Gallagher, D. J. (2011b). *Teaching literacy in the digital age: Inspiration for all levels and literacies*. Stenhouse Publishers.
Gilster, P. (1997). *Digital literacy*. Wiley Computer Publishing.
Gronlund, N. E. (2010). *Assessment of student achievement* (9th ed.). Pearson.
Hague, C., & Payton, S. (2010). Digital literacy across the curriculum. *Futurelab Literature Review*, 7(1), 1–15.
Heitin, L. (2017a). Digital literacy is the new civil right. *Education Week, 37*(13), 8.
Heitin, L. (2017b). K-12 digital literacy skills every student needs to succeed. *Education Week*. <https://www.edweek.org/technology/k-12-digital-literacy-skills-every-student-needs-to-succeed/2017/07>
Hobbs, R. (2013). *Digital and media literacy: Connecting culture and classroom*. Corwin Press.
Iosim, I., Runcan, P., Runcan, R., Jomiru, C., & Gavrila-Ardelean, M. (2022). The impact of parental external labour migration on the social sustainability of the next generation in developing countries. *Sustainability, 14*(8), 4616. <https://doi.org/10.3390/su14084616>
Jenkins, H., Clinton, K., Purushotma, R., Robison, A. J., & Weigel, M. (2006). *Confronting the challenges of participatory culture: Media education for the 21st century*. MacArthur Foundation.
Kajder, S. (2004a). Bringing the outside in: Visual ways to engage reluctant readers. *Journal of Adolescent & Adult Literacy, 47*(4), 304–311.
Kajder, S. B. (2004b). Enter here: Personal narrative and digital video composing. *English Education, 36*(2), 146–158.
Livingstone, S. (2012). Critical reflections on the benefits of ICT in education. *Oxford Review of Education, 38*(1), 9–24.
Marici, M., Clipa, O., Runcan, R., & Iosim, I. (2022). Perceptions of parenting during the COVID-19 quarantine period, in Suceava, the epicenter of COVID-19 outbreak in Romania. *International Journal of Environmental*

Research and Public Health, *19*(23), 16188. <https://doi.org/10.3390/ijerph192316188>

Marici, M., Clipa, O., Runcan, R., & Parghie, L. (2023a). Is rejection, parental abandonment or neglect a trigger for higher perceived shame and guilt in adolescents? *Healthcare*, *11*(12), 1724.

Marici, M., Clipa, O., Schipor, M.-D., Runcan, R., & Andrei, A.-M. (2023b). Offering and asking for help with domestic chores in couple relationships. *International Journal of Environmental Research and Public Health*, *20*(4), 3708.

Marici, M., Runcan, R., Iosim, I., & Haisan, A. (2023c). The effect of attire attractiveness on students' perception of their teachers. *Frontiers in Psychology, Section Educational Psychology*, *13*, 1059631. <https://doi.org/10.3389/fpsyg.2022.1059631>

Martin, A. (2006). The relationship between ICT and literacy: An Australian case study. *Journal of Computer Assisted Learning*, *22*(2), 81–90.

McMahon, T. (2017). Digital literacies in higher education: Exploring textual, technological, and social practices of reading. *Studies in Higher Education*, *42*(2), 229–238.

OECD. (2019). *PISA 2018 results (volume I): What students know and can do*. OECD Publishing.

Pachler, N., Bachmair, B., & Cook, J. (2010). *Mobile learning: Structures, agency, practices*. Springer Science & Business Media.

Ponton, D. M., & Carrington, V. (2020). Young children's experiences of digital play in the early years. *Early Years*, *40*(3), 294–312.

Prensky, M. (2001). Digital natives, digital immigrants part 2: Do they really think differently?. *On the Horizon*, *9*(6), 1–6.

Rheingold, H. (2012). *Net smart: How to thrive online*. MIT Press.

Roblyer, M. D., & Doering, A. H. (2013). *Integrating educational technology into teaching* (6th ed.). Pearson.

Runcan, R., Nadolu, D., & David, G. (2023a). Predictors of anxiety in Romanian generation Z teenagers. *International Journal of Environmental Research and Public Health*, *20*(6), 4857. <https://doi.org/10.3390/ijerph20064857>

Runcan, R., Rad, D., Runcan, P., & Maduta, C. (2023b). A network analysis approach toward adaptive overt narcissism network. *Behavioral Sciences*, *13*(6), 468. <https://doi.org/10.3390/bs13060468>

Sârbu, E. A., Nadolu, B., Runcan, R., Tomiţă, M., & Lazăr, F. (2022). Social predictors of the transition from anomie to deviance in adolescence. *PLoS ONE*, 17(6), e0269236. <https://doi.org/10.1371/journal.pone.0269236>

Selwyn, N. (2016). *Education and technology: Key issues and debates*. Bloomsbury Publishing.

Smith, S. D., Salaway, G., Caruso, J. B., & Katz, R. N. (2009). *The ECAR study of undergraduate students and information technology* (ECAR Research Study, Vol. 6). EDUCAUSE.

Trilling, B., & Fadel, C. (2009). *21st century skills: Learning for life in our times*. John Wiley & Sons.

West, R. E. (2012a). The power of digital literacy. *Journal of Adolescent & Adult Literacy*, *56*(5), 367–370.

West, R. E. (2012b). Using learner-centered teaching strategies to improve students' college success. *Community College Journal of Research and Practice*, *36*(10), 808–818.

Learning Communities and their Benefits on Students' and Teachers' Learning

Sofia-Loredana Tudor

Abstract: The education process naturally impacts students' learning, resulting in both positive and negative feedback on all educational variables. The analysis of the quality or quantity of learning outcomes must be built in the context of the relation *input–processes–output*, a complex system of factors which have as premises the pupil, the family background, social environment, the material resources, etc. Thus, it became essential to quickly approach the didactic process from another perspective, taking into account all educational factors, as a consequence of the reorganization of educational models through technology integration, flexibilization of curricular approaches, the development of learning communities, etc. Consequently, it is necessary to seek solutions to the new educational challenges while scientific analyses based upon empirical data or meta-analyses can provide valuable contributions. What will be the learning outcomes or to which extent can we discourse upon forming specific competences within the present-day educational context? What will be the impact of this process on pupils/students? Studies underline the efficiency of collaborative activities among pupils and between pupils and teachers, in school and outside school. These activities were found to have visible effects amid concerns over a rise in pupils' learning outcomes on one hand and their effects on the well-being of the human resource involved, on the other. The organization and promotion of professional activities in educational communities will offer a higher flexibility and creativity in the management of educational activities.

Keywords: learning community, collaborative learning, teachers' learning community, pupils'/students' learning community.

Introduction

The evolution of the education concept and the reorganization of the educational system facilitated the development of new approaches in the modalities of implementing the educational system. Supplying quality education is a major responsibility through which the decision-makers are challenged to develop strategies and to solve issues in real time within different educational contexts, which implies communication and interaction with those involved in the process, but, above all, a reconstruction of the mission and practices in the school (Constantinescu, 2015).

To that effect, learning communities were developed, implying the creation and functioning of professional learning groups which bring together not only class teachers and pupils but also other members of the community.

A learning community develops following the coordinates of an educational model which will be in accordance with society learning factors. Participation of community members is essential, and each of them will involve directly or indirectly in a learning community and influence learning and development of other members (teachers and pupils). The development of learning communities is based on primary theories of social cohesion, built upon people's need to belong to a group.

The interests for developing learning communities increased in the latest years, as a result of the development of educational theories which advocate the importance of interactive learning in education and the role of educational environment in diminishing academic failure. Learning communities are based on the principles of interactive learning (McIntyre & Wolff, 1998; Senthamarai, 2018; Sailer & Nomner, 2020):

- knowledge is built among all participants by equal learning;
- in collaborative learning, the use of resources (time, space) is more efficient;
- academic goals and responsibilities are shared in achieving activities;
- learning process is collaborative and pupils/students are stimulated to be critical, creative, etc.; their physical and intellectual engagement in interaction with peers and teachers ensures the improvement of educational excellence. Engagement is an active condition which is influenced by interaction or its absence.

Instruction models offer different accents on educational variables, but contemporary approaches highlight the accent on interaction in the educational process. Authentic learning takes place when the student/pupil is involved and responsible actively while the learning process is focused on learning and not on instruction.

School is the environment which will ensure the collaboration among teachers in order to create a team which will work to achieve the assumed mission and objectives (Hattie, 2014). Three categories of human resources function in a school in interinfluence, shaping as such a learning community with multiple roles (Senge et al., 2016):

- Teachers, whose professional formation and development are assumed by school through its mission. Each school must take into account the promotion, development, and safety of its teachers as an acknowledgement of their professional role. They have to be involved in a long-life continuous formation, concerning not only the content of the discipline they teach but also the teaching profession. As such, teachers' professional community which exists and functions at school level develops also at the level of teaching staff professional community;
- Pupils represent the core of school community and their presence in school manifests as a result of their fundamental right, the right to education. In pupils' learning community, the teacher is their guide, contributing to their evolution and to relational progress;
- School managers have responsibilities in creating a learning community at school level, through developing and sharing a cantered vision upon pupils' and teachers' learning.

Learning community: Conceptual delimitations, characteristics, and classification

Generally, a community is a group of persons whose common interest is pedagogical formation, the persons involved being responsible for an optimal development of the educational process. The membership at group level implies certain characteristics in community evolution:

- community/group members share the same vision and common goals and values, for both pupils and teachers;
- relations among members are collaborative and based on positive interaction;
- educational communities convene members with mutual interests, but at the same time they capitalize different styles, since group efficiency is conditioned by an optimal share of tasks;
- group democracy underlines responsible participation and critical and constructive implication.

A learning community is a professional group in which its members interact systematically, being involved in similar activities, having same goals and work together for extended periods of time in order to create common rules and behaviors which facilitate interaction and constructive communication. In the academic field, these communities prove their usefulness through the many possibilities of communication and transfer of some models, both theoretical, but especially applied, considering the complexity of the teaching activity and the many skills that a future teacher must train and practice (Mogonea et al., 2021).

Specialty studies mention six stages of designing the learning process within a learning community (Ashar et al., 2021):

- student/pupil learning – the emphasis is laid on the learning process specific to pupils/students, on psychology of learning elements);
- adult learning – the emphasis is laid on the development of professional learning community of school teachers;
- leadership learning – it defines learning at the level of the educational unit, through the implication of school management;
- organizational learning – it defines learning as an organizational development process, laying the emphasis on the role of learning in change and innovation in organizations;
- school-to-school learning – it is an inter-school learning named network learning, implying different formal and non-formal collaborative modalities among schools' members;
- network-to-network learning – it is the learning at system level, which extends the learning process at the level of local/national/international communities, through the implication of pupils and teachers and also decision makers from the system.

The purpose of learning communities is to facilitate active learning toward the passive one, cooperation toward competition, as well as to stimulate a strong feeling of community among those who align to the same goals in academic and professional formation (Rocconi, 2011).

A learning community is:

- a professional/learning group which capitalize common effort and competences of each person in the group (Negară, 2013);
- a group of persons sharing common values and interests and respecting the same organizational values and norms (Bezede, 2014);

- a group of teachers who share their educational practice critically and pupils' learning outcomes in a continuous, reflective, collaborative, learning-oriented way (Chuang & Ting, 2021).

Analyzed at the level of university programs, learning communities imply a deliberate restructuring of curriculum – in time, credits, and students' learning experiences – of those who are members of a group, with a view to build a learning community and to stimulate explicit connections between students and the contents/disciplines to be studied (Rocconi, 2011).

Analyzed from teachers' perspective, learning communities are considered as a major facilitator in the process of teachers' professional formation, offering important supportive measures in implementing curricular practices, such as support leadership, promotion of school projects, and development of curricular consultancy measures. To this purpose, schools must build up these communities as modalities to promote teachers' collaboration and to ensure their professional development (Chuang & Ting, 2021):

The characteristics of a functional learning community are (Bezede, 2014):

- a common academic goal, accepted by all members of the community;
- mutual support in the learning process of community members;
- community formation is based on values like reliance among members, cooperation, empathy, collaborative spirit, etc.;
- implication of all members (teachers, pupils/students, other members) in learning activities which will contribute to their professional/personal formation.

Much research has focused on teachers' professional learning, arguing that collaborative leadership practices represent an optimal model for teachers' professional learning, and therefore schools must develop practices that will support teachers' learning. Admiraal et al. (2021) defends the necessity of an integrative approach of the learning community in school, defined by some specific elements:

- development of a view focused on group learning;
- creation of continuous learning opportunities for both teachers and pupils;
- promotion of team learning and collaboration among teachers and pupils;

- development of a research, innovation, and exploration culture in teachers;
- use of documentation and information gathering systems useful in the learning process;
- promotion of non-formal and informal learning;
- implementation of efficient learning models.

The importance of management in developing the learning community is for (Ursu, 2020):

- development of equipment facilities in the educational unit, with the necessary logistics for the implementation of collaborative learning (material, space, digital resources) at the level of social community;
- teachers' training for transversal competences development (counselling and mentorship);
- efficient monitoring of the educational process, by setting communication rules and norms with teachers, pupils and parents, and members of social community.

Different analyses of school as an organization endorse the idea of school as a community, describing the necessity to implement the model of a school that is student- and teacher-friendly, ensures the well-being of its members, and offers a healthy and protective environment for an efficient learning.

Also, teachers' well-being is associated with other psychological constructs (satisfaction and positive emotions, endurance, motivation, and professional engagement). The proposed organizational model to ensure teachers' well-being is defined by three positive dimensions (work engagement, happiness at the workplace, and satisfaction at the workplace) and two negative dimensions (workaholism and burnout). (Hascher & Waber, 2021) Other models propose the integration of interactive strategies (playful or dramatic) for the development of the well-being of the members of the learning group (Balaş & Cioban, 2023)

Teaching as an essential role in the exercise of didactic function is based on a set of professional competences. Teachers' performance is characterized by a large number of competences and skills they have to acquire during their professional career. Permanent interaction with pupils, parents, and co-workers generate accumulation of stress and tension insomuch that the well-being (of pupils, teachers, parents) is a *sine qua non* condition for an efficient functioning of educational communities. This condition is directly related to teaching efficiency and to pupils'/students' academic performances (Hattie and Zierer, 2019).

The diversity of learning communities is determined by the existence of different criteria in classification. On this line, we propose the following classification of learning communities:

Relative to the student group we refer to, one can distinguish:

- pupils'/students' learning community,
- teachers' learning community.

In terms of the assumed goal at the community level, we identify:

- the learning community created with a view to form/develop academic competences for pupils/students,
- the learning community created to develop professional competences.

A classification of learning communities can be analyzed from the perspective of formal/informal/non-formal educational environment as it follows:

- formal learning community, made up of members of school organization (pupils, teachers),
- non-formal learning community, made up of members of school organization and members of local community (pupils, teachers, representatives of community, other categories of specialists).

Relative to the educational space for specific activities, we identify:

- the learning community with activities in physical classroom,
- the learning community with online/hybrid activities.

Teachers' learning community versus pupils'/students' learning community

Teachers' learning community

Many researchers have underlined the effect of professional communities upon teachers' collaboration, feedback provision, job satisfaction, and self-efficacy, highlighting the importance of collaboration among teachers through three concepts: collegiality, professional capital, and collaborative professionalism (Hargreaves, 2019; Yoo & Jang, 2022).

The development of teachers' identity, which refers to ideal self as a professional based on relations between self and others, is essential in helping teachers exercise didactic profession that is built on a collaborative culture among teachers and students (Meihami, 2023).

Professional learning communities have become one of the most challenging development modalities for teachers. Schools from different countries look for opportunities to be part of a professional learning community, since their mission is to develop means of improving educational process through implementing advanced educational practices. These are developed through exchanges of experience among teachers who implement different instructional models.

Professional learning communities ask teachers to advance in their profession in order to engage in professional debates that are essential to improve professional practices (Stoll et al., 2006). Professional relationships facilitating contexts of collaboration, debate, and exchange of best practices is a suitable environment for developing relationships on a positive note (Tudor et al., 2023). The mission of a professional learning community is to ensure that all pupils learn through teachers' collaborative and independent practice (Reichstetter, 2006). The transfer of learning in classroom practices depends on teachers' ability to renegotiate professional identity, as a result of their continuous professional development (Flores, 2020).

A professional learning community is comprised of team members who collaborate regularly to satisfy pupils' needs through a common curricular vision. The achievement of this process is conditioned by the following factors: collaborative leadership and structural conditions offered by school, collective challenge and professional self-formation assumption, reflection upon instruction practices of community members, intervention and improvement decisions based on common formative outcomes of pupils' evaluation.

Collaborative practice is exemplified when teachers gather regularly in their continuous experiments to develop pedagogical knowledge and didactic practices. The role of management is fundamental in developing a professional framework which integrates and transfers professional practices. Each person is encouraged to assume responsibility for his own learning and evolution and this is considered a norm of school culture (Thompson et al., 2004; Trust & Horrocks, 2019).

General characteristics of teachers' professional development include collaboration; reflection upon personal professional practices; focus on pupils' learning, as they represent a central element in the mission of school organization; and the will to be part of the community and to act for attaining the assumed objectives (Prenger et al., 2019).

The following variables describe the teachers' professional learning community (Lomos et al., 2011):

- shared objectives – define the extent to which teachers align to school mission and implicitly, to the objectives and principles of professional community;
- reflexive dialogue – refers to the extent to which teachers engage in professional dialogues about relevant educational topics;
- derivatization of practice – refers to the activity through which teachers engage in a self-analysis process of personal or colleagues' professional practices in order to give or receive feedback to improve them;
- collaboration activity refers to the extent to which they engage professionally with other teachers to function at the community level, exercising professional roles and responsibilities;
- collective focus on pupils' learning – refers to teachers' mutual engagement in order to improve pupils'/students' performances and to fulfil the mission of their formation.

The characteristics of the professional learning community (Stoll et al., 2006):

- shared vision and values for community members, pupils and teachers;
- focus on learning, as a professional development process (self-regulated/self-guided learning, etc.) and learning as a process through which pupils build their competences;
- collective responsibility, since community members assume collective responsibility for pupils' learning constantly;
- professional reflective analysis, including the reflective dialogue on educational issues, frequent feedback on teachers' practice;

- collaboration, which supposes teaching staff implication in professional development activities;
- group learning as well as individual learning, collective learning being essential within a community in order to create a dialogue.

Pupils'/students' learning community

The development of pupils'/students' learning community is implicit in school organization which fosters a collaborative culture, where interaction among teachers represents a model of good practice for pupils/students.

Students' learning community is the commonest form of this approach. We identify variants such as students' practical activity community (especially at the level of university programs), international students' learning community (as a result of university mobilities through European projects implementation), online students' community (developed predominantly during recent years, as a result of pandemic effects upon the educational process).

Pupils'/students' learning community develop due to their participation in different learning contexts (local/national/regional/European) and their interaction with different cultural environments. Practical activities communities offer authentic learning experiences which support academic competences.

Learning communities are groups of pupils/students who learn together, share different school tasks, collaborate in projects, and more, and their existence and functioning are based on collaborative interactions, peer feedback, and sharing personal experiences (Marlatt, 2020; Trust & Horrocks, 2019).

The functioning of this community implies a creative and active process, in which the knowledge acquired through it is the result of a reconstruction process where the pupil's/student's active participation is total. It represents an individual as well as a social experience at the same time – it capitalizes pupils' point of view, stimulating self-trust in order to have new ideas and to make decisions, etc. (Cerghit, 2008).

The learning community: advantages for school organization members

At the level of school organization, efficient learning communities target essential problems for organization mission, as it has been proved that student-centered leadership is a key component of efficient study programs. Learning communities are an essential element in the pursuance of institutional quality (Smith & MacGregor, 2009).

Learning communities imply interactive learning through the transfer of knowledge, skills, and attitudes within organizations, bringing a significant contribution concerning:

- alignment of successful practices, procedures, and instruments used within school organization;
- research on areas of interest and sharing results in the community and organization;
- transfer of practices among community members;
- counselling and mentorship from experts in the community.

Learning communities have made a special contribution to teachers' professional formation because they facilitate teachers' involvement in collective actions, engagement with school mission and objectives, and generated shared responsibilities for pupils and teachers. Learning within professional communities will improve teachers' capacities to create a favorable learning environment through integrating innovative practices (Affandi et al., 2019).

The benefits of collaborative action for teachers in the learning community are based on the advantages of professional dialogue and on the stimulation of a critical attitude among them (Rabin, 2020).

The promotion of collaborative learning in school helps teachers find an easier way to develop professional competences and allows them to engage in collaborative actions and to develop learning networks in schools. Professional interaction at the community level in school ensures the capitalization of teachers' expertise through involvement in training of trainer's activities, teachers' implication in development/research activities, teachers' involvement in formation activities, and awareness of professional development opportunities (Senge et al., 2016).

Some studies highlight the benefits of belonging to a learning community as regards the improvement of pupils'/students' academic performances (Hattie& Zierer 2019). The increase in academic performance is fostered by the student's active and social involvement in the learning group and the expansion of their circle of contacts, which can be beneficial for learning.

The mutual interest for certain didactic tasks has positive effects on learning motivation.

On the other hand, collective learning achieved within a professional learning community is a predictor of pupils' performance, as a result of the positive interaction between teachers and pupils and the development of a stimulant educational environment. Studies show that professional learning in a learning community improves teachers' capacity to design a supportive learning environment for pupils and is a significant predictor of pupils' disciplined behavior (Affandi et al., 2019).

The increased interest for learning communities is based mainly on the evidence that participation in a learning community has been related to various academic performances, including transition to university and transition of graduates to the labor market. Effects include satisfaction with the program of studies, perseverance in continuing studies, interest and involvement in school activities, increased peer interaction, stimulation of creative and critical thinking, and a positive perception of student condition (Rocconi, 2011).

Learning communities facilitate students' academic transition through their integration in professional/academic network. Students' positive educational outcomes are associated with their participation in learning communities.

The advantages of being in a learning community include (Hargreaves, 2019; Marlatt, 2020; Yoo and Jang, 2022):

- development of academic and professional motivation, as a result of an extended social interaction;
- creation of academic, social and professional opportunities;
- development of self-regulated skills, through the individual responsibilities of community members in solving differentiated tasks;
- encouragement in accumulating positive academic and social experience;
- development of positive interaction among teachers and pupils/ students, members of school community and members of social community, etc.;
- identification of opportunities to develop other competences (transversal, soft).

Conclusions

Promoting the idea of a learning community will ensure a solid foundation of a school that has the capacity to develop and provide affordable quality for everyone.

A school is primarily a learning organization because it allows teachers to develop pedagogical competences, to engage in collaborative actions, and to develop a learning network inside and outside school. It is the place where pupils/students learn through an assumed and regulated formation process, and the outcomes of this process represent efficiency indicators of quality in education.

References

Admiraal, W., Schenke, W., De Jong, L., Emmelot, Y., & Sligte, H. (2021). Schools as professional learning communities: What can schools do to support professional development of their teachers? *Professional Development in Education*, *47*(4), 684–698. <https://doi.org/10.1080/19415257.2019.1665573>

Ashar, M., Kamdi, W., & Kurniawan, DT. (2021). Professional skills development through the network learning community using an online learning platform. *International Journal of Interactive Mobile Technologies*, *15*(2), 202–210. <https://doi.org/10.3991/ijim.v15i12.21587>

Affandi, L. H., Ermiana, I., & Makki, M. (2019). Effective professional learning community model for improving elementary school teachers' performance. *Advances in Social Science, Education and Humanities Research*, *326*, 315–320. <https://doi.org/10.2991/iccie-18.2019.54>

Balaş, E., & Cioban, S. G. (2023). Developing the well-being of students by using ludic and dramatic methods in the teaching-learning-assessment process. In E. Balaş, A. Roman, & D. Rad (Eds.), *Students' well-being and teaching-learning efficiency during and post-pandemic period* [Bunăstarea studenţilor şi eficienţa predării-învăţării în perioada şi post-pandemie] (pp. 45–62). Peter Lang. https://doi.org/10.3726/b20636.

Bezede, R. (2014). *Valorificarea leadership-ului paideutic în cadrul comunităţilor profesionale de învăţare* [Valorising paideutic leadership in professional learning communities]. Didactica Pro... revistă de teorie şi practică educaţională, (5–6), 16–20. Chişinău: Editura Didactica Pro.

Cerghit, I. (2008). *Sisteme de instruire alternative şi complementare. Structuri, stiluri, strategii* [Alternative and complementary training systems. Structures, styles, strategies]. Polirom.

Chuang, N. C., & Ting, Y. K. (2021). School-based professional learning communities as a means for curriculum development: A case study from Taiwan. *International Journal of Research in Education and Science*, 7(4), 1184–1210. https://doi.org/10.46328/ijres.2408

Constantinescu, M. (2015). Teachers' attitudes toward educational changes in Romania. *Procedia – Social and Behavioral Sciences, 177*, 61–64. <https://doi.org/10.1016/j.sbspro.2015.02.334>

Flores, M. A. (2020). Preparing teachers to teach in complex settings: Opportunities for professional learning and development. *European Journal of Teacher Education, 43*(3), 297–300. <https://doi.org/10.1080/02619768.2020.1771895>

Hattie, J. (2014). *Învățarea vizibilă: ghid pentru profesori* [Visible learning: A teacher's guide]. Trei.

Hattie, J., & Zierer, K. (2019). *Visible learning insights*. Routledge.

Hargreaves, A. (2019). Teacher collaboration: 30 years of research on its nature, forms, limitations and effects. *Teachers and Teaching, 25*(5), 603–621. <https://doi.org/10.1080/13540602.2019.1639499>

Hascher, T., & Waber, J. (2021). Teacher well-being: A systematic review of the research literature from the year 2000–2019. *Educational Research Review, 34*, 100411. <https://doi.org/10.1016/j.edurev.2021.100411>

Lomos C., Hofman R. H., & Bosker R. J. (2011). Professional communities and student achievement – A meta-analysis. *School Effectiveness and School Improvement*, 22(2), 121–148.

Marlatt, R. (2020). Capitalizing on the craze of Fortnite: Toward a conceptual framework for understanding how gamers construct communities of practice. *Journal of Education, 200*(1), 3–11. <https://doi.org/10.1177/0022057419864531>

McIntyre, D. R., & Wolff, F. G. (1998). An experiment with WWW interactive learning in university education. *Computers & Education, 31*(3), 255–264. <https://doi.org/10.1016/S0360-1315(98)00025-6>

Meihami, H. (2023). Exploring the role of professional learning community in EFL student-teachers' imagined identity development. *Journal of Language, Identity & Education*, 24(4), 807–824. https://doi.org/10.1080/15348458.2023.2193336.

Mogonea, F., Popescu, A. M., & Mogonea, F. R. (2021). Communities of practice – ways of interaction between professionals. *Educația din perspectiva conceptului clasa viitorului. Culegere de articole ale conferinței naționale științifice cu participare internațională (NSCIP)*, 42–51. <http://hdl.handle.net/123456789/2893>

Molero, P. P., Ortega, F. Z., Jiménez, J. L. U., & Valero, G. G. (2019). Influence of emotional intelligence and burnout syndrome on teachers well-being: A systematic review. *Social Sciences*, *8*(6), 185. <https://doi.org/10.3390/socsci8060185>

Negară, C. (2013). Aspecte didactice ale creării şi managementului reţelelor de învăţare. *Acta Et Commentationes* (Sciences of Education), *2*(1), 71–75.

Prenger, R., Poortman, C. L., & Handelzalts, A. (2019). The effects of networked professional learning communities. *Journal of Teacher Education*, *70*(5), 441–452. <https://doi.org/10.1177/0022487117753574>

Rabin, C. (2020). Co-Teaching: Collaborative and caring teacher preparation. *Journal of Teacher Education*, *71*(1), 135–147. <www.doi.org/10.1177/0022487119872696>

Reichstetter, R. (2006). Defining a professional learning community. *E & R Research Alert*. <https://webarchive.wcpss.net/results/reports/2006/0605plc_lit_review.pdf

Rocconi, L. M. (2011). The impact of learning communities on first year students' growth and development in college. *Research in Higher Education*, *52*, 178–193. <https://doi.org/10.1007/s11162-010-9190-3>

Sailer, M., & Nomner, L. (2020). The gamification of learning: A meta-analysis. *Educational Psychology Review*, *32*, 77–112. <https://doi.org/10.1007/s10648-019-09498-w>

Senge, P., Cambron-McCabe, N., & Lucas, T. (2016). *Şcoli care învaţă: a cincea disciplină aplicată în educaţie* [Learning schools: The fifth applied discipline in education]. Trei.

Senthamarai, S. (2018). Interactive teaching strategies. *Journal of Applied and Advanced Research*, *3*(1), S36–S38. <http://dx.doi.org/10.21839/jaar.2018.v3iS1.166>

Smith, B. L., & MacGregor, J. (2009). Learning communities and the quest for quality. *Quality Assurance in Education*, *17*(2), 118–139. <https://doi.org/10.1108/09684880910951354>

Stoll, L., Bolam, R., McMahon, A. et al. (2006). Professional learning communities: A review of the literature. *Journal of Educational Change*, *7*, 221–258. <https://doi.org/10.1007/s10833-006-0001-8>

Thompson, S., Gregg, L., &. Niska, J. M. (2004). Professional learning communities, leadership, and student learning. *RMLE Online*, *28*(1), 1–15. <https://doi.org/10.1080/19404476.2004.11658173>

Trust, T., & Horrocks, B. (2019). Six key elements identified in an active and thriving blended community of practice. *TechTrends*, *63*, 108–115. <https://doi.org/10.1007/s11528-018-0265-x>

Tudor, S. L., Langa, C., Stan, M. M., & Lazăr, A. (2023). Teacher's well-being: A premise for the development of the professional community. In E. Soare, & C. Langa (Eds.), *Education facing contemporary world issues – EDU WORLD 2022, European Proceedings of Educational Sciences* (Vol. 5, pp. 1382–1390). European Publisher. <https://doi.org/10.15405/epes.23045.141>

Ursu, L. (2020). *Construirea comunităților educaționale școlare în condițiile învățării mixte* [Building school educational communities in blended learning conditions]. Calitate în educație – imperativ al societății contemporane, 2, 20–24.

Yoo, H., & Jang, J. (2022). Effects of professional learning communities on teacher collaboration, feedback provision, job satisfaction and self-efficacy: Evidence from Korean PISA 2018 data. *Compare. A Journal of Comparative and International Education*. <https://doi.org/10.1080/03057925.2022.2036591>

Social Services for Children in Schools: A Case Study

Alina Costin

Abstract: Starting from Bowen's systemic theory (1954), the family functions as a system, in which the dynamics of relationships are in permanent change; any life event that concerns one of the members will have consequences on the other members of the family (Satir, 1951). There is obvious and indisputable evidence on the impact of potentially traumatic events on a child, and that they invariably negatively affect in the child's functioning as part of the family and at school (Demo & Acock, 1988; Kleinsorge & Covitz, 2012; Jensen & Brownfield, 1983). We use the case study method to create a destabilizing family framework, examine its effects on the child, and highlight the crucial role of psychosocial intervention carried out by the public social services in restoring family homeostasis. We draw attention to the importance of school-community services dialogue to report instances of family dysfunction by observing the child's behavior as a reflection of family dynamics. The implications of the failure of specialist services in not taking over these cases are explored.

Keywords: family, system, school, social dysfunctions, social intervention.

School context for manifested social dysfunctions

The social pressures exerted on schools have led to an expansion and diversification of the their role, especially in responding to the social needs of the family. Thus, the school has turned into an educational and socio-therapeutic center – it is much more than a training and instruction framework and manifests itself as a center of networks of instructive, formative, medical, psychological, and vocational counselling services – it is the space that offers specialized support on all dimensions of training, so that the student can acquire the necessary skills and competences for an autonomous life and independence. In this sense, the well-being of school-aged children is also addressed in the school setting (Bye et al., 2009 ; Constable, 2009; Sherman, 2016), this being the interface between the individual and society. Therefore, social dysfunctions and tensions are manifested in the classroom, and this is also where their central prevention and therapy mode is manifested (Neamtu, 2011).

Studies in social psychology have revealed that schools, although intended to create opportunities for all categories of children, actually perpetuate the social inequalities they take from the social field (Batruch et al., 2019). Students, belonging to different social categories and coming from families with different typologies, histories, and resources, make efforts, sometimes hidden, to manage conflicts or difficulties in the family, sometimes at very high costs (Desai & Thorat, 2016). Intervening in such cases is vital for children's mental health and overall development, and sometimes the only solution for their situation is to be referred to specialists. The school, therefore, represents a very important filter for the case management of families in difficulty.

Bolin and Sorbring (2017) conclude that the operation of a social assistance center in school is perceived by students as a means of self-reporting and requesting help; this result also suggests that, by accessing help services, children acquire extraordinary life skills.

Family as a system

This chapter aims to highlight the impact of various potentially traumatic events in the family on children, and implicitly on their school attendance. Research has shown that the death of a family member, divorce, the birth of a child, substance abuse, and neglect can have very serious effects on the child. In severe cases, these events occur simultaneously and place an immense pressure on the child, which they are unable to manage without external help. Public social assistance services have the responsibility to take over these cases and provide support in order to restore family homeostasis.

The main assumptions of the systemic theory emphasize the fact that the answers to different problems of one of the members are inside the family system. Marital conflict, illness, or death of one of the significant members, or new relationships or new members appearing in the family can disrupt the family functioning, and the child's behavior can be analyzed as a symptom of family dysfunction (Bowen, 1954). The systemic school of psychotherapy also shows that a child's problematic behavior reflects issues within the family system and that the responsibility of restoring order always rests with the adults. The establishment of public social assistance services

(SPAS) at the community level was based precisely on these considerations. Serious situations such as abuse and abandonment can be prevented through timely and emergency interventions carried out in the immediate vicinity of the family.

Drifting parents, unfulfilled parental roles, and children exposed to risks

Difficult life events such as separation, divorce, and the death of a child can seriously destabilize the parent, affecting their functionality and the ability to fulfill parental duties. In these situations, a vast category of other variables such as the existence and support of the extended family, access to specialized services, and above all, individual characteristics of the parent, such as resilience, intelligence, maturity, etc., are important predictors for their ability to adapt to traumatic events and reconstruction of the self and one's own life.

In addition to problems in adaptation, particularly among boys (Morrison & Cherlin, 1995), behavioral disorders (Cherlin et al., 1998), and social stigmatization (Lansford, 2009), children frequently develop coping mechanisms such as regression and denial, generally indicating mental health problems (Strohschein, 2005). Pagani et al. (1997) report behavioral disorders in situations where parents remarry (Macie & Stolberg, 2003), such as anxiety and depression (Tweed et al., 1989; Hoyt et al., 1990), aggression, and speech disorders (Babalis, 2011).

On the other hand, a single parent living in poverty or facing significant challenges in meeting the child's needs (Grall, 2007) can result in the child developing depression, anxiety, disorders (Ross & Wynne, 2010), chronic stress (Dasteel, 1982), disorganization, and panic (Mahoney, 2000).

Children's exposure to their parents' substance use includes risks such as abuse, material, psychological and emotional neglect, and violence (McKeganey et al., 2002). According to Lief (1985), there is not a more disadvantaged category than a child with drug-addicted parents because the parents' absence from the plane of reality, the distortion of their personality, and the pathology determined by consumption irreparably affect parental competence, with risks ranging from the smallest neglect to complete abandonment.

The conflictual environment and constant tensions between students induce self-esteem problems and a disturbed image of life in children

(Raschke & Raschke, 1979). Other theories talk about learning helplessness (Maier & Seligman, 1976) and selective mutism (Kumpulainen et al., 1998). Some studies draw attention to self-esteem issues, relationship difficulties, stress, anger, anxiety, and depression (Downs & Rindels, 2004), as well as aggression and self-control problems (Burton, 1961; Magqamfana & Bazana, 2020; Van Ijzendoorn & De Wolff, 1997) as potential consequences of the father's absence in the family.

Aim and research question

We aim to highlight the impact of some social dysfunctions on school-age children and the importance of social intervention in the school setting, so this chapter respects the format of a descriptive study. The research question is how the intervention of the social worker can restore the homeostasis of a dysfunctional family with serious effects on the child. We use the case study method, specific to qualitative researchers (Heritage & Silverman, 2010).

The study took place in a primary school where the social worker in the SPAS structure carried out part of the interventions together with the school psychologist.

Case study 1
Case description

T., a 7-year-old boy, exhibits behavioral disorders in the school environment (isolation, aggressiveness), has difficulty maintaining attention, and shows hyperactivity—symptoms that indicate neglect (no food at school, sleep deprivation). These symptoms were preceded by a period where T manifests chronic fatigue, very low ability to concentrate and pay attention, and heightened sensitivity. The parents did not respond to the summons, repeatedly ignoring the teacher's requests, therefore, the case was reported to the public social assistance service of the local town hall (SPAS).

Family history

- death of the older brother
- mother's suicide attempt a few months after his death
- alcohol and substance use by the mother

- absent father
- conflictual separation of parents
- child with language disorders diagnosed at the age of 3, found in the records of the service
- Pediatric Neuropsychiatry.

Two years ago, T. suddenly lost his 21-year-old brother to whom he was very close.

A year ago, the parents decide to separate. During the trial, the child's father, Mr. C., accuses the mother, Mrs. F., of not being able to keep the house in order, using narcotic substances, consuming alcohol, being depressed, and having attempted suicide, therefore being unfit to take care of the minor son. The child's paternal grandparents also make similar statements, demanding that the mother be stripped of her parental rights, with the father being granted exclusive guardianship. The judge decides to start a home assistance intervention in order to determine the reality of the situation to decide if the mother's rights should be revoked.

In the meantime, the father starts a relationship with another woman, passes by the child's house every day without stopping by and saying hello, and later requests the withdrawal of parental rights because he doubts the paternity of T.

The goal of the intervention: restoring the balance and stability of the family environment by rehabilitating the mother, restoring her responsibility as a parent, and providing support to the child in order to adapt to the changes and family events that triggered imbalances. We consider empowering the family in order to ensure a healthy climate and conditions for the child.

Intervention objectives

The objectives of the intervention are aimed at the mother and the child. The father, being absent, cannot be co-opted into the intervention program. Steps include:

- Evaluation of the mother's parenting skills;
- Development of child-rearing skills;
- Finding a job for the mother;
- Facilitating access to anger management counselling;
- Enrolling the mother in a parenting course;

- Involvement of maternal grandparents in raising the child;
- Counselling and psychotherapy for the child;
- Enrolment in a summer school and interventions aimed at increasing socialization skills and frustration management;
- Moderation of the relationship with the mother's new partner and emotional preparation for the birth of a brother.

The case is considered difficult due to the complexity of the problems involved in this child's life.

Detailed evaluation of the family situation

a) The first meeting with T. takes place at the beginning of April 2022 – he is friendly and invites me to play with him immediately after Mrs. F. introduces me. The mother proves to be open, willing to collaborate, and to do everything possible for the good of the child. He is often visited at home by the neighbor's grandson, with whom he plays without much difficulty. By going out on a bike, he shows himself to be responsible and exhibits concern for his friend who is more reckless than him.

Considering that at home all the meetings take place without episodes of aggression – other than moments when T. demonstrates low tolerance for frustration, and especially a lot of agitation when he has to do his homework – and information continues to arrive from school about the particularly aggressive behaviors of the child both toward his peers and the teaching and auxiliary staff, I decide to expose him to an environment where there are more children, by taking him to the park. Here T. proves to be an educated child, showing only low tolerance for frustration when playing football with children much older than him. Coincidentally, the teacher who assists him at school is present in the park and is amazed by how well he behaves and how well-educated he is.

b) In fact, T.'s school results are particularly low even though he has an IQ of 119, possesses a rich vocabulary, and often proves to be an intelligent child at home, finding ingenious solutions to achieve his goals.

c). The intervention seems to be in a deadlock phase, failing to determine why the child's behavior changes so drastically at school and how it could be improved.

Considering the aggressive behaviors and low performance at school in May, a short program is decided until 12.30. All his schoolmates and classmates finish the program at 16.30.

d). Mrs. F. is making efforts to rehabilitate herself, after the analyses it turns out that she has given up alcohol and narcotics. After the death of her older son, with whom she managed the bar they owned, Mrs. F. was left without a secure and constant source of income. During the same period, Mrs. F.'s father moved into her home to help her raise the child and provide monetary help. I try to convince her that it is necessary for her to prove that she can manage herself financially, and shortly after our discussion, she manages to move on to a full-time and permanent contract.

e). T. is enrolled in a summer school organized in the city.
The child initially showed reluctance, expressing fear of new experiences and socializing with other children. However, with adequate support, he accepted to postpone and returning without difficulties throughout the summer. Exposure to frustration and discussions with the assigned psychologist worked to improve the child's way of relating to others in the group. In the meantime, the mother enrolled in a psychological and parenting course in order to have the necessary tools to manage her relationship with T. as well as that between the siblings.

f). Mr. A., the mother's new partner, visits T.'s family more often and for longer periods. I often find him playing with T., who seems to have accepted him and tries to imitate him. Mr. A is able to make himself heard by the child without raising his voice and keeping calm.

We try to do the homework for the holidays but T. he gets agitated easily, sulks, and categorically refuses to work, saying that he does not feel capable. I then propose that we do another type of exercise that trains the executive functions, which he does with great pleasure and ease. After a certain period of time, he agrees to move on to homework by setting few rules, together, by mutual agreement that he generally strives to follow.

During the entire period of the interventions, lasting ten months, the child was not aggressive at home, and the relationship between the adults in the family and T. was affectionate, including his paternal grandparents, who took him to their home every other weekend. However, his father never asked to see him even though he passed by the house at least twice a day.

Results

The child's mother tried to implement all the suggestions and fulfill the objectives established together. Ms. F's relationship with Mr. A is stable, in the meantime a child was born, for which T. was emotionally prepared. After the birth of the brother, the maternal grandmother was often present. Mrs. F. devoted time to just being with T., cooking together and spending quality time with him. At first T. kept his distance from the newborn child, but slowly he began to treat him with affection and play with him.

At the start of school, the female teachers saw a notable improvement in T.'s behavior, and he no longer interacts aggressively with his peers or adults. The 10-month-long intervention ended as T.'s family relocated to the city where Mr. A. is from, where he has more activities to manage as an entrepreneur. His mother gradually included him in the new family, and he was being received affectionately by the new relatives. At school, he has a short program lasting four days a week, the number of students per class is smaller, and with a support teacher, the child's behavioral problems have subsequently decreased.

Conclusions

What emerges from this intervention and prompts reflection is that this child has always had vulnerabilities which were further exacerbated by serious losses that are difficult to manage even by an adult. An intensive intervention involving different professional figures working with both the child and the adult members of the family allowed an improvement in the child's condition.

Limits

The study uses a single instrumented case to achieve the proposed goal, however, the case is relevant and constitutes in itself an argument in favor of social interventions in an extremely difficult period from a social point of view.

References

Babalis, T., Xhantakou, Y., Papa, C., & Tsolou, O. (2011). Preschool age children, divorce and adjustment: A case study in Greek kindergarten.

Batruch, A., Autin, F., & Butera, F. (2019). The paradoxical role of meritocratic selection in the perpetuation of social inequalities at school. *In F. Butera & J.-L. Mari (Eds.), The social psychology of inequality* (pp. 123–137). Springer. https://doi.org/10.1007/978-3-030-13725-1_7.

Burton, R. V., & Whiting, J. W. (1961). The absent father and cross-sex identity. *Merrill-Palmer Quarterly of Behavior and Development*, 7(2), 85–95.

Barnard, M., & McIntosh, J. (2002). Paying the price for their parents' addiction: Meeting the needs of the children of drug-using parents. *Drugs: Education, Prevention and Policy*, 9(3), 233–246. https://doi.org/10.1080/09687630210100545.

Bowen, M. (1978). Family Therapy in Clinical Practice. Northvale, NJ: Jason Aronson.

Bolin, A., & Sorbring, E. (2017) The self-referral affordances of school-based social work support: A case study. *European Journal of Social Work*, *20*(6), 869–881. <www.doi.org/10.1080/13691457.2016.1278521>

Constable, R. (2009). The role of the school social worker. In R. Constable, C. R. Massat, S. McDonald, & J. P. Flynn (Eds.), *School social work: practice, policy, and research* (pp. 3–29). Lyceum Books.

Cook, S. W. (1985). Experimenting on social issues: The case of school desegregation. *American Psychologist*, *40*(4), 452–460. <https://doi.org/10.1037/0003-066X.40.4.452 >

Cherlin, A. J., Chase-Lansdale, P. L., & McRae, C. (1998). Effects of parental divorce on mental health throughout the life course. *American Sociological Review*, *63*, 239–249.

Dasteel, J. C. (1982). Stress reactions to marital dissolution as experienced by adults attending courses on divorce. *Journal of Divorce*, *5*(3), 37–47.

De Wolff, M. S., & Van Ijzendoorn, M. H. (1997). Sensitivity and attachment: A meta-analysis on parental antecedents of infant attachment. *Child Development*, *68*(4), 571–591.

Demo, D. H., & Acock, A. C. (1988). *The impact of divorce on children. Journal of Marriage and the Family*, 50(3), 619–648. https://doi.org/10.2307/352629.

Desai, S., & Thorat, A. (2016). Social inequalities in education. In *India Infrastructure Report 2012* (pp. 82–89). Routledge India.

Downs, W. R., & Rindels, B. (2004). Adulthood depression, anxiety, and trauma symptoms: A comparison of women with nonabusive, abusive, and absent father figures in childhood. *Violence and Victims*, *19*(6), 659–671.

Grall, T. S. (2009). *Custodial Mothers and Fathers and Their Child Support: 2007* (Current Population Reports, P60-237). U.S. Census Bureau.

Heritage, J., & Silverman, D. (2010). Conversation analysis: Practice and methods. *Qualitative Research*, 208 –230.

Hoyt, L. A., Cowen, E. L., Pedro-Carroll, J. L., & Alpert-Gillis, L. J. (1990). *Anxiety and depression in young children of divorce. Journal of Clinical Child Psychology*, 19(1), 26–32. https://doi.org/10.1207/s15374424jccp1901_4.

Jensen, G. F., & Brownfield, D. (1983). Parents and drugs: Specifying the consequences of attachment. *Criminology*, *21*(4), 543–554.

Kleinsorge, C., & Covitz, L. M. (2012). Impact of divorce on children: Developmental considerations. *Pediatrics in Review*, *33*(4), 147–155.

Kumpulainen, K., Räsänen, E., & Puura, K. (2001). Psychiatric disorders and the use of mental health services among children involved in bullying. *Aggressive Behavior: Official Journal of the International Society for Research on Aggression*, 27(2), 102–110.

Lief, N. R. (1985). The drug user as a parent. *International Journal of the Addictions*, *20*(1), 63–97.

Macie, K. M., & Stolberg, A. L. (2003). Assessing parenting after divorce: The co-parenting behavior questionnaire. *Journal of Divorce & Remarriage*, *39*(1–2), 89–107.

McKeganey, N., Barnard, M. B., & McIntosh, J. (2002). Paying the price for their parents' addiction: Meeting the needs of the children of drug-using parents. Drugs: Education, Prevention & Policy, 9(3), 233–246. https://doi.org/10.1080/09687630210122508.

Mahoney, D. M. (2000). *Panic and self states: An ethnomethodological approach.* Institute for Clinical Social Work (Chicago).

Maier, S. F., & Seligman, M. E. (1976). Learned helplessness: Theory and evidence. *Journal of Experimental Psychology: General*, *105*(1), 3.

Magqamfana, S., & Bazana, S. (2020). Absent fathers: Psychological and socio-economic implications for black children and directions for future research. *Journal of Psychology in Africa*, *30*(2), 169–173.

Morrison D. R., Cherlin A. J. (1995). The divorce process and young children's well-being: A prospective analysis. *Journal of Marriage and the Family*, *57*, 800–812.

Pagani, L., Boulerice, B., Tremblay, R. E., & Vitaro, F. (1997). Behavioural development in children of divorce and remarriage. *Journal of Child Psychology and Psychiatry*, *38*(7), 769–781.

Ross, L. T., & Wynne, S. (2010). Parental depression and divorce and adult children's well-being: The role of family unpredictability. *Journal of Child and Family Studies*, *19*, 757–761.
Tweed, J. L., Schoenbach, V. J., George, L. K., & Blazer, D. G. (1989). The effects of childhood parental death and divorce on six-month history of anxiety disorders. *The British Journal of Psychiatry*, *154*(6), 823–828.
Strohschein, L. (2005). Parental divorce and child mental health trajectories. *Journal of Marriage and Family*, *67*(5), 1286–1300.
Raschke, H. J., & Raschke, V. J. (1979). Family conflict and children's self-concepts: A comparison of intact and single-parent families. *Journal of Marriage and the Family*, 41(2), 367–374. https://doi.org/10.2307/351693
Lansford, J. E. (2009). Parental divorce and children's adjustment. *Perspectives on Psychological Science*, *4*(2), 140–152.
Sherman, M. C. (2016). The school social worker: A marginalized commodity within the school ecosystem. *Children & Schools*, *38*(3), 147–151.
Van Ijzendoorn, M. H., & De Wolff, M. S. (1997). In search of the absent father – Meta-analyses of infant-father attachment: A rejoinder to our discussants. *Child Development*, *68*(4), 604–609.

The Development of Transversal Competences in Students through Extracurricular Activities

Henrietta Torkos, Evelina Balaş, and Editha Coşarbă

Abstract: This study starts from the hypothesis that at the level of higher education, professional competences – be they general, at the level of a field of studies, or specific, at the level of each study program – must be supplemented and supported by transversal competences, whose importance is currently undisputed. Educational institutions must accept the importance of these competences and the reality of their impact on the professional prospects of students, a field to which they must direct their attention and offer solutions or remedies for the acquisition or development of these transversal competences. This task can no longer remain exclusively the responsibility of the student, the family, or alternative forms of education. Otherwise, the universities will find in the very near future that their own graduates are outclassed in job interviews by candidates from other educational institutions, with a direct impact on the prospects and attractiveness of the university for the future generations of students.

Keywords: transversal competences, higher education, extracurricular activities.

Introduction

All higher education institutions, whether they operate at the national or global level, aim to provide theoretical and practical training that will ensure students have the best chances of success in the future in the labor market under conditions of increasingly intense competition. This competition is manifested, on the one hand, by the increasingly varied educational offers existing at this moment, with the number of higher education institutions and study programs offered, be they bachelor's, master's, or doctorate, witnessing a constant increase. Another factor that determines the need to maintain a higher level of quality and competitiveness for universities is globalization, viewed from the perspective of facilitating access to educational offers at the university level for students from other countries than the one in which the higher education institution operates. Numerous national education systems, both within the European Union and in other countries with a tradition of higher education at a level of excellence, such as the United States, Great Britain, China, or Japan, make efforts to attract foreign students through offering scholarships and credit facilities, providing accommodation and transport conditions, or allowing mutual recognition of diplomas.

On the other hand, competition also manifests itself at the level of graduates of higher education institutions, their number being in constant growth in the last two decades, compensated to some extent by a development of the services and consumer market. However, this trend is valid only for a limited range of the existing professional qualifications in the students' portfolio.

In these conditions, it can be noted that an increasing importance is given, both by universities and by future potential students, to a statistical criterion for the classification of higher education institutions, namely the degree to which their graduates find a job in the first year from the completion of bachelor's/master's studies. Numerous universities already publish such data on their own online webpages, broken down by each specialization offered, as a form of promoting their own educational offer. From the analysis of this statistical information, conclusions can be drawn both regarding the fields of activity that are predominantly eager for specialized labor, and on the other hand, the competitiveness of study programs within the same subject or specialization, between different universities. In many instances, graduating from a major at a prestigious university does not guarantee a high-quality job when the student is competing with graduates from perhaps lesser-rated universities.

A potential answer to this apparent contradiction could be the fact that only specialized training is not enough to ensure success in the labor market, and that the acquisition of transversal competences becomes an often-indispensable condition for the graduate to be able to capitalize on his professional knowledge within a company or institution. In other words, a graduate of a higher education institution who has an impressive set of specialized professional knowledge, but who has difficulties working in a team or who, due to a lack of self-confidence, has reservations in presenting his own opinions in discussions with his hierarchical superiors, or who manifests an attitude devoid of empathy toward colleagues or even the customers with whom he interacts, will find that at a job interview they will not be selected, to the detriment of another graduate, perhaps less professional prepared, but who has the transversal qualities or competences exemplified previously. This reality has long been known by employers, even if it was not theorized and framed in a terminological standard by specialists in the field of education until the relatively recently.

Overview of transversal competences

Competences are defined by the European Parliament and the European Council in the Recommendation (2006/962/EC) on key competences for lifelong learning being a "combination of knowledge, skills and attitudes appropriate to the context and the key competences are those which all individuals need for personal fulfillment and development, active citizenship, social inclusion and employment."

Transposing these recommendations into the national legislation, in the Methodology for creating the National Framework of Higher Education Qualifications in Romania (2012), competence is presented as the ability "to select, combine and use knowledge, skills and other acquisitions (values, attitudes) appropriately, in order to successfully complete a certain category of work or learning situations, as well as for professional or personal development under conditions of effectiveness and efficiency."

If professional competences are developed, especially from the perspective of "knowledge and skills specific to the field and study programs" (Crețu et al., 2019), with the teacher being trained through the acquisition of a wide range of content knowledge (of pedagogical content knowledge, of management knowledge, etc.; Oser, 2013), transversal competences are "value and attitudinal acquisitions that transcend a certain field/study program and are expressed through the following descriptors: autonomy and responsibility; social interaction; personal and professional development" (CNC Methodology, 2012). The importance of the latter is currently being recognized on a wider level, and in relation to the role played, it was stated: "Transversal competences have the role of shaping the individual profile of any professional and include the development and evaluation of acquisitions in the form of values and attitudes, such as: critical thinking, problem solving, collaboration, use of technology, autonomy in learning and communication, etc." (Crețu et al., 2019, p. 187).

Transversal competences encompass what are traditionally known as "soft skills," which involve personal abilities to interact effectively with others, including teamwork, efficient communication, and problem-solving (Ritter et al., 2018). As individuals transition from university to the job market, technical and professional skills alone are insufficient; personal and social competences such as communication, organization, time management, teamwork, and conflict resolution become equally crucial. This significance in a highly competitive context is highlighted by Santos et al. (2020), who noted that social and emotional competences have experienced notable growth, second only to technological competences, emphasizing the need for higher education institutions to effectively integrate these dimensions.

These competences serve as prerequisites for adapting to change and promoting lifelong learning, underscoring the importance for universities to foster students' personal development through academic, personal, social, and professional adjustment (Craşovan, 2016). Employers widely agree that transversal competences are often more highly valued than specific competences during recruitment and selection processes, affirming that soft skills facilitate the entry of new graduates into the labor market (Andrews and Highson, 2008 ; Belchior-Rocha et al., 2022; European Parliament, 2008; Mourshed, 2014; Owen, 2001).

We consider that an eventual attempt to compare the importance of these two types of competences would not be beneficial, even if from the perspective of higher education institutions there was and still is a tendency to favor professional training at the expense of programs designed to develop transversal competences.

In reality, the two sets of competences actually act in a relationship of complete inter-dependence, mutually conditioning and supporting each other, and improving each other. Even if they have not known a theoretical or doctrinal recognition, transversal competences have always existed, for example, the stories about the "distracted genius" of Isaac Newton, the "father of the law of gravity," being known to us since childhood. Concretely, professional competences cannot be expressed and capitalized in the absence of the specific transversal competences necessary for occupying a position in the labor market and, correlatively, the possession of transversal competences in the absence of theoretical training specific to the field of study cannot ensure a successful career in the medium or long term.

The question thus arises, beyond the theoretical definitions, of what such transversal competences actually consist of. The *Glossary of Education Reform*

(2014) defines the term "transversal competences of the 21st century" as a broad set of knowledge, skills, work habits, and character traits that are considered to be of great importance for success in the contemporary world, and transversal competences can be applied in all professional fields and in all educational, civic and career contexts throughout the life of a student, who is a future citizen on the labor market. In 2016, UNESCO published *School and teaching practices for twenty-first century challenges: Lessons from the Asia-Pacific region, regional synthesis report; 2014 regional study on transversal competencies in education policy and practice (Phase II)*, in which an exhaustive list is provided with examples of transversal competences that deserve to be mentioned: You've listed an impressive array of skills and attributes that are crucial in various aspects of life and work. These encompass cognitive abilities like critical thinking, innovative thinking, creativity, and reflective thinking, as well as practical skills such as application skills, presentation skills, reasoned decision-making, and entrepreneurship. Moreover, interpersonal qualities such as communication, leadership, organizational skills, teamwork, collaboration, initiative, sociability, collegiality, self-discipline, enthusiasm, perseverance, self-motivation, compassion, integrity, and commitment are essential for success in personal and professional realms. Furthermore, there are broader perspectives including awareness, tolerance, openness, global citizenship, respect for diversity, intercultural understanding, conflict resolution, civic participation, and respect for the environment. Moreover, aspects related to physical and psychological health, such as a healthy lifestyle, physical fitness, empathy, and self-respect, contribute significantly to overall well-being and success.

Of course, simply going through this list can have a discouraging effect for any education specialist who tries to suggest a transversal competences development program alongside professional training, their number seeming at first sight to be impossible to manage. In reality, however, each individual is different and possesses such transversal competences in different proportions, being to a large extent also a mirror of his personality traits. It is practically impossible to generate a program that aims to maximize all the competences described above, mainly due to time constraints. On the other hand, the presented list is by no means exhaustive, with certain specialized fields on the labor market also on the lookout for other skills apart from those previously mentioned.

However, the number of transversal competences available to a graduate is less important, of relevance actually being the way in which the existing ones interact, intertwine, and act in conjunction, both with each other and together with the specialized professional skills. This interaction practically determines the socio-professional traits of the university graduate and his desirability for potential future employers.

In practice, it is not possible to rank transversal competences, for example, to state that the ability to think innovatively or creativity is a transversal competence preferable to the ability to work in a team. Each field of activity is based on a series of specific transversal competences, which they actively look for in the portfolio of potential employees, followed by preferable but not indispensable competences, and finally competences that are not particularly relevant in that field. It is thus almost impossible to conceive or follow the implementation of a standard model for the development of transversal competences, as the specificity of the individual's set of skills and the interaction between them ultimately determines the level of success in the process of obtaining a job. Development programs should focus first on those transversal competences of a general nature that are beneficial to any person, then on the development of those that are most compatible with the specialized professional competencies that are formed within the university training, and finally, to the extent that the limitations of time and costs allow it, the valorization and maximization of pre-existing individual skills with potential impact on the general portfolio of competences and knowledge.

Considering the diversity and the nature of transversal competences, an attempt to offer formal study programs aimed at their development may have modest or unsatisfactory results. This is the reason why both the educational units in the initial training and the institutions or companies in the continuous training opt for non-formal ways to achieve this goal.

As far as universities are concerned, extracurricular activities are a viable tool for developing some of these competences. The range of possibilities is very wide, with the number and quality of such activities being directly proportional to the material resources allocated within the higher education unit, to the resources in terms of students' time in relation to the formal curriculum, and finally to the degree of involvement of the teaching staff in supporting some such extracurricular programs. On the other hand, the degree of attractiveness of such activities is generally superior to standard forms of professional training, and such programs are, in principle, optional.

Within transversal competences, teachers play a dual role: they evaluate students' progress and engage in self-evaluation. Collaboration and teamwork foster a heightened awareness of the teacher's role in promoting the necessity of lifelong learning. These skills enable graduates to adapt to dynamic and complex realities across formal and non-formal contexts (Langa, 2015).

For this teaching process to succeed, the active involvement of students is crucial, with self-regulation being a central aspect, ideally through interventions in real contexts. An effective strategy involves the adoption of clearly defined assessment criteria, such as rubrics, in interdisciplinary and iterative work. Students benefit from a clear understanding of their learning progression regarding the competences they are expected to acquire (SabariegoPuig, 2015).

Non-formal education contributes to the formation and development of student competences at two levels: as an interactional process in various social contexts and as prescribed curriculum elements. While schools focus on key competences across disciplines, non-formal and informal education play a significant role in lifelong learning and are essential components of education (Tudor, 2016).

Without any intention of ranking the transversal competences, for the reasons explained in detail above, we will try in the following sections to offer some examples of extracurricular activities with an emphasis on the practical form of implementation and on the targeted competence.

Empathy

The definitions of empathy refer to a wide range of emotional states, but specialists consider empathy to be the ability to understand or feel what another person is feeling, from that person's perspective. Putting yourself in someone else's place can be difficult, especially when they are suffering, but it is very useful as it allows you to understand what that person is going through. Empathy is that experience that gives rise to a behavioral tendency to naturally and spontaneously help others and express compassion. At the opposite pole, as an experience, is indifference.

Empathy, from the Ancient Greek ἐμπάθεια (*empatheia*, meaning "physical affection or passion"; that word derives from ἐν (*en*, "in, at") and πάθος (*pathos*, "passion" or "suffering"), is the ability to recognize and, to some extent, share feelings (such as sadness or happiness) that are experienced by another being, even if they do not express them explicitly. A person needs to have a certain degree of empathy before they can be able to feel compassion.

As we stated before, compassion and empathy are transversal competences recognized as such worldwide, whose importance in a person's portfolio of general, specialized, and transversal competences is difficult to quantify because they are strongly dependent on the field of professional activity in which the graduate expects to work.

Certain professions require such a competence as an indispensable condition, such as, for example, the medical field, that of caring for the elderly, of psychologists, etc. On the other hand, certain fields of activity do not pay particular attention to this competence, such as the military, industry, or transport fields. However, both empathy and compassion, seen as a subsequent consequence of empathy, are some of the transversal competences whose acquisition is likely to amplify the positive personality traits of any individual. The desire and willingness to help, provide mutual support, and offer moral support is a quality sought after and appreciated by the vast majority of employers.

Increased attention paid to this competence during university studies can only be beneficial for all parties involved. On the other hand, considering the nature of limited importance of empathy only to certain specific fields of activity, it would be necessary to design some forms of development of this transversal capacity that do not require considerable or significant material and human resources from the educational institution.

The example that we think has the greatest potential for success, considering the criteria set out above, is the encouragement of student involvement in volunteering programs, organized and coordinated by the university. Such activities are already implemented in several higher education institutions, and the benefits perceived by both those involved and the beneficiaries of the volunteer action far exceed the resources or efforts involved.

Concretely, some universities have introduced and organize annually, before the start of the academic year, an "initiation week" for future students who are about to start the first year of undergraduate studies. As part of these activities, the students from the senior years offer the "freshmen" a complete tour of the educational institution, accommodation facilities, libraries, recreational spaces, sports activities, etc. There is thus an interaction between students from several generations, in which information is exchanged, the everyday realities of student life are discussed in a non-formal setting, and support is offered in case of unforeseen situations. This interaction is beneficial both for the new students, who thus get over the impact of starting a new phase in life and professional training, often far from their family and in a foreign city, much more easily, but also for older students involved in this activity, which thus develops the transversal competence of empathy, from which this example started. This type of activity is equally appreciated by the teaching staff and the students' families and, as can be seen, it does not involve any costs or material resources from the university, with the added benefit of increasing the degree of attractiveness of a university that implements such a program of volunteering.

Voluntary involvement of students in such extracurricular activities to provide support to new colleagues or potential colleagues can continue throughout the academic year or even beyond it. Senior students can offer guidance or support in various ways, such as assisting with registration for admissions to various faculties within the university or through individual support and mentoring activities.

These practical methods have the advantage of a minimal involvement of the teaching staff, who already face an increasing overload in terms of the time allocated to the profession and, as we specified above, a cost reduced to a minimum in terms of supporting such programs.

Respect for the environment and understanding of ecosystems

We will try to cover these two transversal competences together, due to the close connection between them, on the one hand, and the possibility of their simultaneous development through specific outdoor education activities that we will refer to next.

Hascher (2010) noted that helping students to feel connected with those around them and involved in their own educational process, as well as fostering a collaborative and cooperative relationship with their family, will allow them to acquire the necessary social and emotional skills for the development of a harmonious personality and thus create the necessary conditions to become a successful member of both the school community and society in general.

The environment has been recognized as a factor that can stimulate creativity and independence and contribute to the free expression of ideas and experiences, all of which are associated with a quality education. The choices made regarding the formal framework in which the educational process takes place, such as place, material and training resources, air quality, access to natural light, etc., all have a direct influence on the learning possibilities of students. It is very important for students to have the opportunity to explore and learn outside the school environment.

Outdoor education is a type of non-formal, active learning that takes place outside the school. The participants learn based on the outdoor activities, the experiences they encounter, and the new and interesting things they discover. The discovery of the environment in a framework assisted by the teaching staff will make the student adopt an attitude of awareness and appreciation toward plants, animals, and air and water quality, which are absolutely necessary for a healthy personal and social development and for a good understanding of the world in which he lives. Outdoor learning has the benefit of increasing students' intrinsic interest in learning generated by curiosity, provides the opportunity to participate in pleasant or attractive lessons, generates an increase in creativity, and activates critical thinking components (Gilbertson, 2006).

The conscious use of this form of education centered on interaction with nature and adventure offers an alternative way to promote health and well-being in general for both direct beneficiaries (participating students) and indirect ones (family members who are influenced). It encourages a healthy lifestyle by creating opportunities for physical activities and freedom of movement and ensures students' contact with the natural world and the environment and the direct perception of natural phenomena. All this provides the prerequisites for the development of an attitude of respect and protection of nature in the students' personality, but also a stimulation of the inclinations toward exploration, experimentation, discovery, in a safe environment due to the constant presence of the teacher in these activities.

The benefits of outdoor education can be grouped on three levels: physical, cognitive and socio-emotional.

Regarding the first category, people who learn in a park or other outdoor environment have developed motor skills superior to those who carry out the same activities in an artificial space and are healthier and happier as a result of direct exposure to the sun, air, and natural light. An increasing number of studies show that learning in nature produces faster and more lasting effects over time. Students of the 21st century spend most of their time indoors, and often the only moment associated with an outdoor activity is the walk to and from school. School can thus remain the last refuge for allocating a fraction of time for outdoor activities.

As far as the cognitive benefits are concerned, spending time in nature has a favorable impact because curiosity is satisfied through direct observation, reception, and research, carried out through educational activities in an environment external to the university building. Outdoor education also promotes the exchange of ideas and encourages the formulation of questions for clarification. Students have an instinctive need to follow, observe, investigate, compare, and experiment in the concrete circumstances offered by the interaction with plants, animals, and the surrounding nature in general. The most intense and lasting cognitive accumulations occur through play and activities in nature.

Finally, outdoor education definitely has positive effects from a socio-emotional point of view. Strong negative emotions such as anger or frustration can be controlled through outdoor interaction. When students suddenly find themselves in a wide space, such as the outdoors, where the atmosphere tends to be relaxing, students communicate much more freely and focus more on interacting with the things and beings around them. Individuals who, inside the classroom, can be categorized as reclusive people open up and reveal themselves when the educational activity moves into nature – they are more relaxed, interact with other people much more easily, and often create socio-emotional ties without any means of external coercion.

Last but not least, it should be stated that outdoor education is likely to facilitate the development of emotional intelligence, seen as the ability to react effectively to the many unforeseen events that will be faced during life or the management of conflict situations that may arise (Balaş et al., 2023).

On the other hand, ecosystems are systems of increased complexity, with multiple interactions and mutual conditioning on the part of the individuals that compose it. The simple observation and attempt to analyze these interactions is likely to develop analytical thinking seen as a transversal competence, to which is added the acquisition of respect for the environment and a superior awareness of the fragility of the ecosystems. The acquisition of such a competence, that of understanding ecosystems, will determine changes in the student's behavior, as a rule, he manifests himself as a much more responsible and sensitive person in relation to the protection of the environment.

The scale reached by strategies to promote an existence centered on respect for the environment, to policies to reduce global warming, the increase in the number of political formations with a "green" agenda, causes certain companies to select their future employees considering their attitude toward the environment as an important criterion. The development of these transversal competences during university studies would thus have the potential to increase the chances of success on the labor market for students involved in such forms of non-formal outdoor education.

Also in this case, the costs in material and human resources involved in carrying out such training activities are not prohibitive and are also counterbalanced by the fact that, in the same open-door environment, the classical didactic activities related to professional training can also be performed.

Teamwork

This type of transversal competence is undoubtedly one of the most sought after, regardless of the field of activity in which the student intends to work after completing university training. Moreover, one can hardly imagine a field in which such competence is not absolutely necessary– maybe only in the case of those activities that exclusively involve individual work, without a meaningful interaction with those around, such as artists and painters, for example. But these exceptions only confirm the initially stated rule.

Due to the importance of the ability to work in a team for the vast majority of companies that have many employees, the development of this transversal competence has enjoyed increased attention from the management of higher education institutions, compared to other competences.

Of course, teamwork is a framework competence that includes several specific transversal competences, such as effective communication, critical thinking, proactiveness, sociability, enthusiasm, perseverance, tolerance, openness, and integrity. The ability to work in a team implies the compatibility of the individual with the team, both regarding the specialty training and the way of organizing work, of values, of the preferred strategies for achieving objectives and existing relations, and socialization between group members. For this reason, in this case, it is not possible to generate a standard program for the development of this competence, but it can be said with sufficient certainty that one of the main characteristics for a person to be able to work in a team is adaptability.

The means of improving this competence at the level of higher education units are particularly varied, with the choice of one or the other options mostly relating to a cost–benefit analysis. These forms of training involve a large number of students, an aspect that is likely to generate additional costs. On the other hand, the projects designed with the objective of developing the ability to work in a team can serve a double purpose: developing teamwork ability and, at the same time, pursuing the development of professional skills specific to the participants' field of study, a situation in which the cost–benefit ratio would oscillate in favor of the former.

Project-based learning offers the advantage of enhancing students' awareness of the interconnectedness of knowledge across different disciplinary areas. This approach also facilitates the development of various transversal competences, including teamwork, problem-solving, acceptance of diverse perspectives, and critical analysis. In addition, by employing project-based learning and other active methodologies, teachers can strengthen their interaction with students, fostering closer engagement and providing more personalized assessment of their progress and competences. This approach also enables teachers to identify students' difficulties and weaknesses more effectively, allowing for the implementation of proactive solutions to prevent or mitigate situations of academic failure (Herrero & Antequera, 2012).

By engaging students in collaborative and cooperative tasks at the level of the instrumental dimension, socio-emotional skills can be developed. Collaborative tasks, especially individual tasks that are important in the individual learning process, focus on the fact that "knowledge can be created in a community whose members actively interact through the exchange of experiences and sum up their symmetric knowledge" (Albulescu & Catalano, 2022).

Combining the two types of tasks, individual and collaborative, is useful because in situations where students' interest is switched from individual to group, individual performance is also consolidated. Cooperative learning and collaborative learning involve the completion of group tasks and students carrying out activities with the aim of maximizing their own learning and that of others. Thus, collaborative and cooperative learning will merge with social and emotional learning. Cooperative learning refers to the contribution to the group product of the class with the individual results of the students, and cooperative learning assumes interaction within the group to achieve a common goal (Albulescu & Catalano, 2022). They can be educated and encouraged to search for and access relevant information together, select and sort the information, and devise new ways of presenting the learning products.

Another example could be from the technical field, where the universities organize various competitions in the fields associated with the specific curriculum of the respective faculty, such as in the field of robotics, aerospace engineering, and the development of computer applications. Such a form of development of transversal competences, which, as we said, takes the form of a competition, presents multiple advantages.

First, any competition, whether it offers some material benefit to the winners or just a track record victory, always has a much higher degree of attractiveness than a program that does not contain any hierarchy of completed works. Young people being especially competitive people, a good part choose to register for such competitions as a means of estimating their own abilities compared to those in their entourage or the immediate environment. Also, the nature of the cooperation within the teams in the situation of such a competitive activity will affect the interaction between teammates: the concentration will be higher, the passions within the group will be intense, the tolerance for failure will be reduced accordingly when the deadline for completing the task is approaching, etc. In other words, an active, lively interaction is basically ensured, and in this educational context, the accumulation of knowledge and skills, whether professional or transversal, is more intense and usually lasts a longer period of time compared to classic teaching activities/learning.

Second, it is possible to design competitions with wider participation, of students from several universities or even from the private, non-academic environment, an aspect that would also exponentially increase the degree of competitiveness and subsequent attractiveness.

This form of extracurricular training involves significantly higher costs compared to the other activities exemplified previously, the competence of teamwork itself being one with multiple components that can justify these additional material and human costs. A factor likely to alleviate this disadvantage would be the attraction of sponsors or the involvement of external partners in the logistical organization of these competitions.

Entrepreneurship

Starting from the last idea expressed, that of a collaboration with external partners, be they private or public institutions, we will try to offer an example of the development of another transversal competence, namely the entrepreneurial spirit.

This competence is pursued mainly by employers in the economic-financial fields, but it is one with a distinct characteristic compared to the others analyzed. Acquiring such a competence at the highest possible level will allow the student, the future graduate, to no longer be dependent on the fluctuations of the labor market regarding existing jobs at a given time and, either alone or in association with other people, start his own company. It is an approach that involves a series of risks both from the point of view of material investments but also of time, emotional resources, etc. Considering this specific character, a form of extracurricular activity for the development of this transversal competence, must takes place in a much more formalized framework.

It is necessary to have a good theoretical training doubled by a practical training under the monitoring and with the support of people who have the necessary skills and expertise to offer such support. Material costs are usually high and often exceed the possibilities of a single educational institution.

One of the ways in which such a program for the development of entrepreneurial competences was put into practice was the design and implementation of projects in a public–private partnership, with funding provided from the European Union budget. For example, one such project aimed to develop and deliver a limited number of new educational offers with innovative content in tertiary university education, by matching them with the needs of the labor market in competitive economic sectors and areas of smart specialization in which the trained teaching staff were also involved in the project, together with social partners from the private sector in order to develop new educational offers in the project, with a predominant application component correlated to the needs of the labor market in the economic sectors/fields addressed by the project. A particularly important role in this educational offer was played by the practical, applied part of an entrepreneurial nature with the involvement of the external partners, where experts from both the private and the public sectors presented the students with different practical cases, simulations, and case studies for everyday practice. The completion of the entrepreneurial program was achieved by the presentation of a business plan by the beneficiaries of the entrepreneur scholarships in front of a mixed commission made up of representatives of teaching staff and partners from the public and private institutions.

Within such a project, the higher education institution assumes responsibility for providing the framework and theoretical training. For example, through the Introduction to Entrepreneurship course, students were offered the opportunity to learn how to start a business, develop it, and quickly adapt to changes in the external environment, giving them the ability to make decisions in accordance with a certain organizational context and assume responsibility for specific tasks. Through its contents, a second module had a pronounced pragmatic character, contributing to the training of entrepreneurs/specialists in the financial-accounting field, appropriate for the level of private commercial companies, but also for the level of financial, credit, or insurance institutions. Finally, the third module of the entrepreneurial training course was designed to complete the basic knowledge of an entrepreneur, accumulated following the completion of the first two modules, ensuring at the same time his ability to develop his own business plan.

It should be mentioned that following the completion of this type of project, the university has the freedom to include the newly proposed educational content in the study programs with the status of optional or facultative subjects.

Conclusions

The development of transversal competences in the course of initial training within universities or other higher education institutions is currently more relevant than in the past, because the world evolves very quickly, and formal learning and training no longer always meet the needs of people who have to quickly retrain in their professional life due to changes initiated by what is already commonly referred to as the Fourth Industrial Revolution. Therefore, people turn to non-formal or informal learning environments to acquire the skills and competences they need.

Of course, the development of transversal competences does not necessarily involve the organization of training programs at the level of higher education institutions, but understanding and offering such programs can provide multiple benefits to students who are about to enter a university program for the first time. As we mentioned in the Introduction, universities must be concerned about how their graduates transition into the labor market, as the success of their students serves both as a measure and a mirror of the university they graduated from.

References

Albulescu, I., & Catalano, H. (2022). *Învățarea prin activități de grup* [Learning through group activities]. Didactica Publishing House.

Andrews, J., & Highson, H. (2008). Graduate employability, 'soft skills' versus 'hard business knowledge': A European study. *Higher Education in Europe*, *33*, 411–422.

Balaş, E., Torkos, H., & Egerău, A. (2023). Achieving well-being in primary school by enrolling in outdoor learning situations. In E. Balaş, A. Roman, & D. Rad (Eds.), *Students' well-being and teaching-learning efficiency during and post-pandemic period* [Bunăstarea studenţilor şi eficienţa învăţării predării în perioada şi post-pandemie] (pp. 116–127). Berlin, Germany: Peter Lang. ISBN 9783631899663.

Belchior-Rocha, H., Casquilho-Martins, I., & Simões, E. (2022). Transversal competencies for employability: From higher education to the labour market. *Education Sciences*, 12(4), 255. <https://doi.org/10.3390/educsci12040255>

CNC. (2012). *Ghid pentru aplicarea metodologiei de construcție a Cadrului Național al Calificărilor în învățământul superior* [Guide for the application of the methodology for the construction of the National Framework of Qualifications in Higher Education]. Bucureşti: Autoritatea Naţională pentru Calificări.

Craşovan, M. (2016). Transversal competences or how to learn differently. In M. Micle, & C. Mesaros (Eds.), *Communication today: An overview from online journalism to applied philosophy* (pp. 171–178). Trivent Publishing.

Creţu, D. M. (Ed.). (2019). *Predarea şi învăţarea în învăţământul superior. Aspecte teoretice şi practice* [Teaching and learning in higher education: Theoretical and practical aspects]. Bucureşti: Editura Universitară.
European Parliament. (n.d.). *Council Recommendation of the European Parliament* (2006/962/EC). <https://eurlex.europa.eu/legalcontent/EN/TXT/PDF/?uri=CELEX:32006H0962&from=EN>
European Parliament. (2008). Council recommendation of the European Parliament and of the Council of 23 April 2008 on the establishment of the European Qualifications Framework for lifelong learning. *Official Journal of the European Union*, C 111, 23 April.
Gilbertson, K. (2006). *Outdoor education. Methods and strategies*. Human Kinetics.
Glossary of Education Reform (2014). 21st century skills. <https://www.edglossary.org/21st-century-skills>
Hascher, T. (2010). Wellbeing. In P. Peterson, E. Baker, & B. McGaw (Eds.), *International encyclopedia of education* (3rd ed., Vol. 6, pp. 732–738). Elsevier.
Herlo, D. (Ed.), Egerău, A., Balaş, E., Dughi, T., Bran, C., & Roman, A. (2020). *Devenire în profesorat* [Becoming a teacher]. Cluj-Napoca: Presa Universitară Clujeană. ISBN 978-606-37-0799-5.
Herrero, M., & Antequera, M. A. (2012). The integrated project as a learning experience. *Journal of Technology and Science Education*, *2*, 13–21.
Langa, C. (2015). The contribution of transversal competences to the training of the educational sciences specialist. *Procedia – Social and Behavioral Sciences*, *180*, 7–12.
Ministry of National Education (2017). *The methodology for creating the National Framework of Higher Education Qualifications in Romania*. <https://www.edu.ro/sites/default/files/ORDIN%203475-2017.pdf>
Mourshed, M., Patel, J., & Suder, K. (2014). *Education to employment: Getting Europe's youth into work*. McKinsey Centre for Government.
Oser, F. (2013). I know how to do it, but I can't do it: Modeling competence profiles for future teachers and trainers. In S. Blömeke, O. Zlatkin-Troitschanskaia, C. Kuhn, & J. Fege (Eds.), *Modeling and measuring competencies in higher education: Tasks and challenges* (pp. 45–59).
Owen, E. (2001). What key skills do employers need? *Journal of Geography in Higher Education*, *25*, 121–126.
Ritter, B. A., Small, E. E., Mortimer, J. W., & Doll, J. L. (2018). Designing management curriculum for workplace readiness: Developing students' soft skills. *Journal of Management Education*, *42*, 80–103

SabariegoPuig, M. (2015). La evaluación de competencias transversales a través de lasrúbricas [The evaluation of transversal competences through rubrics]. *ATTIC*, *14*, 50–58.

Santos Rego, M.A., Ferraces, M. J., Mella, I., & Vázquez Rodríguez, A. (2020). University, civic-social competences and the labor market. *Revista Española de Pedagogía*, *78*, 213–232.

Tudor, S. L. (2016). The role of non-formal and informal education in competences training – Transversal competences. In *Proceedings of the 8th International Conference on Electronics, Computers and Artificial Intelligence (ECAI)* (pp. 1–6). <https://doi.org/10.1109/ECAI.2016.7861143>

UNESCO (2016). *School and teaching practices for twenty-first century challenges: Lessons from the Asia-Pacific region, regional synthesis report; 2014 regional study on transversal competencies in education policy and practice (Phase II)*. <https://unesdoc.unesco.org/ark:/48223/pf0000244022>

Pedagogical Implications of the Adoption of Educational Technologies in Initial Teacher Training

Nadia Barkoczi and Alina Felicia Roman

Abstract: The pedagogical implications of the adoption of technology focus on the instrumentality of learning, teaching and assessment, the construction of a knowledge pathway using digital resources, and the measurement of learning in terms of training and competence development. The initial training of teachers in higher education institutions, in the context of the digitization of education and through the designed content, aims at changes in the way of building the profile of the future teacher in terms of teaching competences integrating the digital component and through a new way of preparing students for a teaching career. Teacher training programs are on the threshold of transformation brought about by modern, interactive teaching methods, emphasizing the importance of advanced learning. This in turn involves the use of digital technologies, which have the potential to amplify the active, participatory, and personalized nature of pedagogy, and outlines the design and implementation of learning activities based on interactive teaching strategies in flexible learning spaces where, through interactions and challenges, creativity, imagination, motivation are stimulated, contributing significantly to the well-being of educational agents.

Keywords: pedagogy, adoption of educational technologies, initial teacher training, flexible learning spaces.

Introduction

Innovation in the learning–teaching–assessment process traces new directions in the course of learning activities over time, with the ultimate goal being to impart education to citizens living in an information society with regard to developing a sense of creativity, the power to drive change, and manage, analyze, and work with information (Süer & Oral, 2021). Research on the adoption of technology in education focuses on the attitude of educational agents toward change, but also on conditions that increase or decrease the likelihood that they will accept the new educational technology that generates reconfigurations of the teaching strategy and innovations in pedagogy. Time is one of the factors that will support them in identifying the relevance of use, the limitations of adopting educational technologies being determined by the lack of available information about the new technology, how it can be used and what results it returns. The challenges of digitalization of education arising from the adoption of innovative technologies are primarily aimed at educational agents who need to adapt to change (European Commission, 2018; Barkoczi & Roman, 2023). Open education promotes the harmonious blending of competence-oriented and content-oriented approaches through the use of open educational resources (OER), which focuses on teaching materials. A practice-oriented approach plays a primary role, with open educational practices encouraging collaboration for the creation and exchange of knowledge between teachers as practitioners and between teachers and students, the latter being future practitioners. In relation to the adoption of technology, educational agents can be divided into digital natives, those who value digital technologies looking for the possibility of using them, and digital immigrants, those who adopt technology out of the need to adapt to all those changes that have occurred with it. In terms of technology diffusion, this classification can be correlated with that of innovators and imitators as adopters of innovative products.

Diffusion of educational technologies

Adoption, described as the mental process of an educational agent from the moment they first hear about a new technology to the moment they use it, is part of technology diffusion defined as the process by which new technology is transmitted over time between members of a social system (Rogers, 2003; Kotler & Keller, 2008). The four main elements that influence the spread of new ideas – innovation itself, communication channels, time, and the social system – can also be identified in education sector. In order to reduce the time needed to make the adoption decision, educational technology must the following five characteristics determined by the subjective perception of the educational agent (Rogers, 2003): (i) relative advantage, whereby technology must have advantages over other educational technologies already on education and provide benefits to the educational agent; (ii) compatibility, whereby technology must correspond to the lifestyle of the educational agent; (iii) complexity, whereby the degree of complexity of the new technology must not be too high in order to be easily assimilated by the educational agent; (iv) testability, making it easier for testable educational technologies to succeed; (v) observability, whereby the more readily observable the technology, the more potential educational agents see that the product has been experimented with, increasing their interest and reducing adoption time.

Valdés et al. (2021) consider that a paradigm shift is needed, given that the adoption of technology generated by the configuration of technology affects the learning environment and allows the generation of more learning experiences both through the modernization of teaching materials and through the training process in general. In the scientific literature we encounter five stages of educational technology diffusion: awareness, conviction, decision, implementation, and confirmation (Frei-Landau et al., 2022; Kotler & Keller, 2008). At the stage of awareness, the learner is informed about educational technology, assimilates new cognitive knowledge, and designs a process for training skills to use it. The educational agent lacks information. In order to increase the likelihood that the technology will be adopted, a sufficient level of knowledge is required to use it independently. At the basis of conviction are emotions, being the stage at which the attitude toward innovation is formed. When uncertainty intervenes, the educational agent can be influenced by the opinion of others to use the innovative tool. At this stage, it is necessary to go through three substages: (i) arousing interest, through which the educational agent is interested in seeking information about the new technology; (ii) evaluation, whereby the educational agent considers whether or not to attempt innovation; and (iii) determination to try, whereby the educational agent tries innovation to estimate the positive or negative meaning of its value. The third stage is when the educational agent decides whether to adopt or reject the technology, with the likelihood of adoption increasing with the number of previous opportunities to try it. Three types of reasons influencing the adoption decision are mentioned in the scientific literature: (i) personal desire, (ii) peer pressure, and/or (iii) authority pressure. At the implementation stage, the individual uses innovation and examines the results. A key role is played by: (i) user feedback, (ii) in-use assistance that helps reduce uncertainty among new users, and (iii) reinvention, whereby users adapt and modify the digital tool according to their needs. Confirmation is the stage at which users reflexively assess the professional usefulness of the new technology and the results of its use (Frei-Landau et al., 2022; Kotler & Keller, 2008).

It was considered that, in order to adopt a technology, it was necessary to adapt the general pattern of consumer behavior to the specific context of lifestyle and decision-making, by identifying the route to be taken to increase satisfaction with the new product. This model can be translated into the field of education, as can be seen in Figure 16.1, given that for the adoption and use of new technologies it is necessary to identify the professional needs of the teacher, its attitude toward change, the choices that can be influenced and influence the teaching style and, last but not least, the experiences in using new technologies.

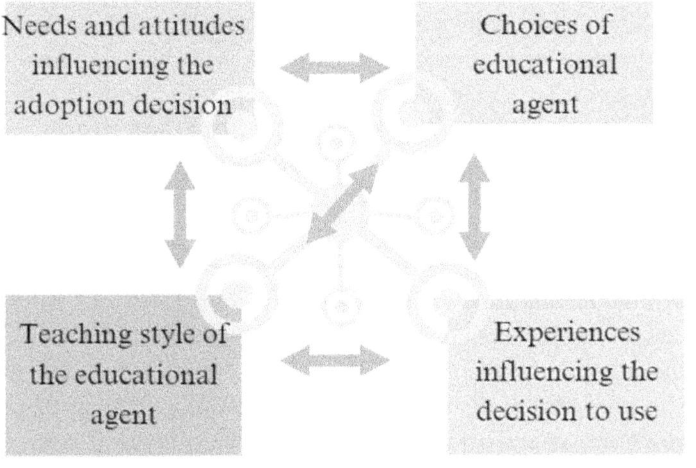

Figure 16.1 Directions in the route to increase the degree of satisfaction of the use of educational technology in the context of the teaching style and the adoption decision

In the diffusion of innovation, information sources play a key role in how technology is viewed as a necessity. When educational agents are faced with using something unknown, they need familiar knowledge to see the usefulness of the new product. The family is often a credible source of information regarding trust in the use of technology, which plays an influential role in the adoption decision (Coşarbă et al., 2021; Costin and Roman, 2020). Solomon (2009) states that there are several reasons, both positive and negative, that place the educational agent in situations of trust or distrust related to the new technology. The degree of uncertainty in the adoption of educational technologies can be diminished by allocating more resources in technology development, and the performance of the education system could decrease or increase, respectively, based on increasing or decreasing uncertainty about the use of technology (Barkoczi, 2022). The literature addresses the issue of motivational conflicts that have been classified into: (1) conflict of two positive reasons; (2) conflict between a positive and a negative motive; and (3) conflict between two negative reasons. The resolution of any type of conflict listed above is possible when the educational agent has to choose between two educational technologies that possess both qualities and defects and can take place by reducing cognitive dissonance. The conflict is resolved when there is enough information to confirm the choice made (Solomon, 2009). The behavior of technology adopters for personal interests differs from that for teaching, and the use of technologies in personal life cannot automatically qualify the educational agent as an adopter of new educational technologies.

Factors influencing the adoption of new technologies in the educational practices of future teachers

Experiences that drive pedagogical change under the impact of technology adoption in educational institutions periodically accumulate a comprehensive set of responses on how to identify resonances between the content imposed by the curriculum, learning spaces, and digital tools that determine students – that is, future teachers – to get involved in projects allowing them, based on curiosity, to find solutions to complex problems to develop critical thinking, imagination, creativity, and lifelong learning. In educational practices, there are several factors of attraction or rejection that develop the experiences described above – factors that are identified in the process of designing, teaching, or delivering Education 4.0 (Scepanovič, 2019). Some examples of factors of attraction or rejection include digital learning, personalized learning, social learning, or machine learning on one side, and resources, including technological ones, existing infrastructure, services within smart connected infrastructure, and time, on the other.

Holotescu and Gosseck (2020) address open educational practices as results of adoption and ranks adopters of OER according to the time it takes to accept the use and management of educational technologies. The opinions of trainee teachers on the use of technology depend on the lens through which they see the adoption of technology, which, followed by open educational practices, can contribute significantly to the formation of digital competences, creativity, and critical thinking that is necessary for future teachers (Rad et al., 2023; Barkoczi, 2022). Some of the factors influencing teachers' adoption of technology include (i) personal characteristics, represented by education level, age, gender, professional experience, experience in using computers for educational purposes; (ii) attitude, in the sense that if teachers perceive that technology does not meet their needs or those of their students, it is more than possible that they will not want to integrate technology into teaching–learning–assessment; (iii) digital competences as part of competences for the teaching profession being significant for integrating communication and information technologies in the teaching–learning–assessment process; (iv) teachers' workload involving constant maintenance and updates of courses, communication with students, formation and development of new competences to those trained, and continuous search for sustainable teaching strategies, etc.; (v) institutional characteristics and accessibility to the digital infrastructure of the school; (vi) professional development as a key factor for the successful integration of digital devices into classroom teaching; and (vii) accessibility to open educational resources (Buabeng-Andoh, 2012).

The adoption of OER is achieved over time depending on the teacher's digital skills profile, the didactic content in the curriculum, and the social influences of educational agents. In this regard, Rodés and Gewerc (2021) propose a conceptual model that includes four stages of the adoption of OER, and therefore of open educational practices, in initial teacher education, as represented in Figure 16.2. Teachers' personal histories and understanding of their own social representations regarding the use, storage, and sharing of OER are bases for identifying subjective factors that determine the adoption of educational technologies and open educational practices (Rodés & Gewerc, 2021). One of the objective factors of OER adoption is curriculum analysis which, by focusing on competences, requires the teacher to create learning situations using diversified learning resources, including adopting and using OER. In order to provide learning support, in addition to creating their own learning resources, and identifying and rigorously selecting existing teaching resources as a resource developer, the teacher adopts and adapts OER to specific learning conditions, individualized needs and interests of students (Ministry of Education, 2021).

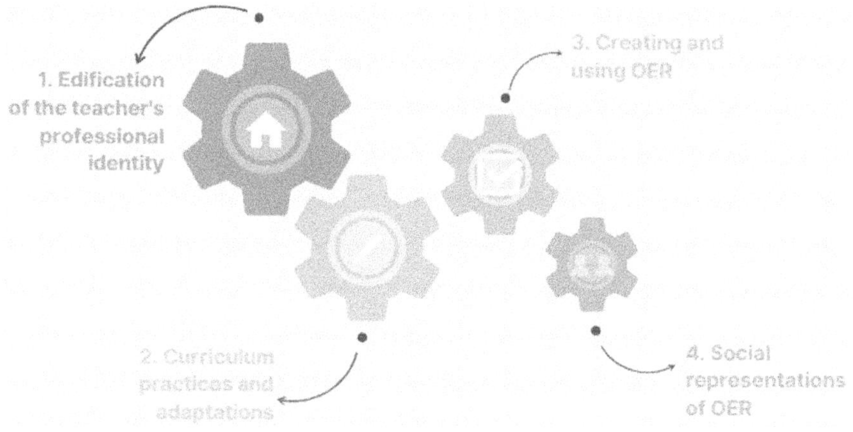

Figure 16.2 Conceptual model of OER adoption
Source: Adapted from Rodés and Gewerc (2021).

Cox and Trotter (2017) designed the OER adoption pyramid that provides a more in-depth analysis of subjective factors in the above-represented model, aiming to identify and understand the context in which individual adoption of OER is possible (Figure 16.3). The levels of this pyramid start from the bottom up, from access to adequate physical infrastructure, such as electricity, internet connectivity, and computer devices, to permission to use or create OER, granted by the copyright on teaching materials produced at the level of the institution. Awareness about the concept of OER represents the third level, followed by that of digital competences for adoption, the educational agent requiring training for their development and willingness to use, believing that their educational materials are relevant and have the necessary quality from a pedagogical point of view. The volition represents the top of the pyramid, being considered the key to the degree of determination of OER adoption, which contributes to shaping pedagogical values according to the social context and institutional culture of the educational agent (Cox & Trotter, 2017).

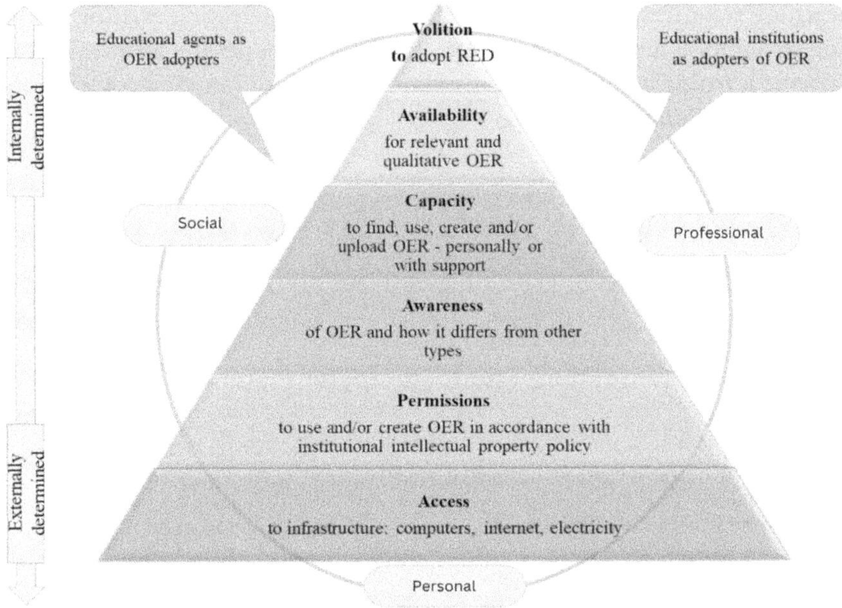

Figure 16.3 OER adoption pyramid
Source: Adapted from Cox and Trotter (2017).

Alhumaid et al. (2023) consider that among the main factors that can influence adoption, such as motivation to learn, desire for interconnection, school environment, and acquisition of knowledge, the individual traits of educational agents, such as the capacity for critical thinking and the ability to think logically, play a key role. The authors analyze studies from the scientific literature on the adoption of artificial intelligence in education and conclude that, if used rationally in various educational contexts, there is a shift in the general attitude toward the use of new technologies, and a possibility for improvement in teaching–learning–assessment strategies as well how, what, and when students learn.

Pedagogy–space–technology framework in initial teacher education

Accessible education provides higher education institutions imparting initial teacher education and beyond with an open education ecosystem that takes into account that technology, robotics, artificial intelligence, 3D printing, and other innovations are advancing at a rapid pace through: (i) unprecedented connectivity between humans via mobile phones, connectivity which, in terms of processing and storage, provides unlimited access to knowledge; (ii) technological innovations that increase the cost of education; (iii) enormous disruptive potential for the "development of professional competencies in universities, including transversal (soft) and disciplinary (hard) ones, ... enabling students to face situations, challenges or problems that require the development of knowledge and efficient know-how" (Miranda et al., 2021, p. 4; Moreno-Charris et al., 2022; Peters, 2019). Gracyalny and Hurtienne (2023) state that the integrated active learning ecosystem can be achieved through quality professional training of teachers through which they are able to interconnect competence-centered pedagogy with the adoption and integration of technology in the teaching act and with the flexibility of learning spaces reflected in the technical and technological infrastructure of the educational institution, as can be seen in Figure 16.4. The pedagogy–space–technology framework was built through the design, use, and evaluation of active learning spaces within which stakeholders assume a critical and holistic grounded approach: (i) toward pedagogy, by addressing the expanded space of technology as a place for teaching activities; (ii) toward design of space, furniture and efficient use of space integrating technology and encouraging a particular type of pedagogy; (iii) toward classroom design that facilitates collaborative learning where teachers not only engage students in discussions but ask them to share what they have learned with the whole class, provide feedback, encourage other students to give feedback, analyze learning processes and outcomes; and (iv) toward effective integration of technology that expands space and improves pedagogy (Lee et al., 2018).

Creating the conditions for learning to take place in flexible learning spaces requires teachers to draw on material resources, including technology and pedagogical solutions through which students build their own knowledge system and appropriate learning styles and learning environments in which they experience increased autonomy to make various choices about their learning in a way that encourages self-assessment, social collaboration, and interaction (Kariippanon et al., 2018; Maier, 2020; Mulcahy et al., 2015). The digital learning space sits at the intersection of physical, online, and hybrid spaces and creates an environment to develop the competencies of learners, especially the digital competencies of teachers, by investing confidence and skills in the use of digital technology to support their teaching, along with a spirit of innovation to ensure that all learners can participate in digital education (Bygstad et al., 2022; European Commission, 2023). In this environment, the physical and institutional boundaries of educational establishments can be open and in continuous interaction with society.

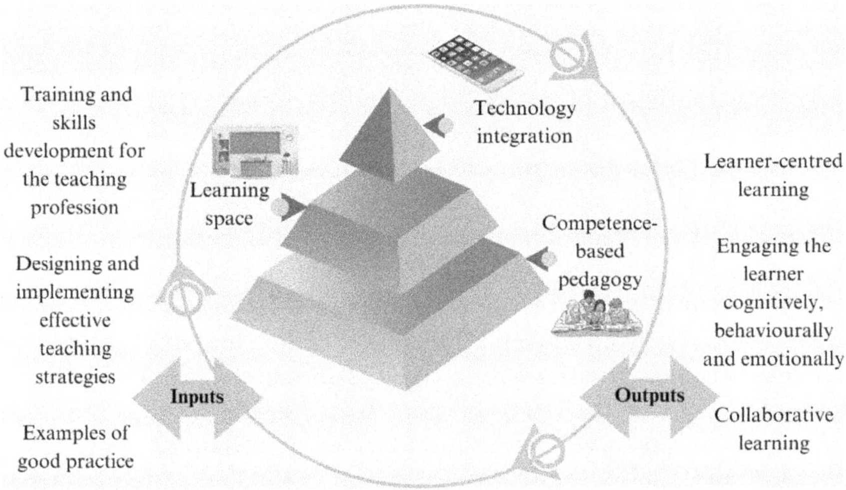

Figure 16.4 Integrated active learning system
Source: Adapted from Gracyalny and Hurtienne (2023).

Conclusions

The competence profile of the teacher is shaped in the context of the development of competences complementary to emerging technologies through specific training programs that can give a positive meaning to the impact of new technologies, adaptation to the digital context, current working conditions, and social inclusion. Through the issues addressed in this chapter, we identify the guidelines of Humbold's theory that students, teachers, and researchers reverse their roles in different learning situations and become more aware that professional preparation for teaching careers requires scientific knowledge at the intersection of pedagogical knowledge, computational thinking, and experiential learning. Teaching skills and teaching–learning–assessment methods can be developed through the adoption of technology in flexible learning spaces and in various forms of organizing teaching activities that provide training in skills for the teaching profession and a learning environment with opportunities to enhance problem-solving skills, critical thinking, and creativity.

Digital transformation for initial teacher education involves rethinking the role and impact of technologies and redesigning a new approach to prepare students for a teaching career with new skills and teaching–learning–assessment strategies. The adoption of advanced learning technologies and their integration into the educational process has led to the improvement of advanced learning mechanisms in education in general and in initial teacher education in particular. In order to reduce the time needed to adopt new technologies, such as OER, artificial intelligence, or robotics, it is necessary to analyze their complementarity with human competences and vice versa, with teachers needing to attend training courses on digital competences and recommendations to support their choice. These recommendations can come from external or internal information sources. In this context, a new research direction would be to identify the type of adopter of new educational technologies, innovator, or imitator, based on the type of information sources.

Future teachers need to rethink their pedagogical approach in an innovative way that integrates emerging educationally appropriate technologies. They need to be trained in the competences needed to master technology and integrate it into classroom work, use active learning strategies, know and implement educational innovations, and operate in a collaborative environment. Higher education institutions, through their initial teacher training programs, need to update their educational models and build, with the involvement of all educational stakeholders, flexible learning spaces, focusing on developing competences for the teaching profession, including digital ones, and encouraging students, as future teachers, to become lifelong learners with flexibility and tolerance for change.

References

Alhumaid, K., Naqbi, S. A., Elsori, D., & Mansoori, M. A. (2023). The adoption of artificial intelligence applications in education. *International Journal of Data and Network Science*, 7(1), 457–466. <https://doi.org/10.5267/j.ijdns.2022.8.013>

Barkoczi, N. (2022). Impactul culturii învăţării asupra utilizării instrumentelor digitale [The Impact of Learning Culture on the Use of Digital Tools]. *Buletin Ştiinţific, Fascicula Filologie, Seria A* [Scientific Bulletin, Philology Fascicle, A Series], *XXXI*, 335–342. http://bslr.ubm.ro/files/2022/22.Barkoczi_Nadia_BSLR_2022.pdf.

Barkoczi, N., & Roman, A. F. (2023). The use of educational technologies in the students' pedagogical practice activities. *European Proceedings of Educational Sciences*, 224–234. <www.doi.org/10.15405/epes.23056.21>

Buabeng-Andoh, C. (2012). Factors influencing teachers' adoption and integration of information and communication technology into teaching: A review of the literature. *International Journal of Education and Development Using ICT*, *8*(1). <https://www.learntechlib.org/p/188018/>

Bygstad, B., Øvrelid, E., Ludvigsen, S., & Dæhlen, M. (2022). From dual digitalization to digital learning space: Exploring the digital transformation of higher education. *Computers & Education*, 182, 104463. <https://doi.org/10.1016/j.compedu.2022.104463>

Costin, A., & Roman, A. (2020). Discussing with the parents of high school students: What do they know about drugs? *Postmodern Openings*, 11(1), 1–19. <https://doi.org/10.18662/po/105>

Coşarbă, E., Roman, A. F., & Costin, A. (2021). Parents' perception regarding the concerns, competencies and perspectives of involvement in non-formal activities. *Technium Social Sciences Journal*, 26(1), 177–185. <https://doi.org/10.47577/tssj.v26i1.5115>

Cox, G., & Trotter, H. (2017). An OER framework, heuristic and lens: Tools for understanding lecturers' adoption of OER. *Open Praxis*, 9(2), 151. <https://doi.org/10.5944/openpraxis.9.2.571>

European Commission. (2023). *Special report 11/2023: EU support for the digitalisation of schools*. European Court of Auditors.

European Commission. (2018). *Carierele cadrelor didactice în Europa: acces, progres şi sprijin. Raport Eurydice* [Teachers' careers in Europe: access, progression and support. Eurydice Report]. Publications Office of the European Union

Frei-Landau, R., Muchnik-Rozanov, Y. & Avidov-Ungar, O. (2022). Using Rogers' diffusion of innovation theory to conceptualize the mobile-learning adoption process in teacher education in the COVID-19 era. *Education and Information Technologies*, *27*, 12811–12838. <https://doi.org/10.1007/s10639-022-11148-8>

Gracyalny, J. R., & Hurtienne, L. E. (2023). The perceived effect of learner-centered pedagogy in secondary active learning spaces and impact on student engagement. *Journal of Learning Spaces*, *12*(1), 1. <https://libjournal.uncg.edu/jls/article/view/2296>

Holotescu, C., & Gosseck, G. (2020). Educaţie deschisă. Resurse educaţionale deschise şi cursuri online masive deschise [Open education. Open educational resources and massive open online courses]. In C. Ceobanu, C. Cucoş, O. Istrate, & I.-O. Pânişoară (Eds.), *Educaţia digitală* [Digital education] (pp. 207–222). Polirom

Kariippanon, K. E., Cliff, D. P., Lancaster, S. L., Okely, A. D., & Parrish, A.-M. (2018). Perceived interplay between flexible learning spaces and teaching, learning and student wellbeing. *Learning Environments Research*, *21*(3), 301–320. <https://doi.org/10.1007/s10984-017-9254-9>

Kotler, P., & Keller, K. L. (2008). *Managementul marketingului* [Marketing management] (5th ed.). Editura Teora [Teora Publishing House].

Lee, D., Morrone, A. S., & Siering, G. (2018). From swimming pool to collaborative learning studio: Pedagogy, space, and technology in a large active learning classroom. *Educational Technology Research and Development*, *66*(1), 95–127. <https://doi.org/10.1007/s11423-017-9550-1>

Lehr, S. (2008). Wilhelm von Humboldt and the shaping of the German university. *European Journal of Education*, 43(1), 131–147. https://doi.org/10.1111/j.1465-3435.2008.00338.x.

Maier, M. (2020). Repere în formarea continuă a cadrelor didactice din învăţământul preuniversitar [Highlights in the Continuous Training of Teachers in Pre-university Education]. *Buletin Ştiinţific, Fascicula Filologie, Seria A* [Scientific Bulletin, Philology Fascicle, A Series], *XXIX*, 351–357. <http://bslr.ubm.ro/files/2020/29.Maier_Monica_(351-357)_BSLR_2020.pdf>

Ministerul Educaţiei Naţionale [Minister of National Education]. (2021). *Repere pentru proiectarea, actualizarea şi evaluarea Curriculumului naţional. Document de politici educaţionale* [Guidelines for designing, updating and evaluating the national curriculum. Educational policy document]. <http://legislatie.just.ro/Public/DetaliiDocumentAfis/237529>

Miranda, J., Navarrete, C., Noguez, J., Molina-Espinosa, J.-M., Ramírez-Montoya, M.-S., Navarro-Tuch, S. A., Bustamante-Bello, M.-R., Rosas-Fernández, J.-B., & Molina, A. (2021). The core components of Education 4.0 in higher education: Three case studies in engineering education. *Computers & Electrical Engineering*, *93*, 107278. <https://doi.org/10.1016/j.compeleceng.2021.107278>

Moreno-Charris, A., Castillo, A. E., Rodríguez, C. R., Palacio De La Cruz, S., Tovar, O. O., & Ortega, F. A. (2022). Internationalization of higher education institutions through marketing orientation. *Procedia Computer Science*, *210*, 328–332. <https://doi.org/10.1016/j.procs.2022.10.159>

Mulcahy, D., Cleveland, B., & Aberton, H. (2015). Learning spaces and pedagogic change: Envisioned, enacted and experienced. *Pedagogy, Culture & Society*, *23*(4), 575–595. <https://doi.org/10.1080/14681366.2015.1055128>

Peters, M. A. (2019). Technological unemployment: Educating for the Fourth Industrial Revolution. In M. W. Apple (Ed.), *The Chinese dream: Educating the future* (pp. 123–135). Routledge.

Rad, D., Egerău, A., Roman, A., Dughi, T., Kelemen, G., Balaş, E., Redeş, A., Schipor, M.-D., Clipa, O., Mâţă, L., Maier, R., Rad, G., Runcan, R., & Kiss, C. (2023). On the technology acceptance behavior of Romanian preschool teachers. *Behavioral Sciences*, 13(2), Article 2. <https://doi.org/10.3390/bs13020133>

Rodés, V. and Gewerc, A. (2021). A Latin American critical conceptual model on the adoption of open educational resources. *Journal of Interactive Media in Education*, 22(1), 1–16. <https://doi. org/10.5334/jime.680>

Rogers, E. M. (2003). *Diffusion of innovations* (5th ed.). Free Press.

Scepanovič, S. (2019). The Fourth Industrial Revolution and Education. *2019 8th Mediterranean Conference on Embedded Computing (MECO)*, 1–4. <https://doi.org/10.1109/MECO.2019.8760114>

Solomon, M. R. (2009). *Consumer behavior: Buying, having, and being* (8th ed.). Pearson.

Süer, S., & Oral, B. (2021). Investigation of classroom teachers' views towards innovative pedagogical practices. *Participatory Educational Research*, *8*(4), 253–273.

Valdés, K. N., Alpera, S. Q., & Cerdá Suárez, L. M. (2021). An institutional perspective for evaluating digital transformation in higher education: Insights from the Chilean case. *Sustainability*, *13*(17), Article 17. <https://doi.org/10.3390/su13179850>

Exploring the Impact of Parental Migration on Elementary School Children: Challenges, Resilience, and Educational Strategies

Ancuta Florentina Răpăcău and Dana Rad

Abstract: This chapter delves into the multifaceted impact of parental migration on elementary school children, particularly focusing on the challenges they face, their resilience mechanisms, and the educational strategies that can effectively support their well-being and development. With an increasing number of parents working abroad, the separation and geographical distance have significant implications for young children. The chapter aims to shed light on the emotional, psychological, and social dimensions of this phenomenon, considering its potential consequences on academic performance, mental health, and socioemotional development. Furthermore, the chapter explores the coping strategies and resilience factors exhibited by these children, highlighting the importance of family, community, and school support systems. By analyzing existing literature and research findings, the chapter aims to provide insights into practical and evidence-based educational approaches that can enhance the adjustment and holistic development of elementary school children affected by parental migration.

Keywords: parental migration, elementary school children, challenges, resilience, educational strategies, academic performance, mental health, socioemotional development, coping strategies, family support, community support, school support.

Introduction

In recent decades, the phenomenon of parental migration has emerged as a defining feature of global migration patterns. It reflects the aspirations of countless individuals who seek better economic prospects and employment opportunities in foreign lands, often leaving their families behind (Castles, 2010). This sociocultural phenomenon has significant implications not only for the migrating adults but also for their families, particularly their elementary school-aged children. The impact of parental migration on children, who remain in their home countries while their parents seek livelihoods abroad, constitutes an area of growing concern within the field of child development and education (Suárez-Orozco et al., 2015).

The global prevalence of parental migration is staggering. Millions of children worldwide experience separation from one or both parents as a result of international migration. According to the International Organization for Migration (IOM), the number of international migrants exceeded 272 million in 2019, with a significant proportion consisting of individuals who are parents or caregivers to school-aged children (IOM, 2020). Consequently, understanding the multifaceted effects of parental migration on elementary school children has become increasingly urgent and critical.

The experiences of elementary school children whose parents migrate are marked by a unique set of challenges, which encompass emotional, psychological, and social dimensions. These challenges can have profound and lasting consequences on various aspects of the children's lives, including their academic performance, mental health, and socioemotional development (Cebotari & Mazzucato, 2017). It is essential to recognize that the effects of parental migration extend beyond mere geographical separation; they reach deep into the emotional cores of these children, shaping their identities, perceptions, and aspirations (Hoang at al., 2015).

The implications of parental migration are inherently complex. On one hand, migration may offer families access to improved economic conditions and opportunities for upward mobility, potentially enhancing their overall well-being (Antman, 2011). On the other hand, the geographical distance between parents and children can introduce a myriad of stressors, including the absence of parental figures during crucial developmental stages, feelings of abandonment, and the challenge of maintaining familial bonds across borders (Cortes, 2008).

These intricacies underscore the need for comprehensive research and nuanced exploration of the impact of parental migration on elementary school children. The experiences of these children are not homogenous; they vary depending on factors such as the age of the child, the duration of parental absence, the quality of communication between parents and children, and the presence of supportive social networks (Asis, 2006).

This chapter aims to delve deeply into the multifaceted impact of parental migration on elementary school children. It seeks to provide a comprehensive understanding of the challenges these children face, their resilience mechanisms, and the educational strategies that can effectively support their well-being and development. By analyzing existing literature and research findings, the study aims to offer insights into practical and evidence-based educational approaches that can enhance the adjustment and holistic development of elementary school children affected by parental migration.

Specifically, the objectives of this study are as follows:

- To examine the emotional, psychological, and social dimensions of parental migration and its potential consequences on academic performance, mental health, and socioemotional development of elementary school children.
- To explore the coping strategies and resilience factors exhibited by elementary school children affected by parental migration, with a particular focus on the role of family, community, and school support systems (Suárez-Orozco et al., 2015).
- To analyze existing literature and research findings to provide insights into practical and evidence-based educational strategies that can effectively support the adjustment and development of these children (Cebotari et al., 2017).

In doing so, this study aims to contribute to the growing body of knowledge on the impact of parental migration on children and to provide valuable guidance for educators, policymakers, parents, and practitioners who work with these young learners. Ultimately, the study underscores the importance of addressing the unique challenges faced by elementary school children in the context of parental migration and emphasizes the potential for resilience and positive development within this population.

Literature review

The global prevalence of parental migration has led to an increasing body of literature that examines its multifaceted effects on elementary school children. This section provides an overview of key findings in the existing literature and highlights the emotional, psychological, and social dimensions of parental migration, as well as its potential consequences on academic performance, mental health, and socioemotional development.

One of the central themes in the literature on parental migration is the emotional toll it can take on elementary school children. The absence of one or both parents can lead to feelings of abandonment, loneliness, and confusion (Chávez, 2012). Cortes (2008) emphasizes the emotional complexity of this experience, highlighting that children often experience a range of emotions, including sadness, anger, and longing, as they navigate the absence of their primary caregivers.

Psychological challenges also manifest as children grapple with issues related to identity and self-concept. Hoang et al. (2015) argue that parental migration can influence children's perceptions of themselves and their roles within the family unit. They may question their place in the family hierarchy and the significance of their contributions to the family's well-being. This exploration of identity can have lasting effects on their self-esteem and self-efficacy (Suárez-Orozco et al., 2015).

The social dimensions of parental migration are equally complex. Children affected by parental migration often encounter challenges related to peer relationships and community integration (Asis, 2006). Stigmatization and discrimination based on having migrant parents can lead to social isolation and hinder their ability to form positive social connections. However, the presence of supportive social networks and culturally sensitive community resources can mitigate some of these challenges (Cebotari & Mazzucato, 2017).

Parental migration can have significant implications for the academic performance of elementary school children. Antman (2011) found that children who experience parental migration may encounter academic difficulties, including lower educational attainment and reduced school engagement. The absence of parental support and supervision can affect their motivation, study habits, and overall performance in school. These academic challenges may persist throughout their educational journey.

The literature also highlights the potential effects of parental migration on the mental health of elementary school children. Suárez-Orozco et al. (2015) found that these children are at an increased risk of experiencing symptoms of anxiety, depression, and emotional distress. The stressors associated with parental absence, coupled with the adjustments to new family dynamics and responsibilities, contribute to the mental health vulnerabilities of these young learners.

Socioemotional development is another critical aspect affected by parental migration. The absence of one or both parents can impact children's ability to form secure attachments and develop healthy relationships (Cebotari &

Mazzucato, 2017). In addition, the potential stigma associated with having migrant parents can affect their self-esteem and sense of belonging within their peer groups and communities.

In summary, the existing literature underscores the emotional, psychological, and social challenges faced by elementary school children due to parental migration. These challenges can have far-reaching consequences on various aspects of their lives, including academic performance, mental health, and socioemotional development. Understanding the nuanced experiences of these children is essential for developing effective strategies to support their well-being and development.

Impact on elementary school children

Parental migration significantly impacts elementary school children across multiple dimensions, with emotional and psychological effects being particularly pronounced. These effects include feelings of abandonment, separation anxiety, loneliness, and confusion (Du et al., 2023). The absence of one or both parents can lead to a profound sense of loss and longing, as children navigate life without their primary caregivers (Asis & Ruiz, 2009). Psychological challenges also manifest as children grapple with issues related to identity and self-concept. They may question their place within the family hierarchy, the significance of their contributions to the family's well-being, and their roles as sons or daughters (Mazzucato et al., 2015).

Social challenges are equally prominent, affecting children's peer relationships, identity formation, and cultural adaptation. Children affected by parental migration often experience stigmatization and discrimination based on having migrant parents, leading to social isolation and hindering their ability to form positive social connections (Creighton et al., 2018). Identity exploration takes on a unique complexity as children redefine their roles and sense of belonging within their families and communities.

Furthermore, the academic performance of elementary school children can be significantly disrupted by parental migration. Mazzucato and Schans (2011) found that these children may face academic difficulties, including lower educational attainment and reduced school engagement. The absence of parental support and supervision can affect their motivation, study habits, and overall performance in school. While these academic challenges may persist throughout their educational journey, there are strategies to mitigate them, such as teacher support, tailored academic programs, and counseling services (Hoang et al., 2015).

Socioemotional development is another critical aspect affected by parental migration. The absence of one or both parents can impact children's ability to form secure attachments, develop healthy relationships, and cultivate interpersonal skills (Creighton et al., 2018). In addition, the potential stigma associated with having migrant parents can affect their self-esteem and sense of belonging within their peer groups and communities (Mazzucato et al., 2015).

Resilience and coping mechanisms

Despite the challenges posed by parental migration, many elementary school children exhibit remarkable resilience and employ coping mechanisms to navigate their unique circumstances.

Family support: Remaining family members and extended family networks play a pivotal role in providing emotional and practical support. Siblings, grandparents, aunts, uncles, and cousins often step in to provide care, guidance, and a sense of continuity (Suárez-Orozco & Suárez-Orozco, 2009). Strong family bonds and communication can mitigate feelings of abandonment and help children maintain a sense of belonging.

Community support: Involvement in community activities, clubs, and organizations offers a sense of belonging and social support (Mazzucato et al., 2015). Participation in extracurricular activities can provide a sense of purpose and connection to peers who share similar experiences. Culturally sensitive community resources and services can help children and families adapt to their new circumstances while preserving their cultural identity (Asis & Ruiz, 2009).

School support: Schools can play a critical role in supporting children affected by parental migration. Positive teacher–student relationships, mentorship programs, and counseling services can provide emotional and academic support (Hoang et al., 2015). Peer support groups and activities that promote cross-cultural understanding and inclusivity can help children feel more integrated within the school community (Du et al., 2023).

By drawing on family, community, and school support systems, elementary school children can develop resilience and coping mechanisms that enable them to navigate the emotional, psychological, and social challenges associated with parental migration.

Educational strategies and interventions

In light of the multifaceted challenges faced by elementary school children affected by parental migration, implementing effective educational strategies and interventions is paramount. These approaches aim to create a supportive and inclusive school environment, address emotional and psychological challenges, promote cultural awareness, and strengthen communication between parents and teachers.

Schools play a crucial role in fostering a sense of belonging and support for children with migrant parents. Creating a welcoming and inclusive school environment is essential to ease their transition and adaptation (Schwartz, 2017). School staff, including teachers and counselors, can be trained to recognize the unique needs of these children and provide them with emotional and academic support. Initiatives such as multicultural fairs, inclusive curricula, and celebrating diverse cultural backgrounds can promote inclusivity within the school community (Yue, 2020).

Addressing the emotional and psychological challenges of these children requires psychoeducational programs that provide them with coping strategies and emotional regulation skills (Lu et al., 2012). These programs can include group counseling sessions, art therapy, or mindfulness practices. By offering a safe space for children to express their feelings and concerns, schools can help them develop resilience and better navigate the emotional complexities of parental migration (Xu, 2020).

Promoting cultural awareness and understanding is vital for both children with migrant parents and their peers. Cross-cultural education programs can teach students about the diverse cultures and backgrounds represented in their school community (Yue, 2020). This not only reduces stigmatization and discrimination but also fosters empathy and respect among students. Schools can invite parents with migrant backgrounds to share their experiences, helping to bridge the cultural gap and create a more inclusive environment (Gao, 2020).

Effective communication between parents and teachers is crucial for monitoring the well-being and progress of children with migrant parents. Schools can facilitate regular meetings, workshops, or conferences that encourage parents to engage with teachers and discuss their children's needs (Lu et al., 2012). This collaboration enables teachers to gain insights into the child's home environment, cultural context, and specific challenges, allowing for tailored support and interventions.

By implementing these strategies within the educational system, schools can provide essential support for elementary school children affected by parental migration. These efforts not only enhance the children's academic success but also contribute to their emotional well-being and socioemotional development, ultimately fostering a more inclusive and supportive learning environment.

Policy implications and recommendations

Addressing the challenges faced by children of migrant parents necessitates a comprehensive and collaborative effort involving schools, communities, and governments. To provide comprehensive support and enhance the overall well-being of these children, it is crucial to develop policy initiatives and recommendations that take into account their unique needs and circumstances. This section explores various aspects of these efforts, including policymaker recognition, collaboration between schools and communities, the importance of flexible immigration policies, and the prioritization of research-informed interventions.

Policymakers play a pivotal role in shaping the support systems available to children with migrant parents. To effectively address the challenges faced by these children, it is imperative that policymakers recognize the specific issues and vulnerabilities associated with parental migration (Suárez-Orozco & Suárez-Orozco, 2009). By acknowledging these challenges, policymakers can prioritize the well-being of these children in policy agendas and allocate resources accordingly.

This recognition should serve as the foundation for the development of targeted policies and programs tailored to the unique needs of this population. Policymakers should emphasize the importance of adopting a holistic approach that encompasses various aspects of well-being, including education, social services, and mental health support (Xu, 2020). A comprehensive policy framework can address the multidimensional impact of parental migration on children and promote their healthy development.

Effective support for children affected by parental migration necessitates collaboration between schools, local communities, and governments. Schools serve as central hubs for education and support, making them key partners in addressing the challenges faced by these children. Collaborative efforts should extend beyond school boundaries to encompass broader community engagement.

Communities can play a crucial role in establishing support networks and community centers that offer resources and services tailored to the needs of these children. These centers can provide counseling services, extracurricular activities, and culturally sensitive programs. Such initiatives can create safe spaces for children to express their feelings, build relationships, and receive academic assistance.

Governments, at various levels, should actively support these collaborative endeavors. Financial support is essential for initiatives such as teacher training, mental health services, and the development of culturally sensitive educational materials (Hou, 2019). Adequate funding ensures that schools and communities can implement effective programs and provide essential services.

Moreover, policymakers should consider the development of flexible immigration policies that facilitate family reunification and reduce the duration of parental separation. Lengthy periods of separation can have detrimental effects on children's well-being (Rad et al., 2022; Redeş et al., 2023). Policies that prioritize family unity can alleviate some of the challenges associated with parental migration and promote the healthy development of these children.

To improve the overall well-being of children with migrant parents, policymakers and educational institutions should prioritize research-informed interventions (Creighton et al., 2018). Evidence-based approaches are essential for guiding policies and initiatives that effectively address the challenges faced by these children.

Investing in research that assesses the effectiveness of various support strategies is crucial. For example, studies can evaluate the impact of psychoeducational programs, cross-cultural education initiatives, and other interventions on the well-being and development of these children. Evidence-based research can inform the design and implementation of policies and interventions that align with best practices (Schwartz, 2017; Rad et al., 2022; Rad et al., 2023; Redeş et al., 2023).

Continuous evaluation and adaptation of these programs are essential to ensure their long-term effectiveness. Ongoing research and assessment can identify areas for improvement and inform policy adjustments. Moreover, collaboration between researchers, policymakers, educators, and communities can facilitate knowledge sharing and the dissemination of best practices in supporting children affected by parental migration.

In summary, addressing the challenges faced by children with migrant parents requires a comprehensive and multifaceted approach. Policymakers must recognize these challenges and prioritize the well-being of these children in policy agendas. Collaborative efforts between schools, communities, and governments can provide the necessary support and resources. In addition, research-informed interventions should guide policies and initiatives aimed at improving the overall well-being of these children. By adopting these strategies, we can work toward ensuring that children affected by parental migration receive the support they need to thrive academically, emotionally, and socially.

Conclusion

In conclusion, the impact of parental migration on elementary school children is a complex and multifaceted issue that demands our attention and concerted efforts to address. This chapter has delved into the emotional, psychological, and social challenges that these children face due to parental migration, as well as the remarkable resilience they demonstrate in response to these challenges. In addition, it has examined a range of educational strategies and interventions that can play a pivotal role in supporting the well-being and holistic development of these young learners.

Understanding the unique experiences of children affected by parental migration is paramount. The challenges they encounter extend beyond mere geographical separation; they reach deep into the emotional and psychological dimensions of their lives. These children may grapple with feelings of abandonment, loneliness, and confusion. They may also navigate issues related to identity and self-concept, questioning their place within their families and the significance of their contributions. The social dimensions of their experiences may involve challenges in forming peer relationships and adapting to new cultural environments. This nuanced understanding of their experiences underscores the need for tailored support systems (Chávez, 2012; Graham et al., 2015; Suárez-Orozco et al., 2015).

This chapter has outlined various educational strategies and interventions that can significantly contribute to the well-being and development of elementary school children affected by parental migration. Creating a supportive school environment is foundational, as schools play a pivotal role in fostering a sense of belonging and support. Initiatives such as multicultural fairs, inclusive curricula, and celebrating diverse cultural backgrounds can promote inclusivity within the school community. Furthermore, psychoeducational programs provide children with coping strategies and emotional regulation skills, offering a safe space for them to express their feelings and concerns. Cross-cultural education initiatives promote cultural awareness and understanding among students, reducing stigmatization and discrimination. Strengthening parent–teacher communication is vital for monitoring the well-being and progress of these children, allowing for tailored support and interventions (Schwartz, 2017; Xu, 2020; Li, 2018; Han et al., 2018).

Addressing the challenges faced by children of migrant parents requires collaborative efforts from policymakers, schools, communities, and governments. Policymakers must recognize the specific needs of these children and prioritize their well-being in policy agendas. This recognition can lead to the development of targeted policies and programs that address the unique needs of this population, emphasizing a holistic approach combining education, social services, and mental health support. Schools should collaborate with local communities and governments to provide comprehensive support, and communities can establish support networks and community centers. Governments can allocate funding for teacher training, mental health services, and culturally sensitive educational materials. Flexible immigration policies that facilitate family reunification and reduce the length of parental separation should also be considered (Suárez-Orozco & Suárez-Orozco, 2009; Hou, 2019).

Policymakers and educational institutions should prioritize research-informed interventions to improve the overall well-being of children with migrant parents. Investing in research assessing the effectiveness of various support strategies can guide evidence-based policies and interventions. Continuous evaluation and adaptation of these programs are essential to ensure their effectiveness over time. Policymakers should also acknowledge the importance of research in shaping immigration policies that consider the welfare of children (Creighton et al., 2018; Schwartz, 2017; Rad et al., 2022; Rad et al., 2023; Redeş et al., 2023).

In conclusion, we call for continued research, policy development, and practical interventions in this area to ensure that children with migrant parents receive the support they need to thrive academically, emotionally, and socially. Acknowledging and addressing the impact of parental migration on elementary school children is not only a moral imperative but also a necessary step toward fostering a more inclusive and supportive educational system. By recognizing the unique challenges and potential of these children, we can pave the way for a brighter future, where every child has the opportunity to reach their full potential, regardless of their family's migration status.

References

Antman, F. (2011). The intergenerational effects of paternal migration on schooling and work: What can we learn from children's time allocations? *Journal of Development Economics*, *96*(2), 200–208.

Asis, M. (2006). Living with migration: Experiences of children left-behind in the Philippines. *Asian Population Studies*, *2*(1), 45–67.

Asis, M., & Ruiz, N. G. (2009). Who is left behind? Understanding the effects of parental migration on Filipino children. *Asian and Pacific Migration Journal*, *18*(4), 441–462.

Castles, S. (2010). Understanding global migration: A social transformation perspective. *Journal of Ethnic and Migration Studies*, *36*(10), 1565–1586.

Cebotari, V., & Mazzucato, V. (2017). The role of migrant remittances and parental migration in schooling and child work: Evidence from Kosovo. *Journal of Ethnic and Migration Studies*, *43*(8), 1282–1303.

Chávez Hernández, N. (2012). *La gestión por competencias y ejercicio del coaching empresarial, dos estrategias internas para la organización* [Competency management and business coaching practice: Two internal strategies for the organization]. Pensamiento & gestión, (33), 140–161.

Cortes, R. (2008). *Children and women left behind in labour sending countries: An appraisal of social risks*. United Nations Children's Fund (UNICEF), Policy, Advocacy and Knowledge Management Section, Division of Policy and Practice.

Creighton, M. J., Goldman, N., Teruel, G., & Rubalcava, L. N. (2018). Parental migration and Mexican children's early educational attainment. *Demography*, *55*(2), 555–580.

Du, K., Yang, T., Zhao, J., & Guan, H. (2023). The impact of parental migration on left-behind children's vision health in rural China. *BMC Public Health, 23*(1), 1–11.

Gao, Y., Li, L. P., Kim, J. H., Congdon, N., Lau, J., & Griffiths, S. (2010). The impact of parental migration on health status and health behaviours among left behind adolescent school children in China. *BMC Public Health, 10*, 1–10.

Graham, E., Jordan, L. P., Yeoh, B. S., Lam, T., Asis, M., & Su-Kamdi. (2015). Parental migration and the mental health of those who stay behind to care for children in South-East Asia. *Social Science & Medicine*, 132, 225–235. https://doi.org/10.1016/j.socscimed.2014.10.060.

Han, X., Yu, P., Liu, Z., Sun, M., & Li, P. (2018). Hierarchical relation extraction with coarse-to-fine grained attention. In Proceedings of the 2018 conference on empirical methods in natural language processing (pp. 2236–2245).

Hoang, L. A., Lam, T., Yeoh, B. S., & Graham, E. (2015). Transnational migration, changing care arrangements and left-behind children's responses in South-east Asia. *Children's Geographies, 13*(3), 263–277.

Hou, F., Lu, Y., & Schimmele, C. (2019). Recent trends in over-education by immigration status. Analytical Studies Branch Research Paper Series, No. 436. Statistics Canada Catalogue No. 11F0019M. Ottawa: Statistics Canada.

IOM (International Organization for Migration). (2020). *World migration report 2020*. International Organization for Migration.

Li, M. (2018). Left-behind children, migrant children, and children with migrant parents in China. *Children and Youth Services Review, 88*, 106–112.

Lu, Y. (2012). Education of children left behind in rural China. *Journal of Marriage and Family, 74*(2), 328–341.

Mazzucato, V., & Schans, D. (2011). Transnational families and the well-being of children: Conceptual and methodological challenges. *Journal of Marriage and Family, 73*(4), 704–712.

Mazzucato, V., Cebotari, V., Veale, A., & White, A. (2015). International parental migration and the psychological well-being of children in Ghana, Nigeria, and Angola. *Social Science & Medicine, 132*, 252–259.

Rad, D., Magulod Jr, G. C., Balas, E., Roman, A., Egerau, A., Maier, R., ... & Chis, R. (2022). A radial basis function neural network approach to predict preschool teachers' technology acceptance behavior. *Frontiers in Psychology, 13*, 880753.

Rad, D., Redeş, A., Roman, A., Egerău, A., Lile, R., Demeter, E., ... & Chiş, R. (2023). The use of theory of planned behavior to systemically study the integrative-qualitative intentional behavior in Romanian preschool education with network analysis. *Frontiers in Psychology*, *13*, 1017011.

Redeş, A., Rad, D., Roman, A., Bocoş, M., Chiş, O., Langa, C., ... & Baciu, C. (2023). The effect of the organizational climate on the integrative–qualitative intentional behavior in Romanian preschool education – A top-down perspective. *Behavioral Sciences*, *13*(4), 342.

Schwartz, S. J. (2017). The importance of studying immigrant youth and families in the twenty-first century. In S. J. Schwartz & S. Unger (Eds.), *Oxford handbook of acculturation and health* (pp. 1–8). Oxford University Press.

Suárez-Orozco, C., & Suárez-Orozco, M. M. (2009). *Children of immigration*. Harvard University Press.

Suárez-Orozco, C., Suárez-Orozco, M. M., & Todorova, I. (2015). *Learning a new land: Immigrant students in American society*. Harvard University Press.

Xu, L. (2020). The impact of parental migration on the well-being of left-behind children in rural China: A meta-analysis. *Children and Youth Services Review*, *119*, 105672.

Yue, A., Bai, Y., Shi, Y., Luo, R., Rozelle, S., Medina, A., & Sylvia, S. (2020). Parental migration and early childhood development in rural China. *Demography*, *57*(2), 403–422.

Endnotes

1 Digital Education Action Plan 2021-2027
2 A Europe fit for the Digital Age
3 Next Generation EU
4 DigComp Implementation Guides
5 https://ro.wikipedia.org/wiki/Siri

www.ingramcontent.com/pod-product-compliance
Ingram Content Group UK Ltd.
Pitfield, Milton Keynes, MK11 3LW, UK
UKHW021922120926
8556IPUK00042BA/1123

9 783631 922293